The New York Mets

Selected Other Works by Richard Grossinger

Book of the Cranberry Islands

Book of the Earth and Sky

The Continents

Embryogenesis: Species, Gender, and Identity

Embryos, Galaxies, and Sentient Beings: How the Universe Makes Life

Homeopathy: The Great Riddle

The Long Body of the Dream

New Moon

The Night Sky: The Science and Anthropology of the Stars and Planets

On the Integration of Nature: Post-9/11 Biopolitical Notes

Out of Babylon: Ghosts of Grossinger's

Planet Medicine: Origins

Planet Medicine: Modalities

The Provinces

The Slag of Creation

Solar Journal: Oecological Sections

The Unfinished Business of Doctor Hermes

Waiting for the Martian Express: Cosmic Visitors, Earth Warriors, Luminous Dreams

As Editor or Co-editor

The Alchemical Tradition in the Late Twentieth Century

Baseball I Gave You All the Best Years of My Life

Ecology and Consciousness

Into the Temple of Baseball

Nuclear Strategy and the Code of the Warrior

The Temple of Baseball

The Dreamlife of Johnny Baseball

The New York
Mets

Ethnography, Myth, and Subtext

Richard Grossinger

Foreword by Mike Vaccaro

Frog, Ltd.
Berkeley, California

Published by Frog, Ltd.

Frog, Ltd. books are distributed
by North Atlantic Books
P.O. Box 12327
Berkeley, California 94712

Cover photo by Jeffrey Zelevansky
Cover design by Paula Morrison
Book design by Brad Greene
Printed in the United States of America

Baseball cards © The Topps Company, Inc., New York, NY.

North Atlantic Books' publications are available through most bookstores. For further information, call 800-337-2665 or visit our website at www.northatlanticbooks.com.

Substantial discounts on bulk quantities are available to corporations, professional associations, and other organizations. For details and discount information, contact our special sales department.

The New York Mets: Ethnography, Myth, and Subtext is sponsored by the Society for the Study of Native Arts and Sciences, a nonprofit educational corporation whose goals are to develop an educational and crosscultural perspective linking various scientific, social, and artistic fields; to nurture a holistic view of arts, sciences, humanities, and healing; and to publish and distribute literature on the relationship of mind, body, and nature.

Library of Congress Cataloging-in-Publication Data

Grossinger, Richard, 1944–
    The New York Mets : ethnography, myth, and subtext / by Richard Grossinger.
        p. cm.
    ISBN 978-1-58394-205-5
    1. New York Mets (Baseball team) 2. New York Mets (Baseball team)—History.
I. Title.
    GV875.N45G76 2008
    796.357′64097471—dc22
                                                      2007009744
                                                      CIP

1 2 3 4 5 6 7 8 9 VERSA 14 13 12 11 10 09 08 07

for Leopold Grossinger
if he chooses . . .

Table of Contents

"Baseball is a lot like life. The line drives are caught, the squibs go for base hits. It's an unfair game."—Rod Kanehl

"It's a bit hard to realize that the one time you were a real poet in your life was when you were only twenty-five years old, sprawled out in right center field at Shea Stadium, praying that you catch a line drive off Brooks Robinson's bat. In everything I've done in my life since then, I've tried to recapture that feeling, that sense of true poetry. But perhaps it only happens once."—Ron Swoboda

"In a corner of my mind I will stand forever with my bat cocked, waiting for the two-one pitch from Calvin Schiraldi. It is the bottom of the tenth inning, two out . . . nobody on base."—Gary Carter, *A Dream Season* with John Hough, Jr.

"Baseball's a frustrating game at times, other times it's exciting, and then again strange, even kind of deep. Spending your life in it, you'll find insecurity, joy, boredom, friendship, mistrust, surprise, despair, hope, and pain. So much happens—you just have to be conscious of the fact that you're not in control of any of it, and from that point on it all does make sense, in a funny kind of way."—Terry Leach, *Things Happen for a Reason* with Tom Clark

"This guy's AWFUL. . . . Christ almighty where can you sign up to get paid 15 million dollars to get nobody out?"—TheMaineMan in nj.com Mets forum, commenting on Tom Glavine, 06/16/07

"I'm the king of all bling,/Came to lay down the evidence,/Not George Bush, but L Millz be the President."—Lastings Milledge

Foreword

There has always been something rebellious, something iconoclastic, something a little *different*, about the men and women of New York City and the world who lend their hearts to the New York Mets. In the very beginning, in 1962, the original Mets fans made a specific choice: they could easily have accepted the status quo, they could have followed the Yankees, who were still involved in an unprecedented run of excellence in which they would win twenty-nine pennants and twenty world championships in the forty-four seasons spanning 1921 to 1964. Mets fans could not tolerate such monopolistic, monolithic thoughts, however, and they summarily rejected the single most successful franchise in the history of North American sport in favor of a team that would soon lose three out of every four games they would play in their maiden, abbreviated, 160-game season, a team that would not only finish sixty and a half games out of first place, but fully *eighteen games* out of *ninth place*.

"You'll never, ever, ever see that again, a group of fans who willingly decided to follow a team that couldn't have been more brutal," the late Richie Ashburn once told me. Ashburn had been a Hall of Fame player with the Phillies, and his one season with the '62 Mets—in which he not only made the All Star Game but also became the Mets' first bona fide .300 hitter (he finished at .306)—was enough to convince him he'd have a happier time of things in a broadcast booth than a dugout. "It was hard on us players because you can't help but be beaten down by the losing. But those fans . . . Jesus, I'm not sure why, but they sure couldn't get enough of us."

More than four decades later, early in his first full season with the Mets in 2005, David Wright invited me to sit next to him at his locker at Tradition Field, the Mets' spring-training home in Port St. Lucie, Florida, because he wanted to ask me a question.

"I know why I was a Mets fan as a kid," he told me. "I grew up in Virginia. The Mets' farm team was in Norfolk. These were the guys I grew up rooting for, and I'd follow them all when they moved onto the Mets. But there's a few million people who have a choice between the Mets and the Yankees in New York. You'd think it would have been easy for them all just to say, 'The heck with it, I'm rooting for the Yankees.' But it doesn't work out that way. Why is that?"

It's a great question. It's a complicated question. Surely there is a segment of Mets fan out there who came to their primary rooting interest by less-than-honorable means, which means they jumped on the bandwagons of 1969, 1986, 2000, or 2006, by sensing which way the New York baseball winds were blowing and made the easiest call. These fans are notable mostly because they too easily can recite the words to "The Curly Shuffle" and by the fact that when things inevitably began to ebb for the Mets after those first three magic-graced seasons—the way they inevitably will end someday in the wake of 2006—you couldn't see them. You couldn't hear them. When times are good these are the loudest, most obnoxious of the lot. They are the ones who chant anti-Yankee oaths in the bowels of Shea Stadium. They are the ones who wear their hats and their jerseys and their warm-up jackets. All of which go in the closet at the first whiff of a six-game losing streak.

The majority of Mets fans not only differ from these fickle frauds. They abhor the very thought of acting this way. The prime core of the fan base include people like Richard Grossinger, the author of this splendid book, who came of age as a Mets fan at a time when the mere thought of being competitive seemed laughable, let alone competing for a championship. Never has such a leap of faith been more richly rewarded, of course, because this was the generation who got to taste the miracles of 1969 and '73. Another sort of Mets fan was born during the acrid days following the fall of those first Mets champions and preceding the rise that culminated with the '86 champs; I fall into that category. Lastly there is a growing number of Mets fans who toiled with the team during their most recent foray into the heart of baseball darkness, during the seasons 2002, 2003, and 2004. These are the fans who weren't at all offended by the way the Mets' 2006 season ended so abruptly, with the bat remaining forever on Carlos Beltran's shoulder as he stared at strike three; instead, these were the wide-eyed kids who woke up the next morning, checked the calendar on the family refrigerator, and started counting the days until the start of spring training.

These are the fans for whom Richard Grossinger writes, the people whose own baseball journeys are reflected in his. People who aren't Mets fans may not understand at first, because they always look at Mets fans as something a shade below freaky. Why, indeed, would you root for the Mets when the Yankees are so readily available? A friend of mine has taken that question a step further.

"I almost hope my kids grow up rooting for the Yankees," John says, "because I wonder if forcing them to root for the Mets can't technically be considered some form of child abuse, and when they get older they may choose to cut me off."

Funny thing: I was a kid who went the other way. I could easily have decided to grow up a Yankees fan and it would have been fine, because I would have been a legacy, my father having bled pinstripes his whole life, and his father having done the same before him (mostly because of the Yankees' proclivity for signing, and developing, a pleasing plethora of Italian-surnamed stars over the years, from Lazzeri to Crosetti to DiMaggio to Rizzuto to Pepitone). Yet I chose another path. Maybe it was just a more innocent choice of rebellion, rather than dropping out of school, or smoking pot, or running with the wrong crowd. I don't know. What I do know is, I was two years old when Jerry Koosman induced Davey Johnson to fly out to Cleon Jones to end the '69 World Series, so I wasn't on that bandwagon. I was six when the Mets made their giddy charge to the World Series in 1973, and while those are my first memories of baseball (even my father the Yankees fan rooted for the Mets in those days), I was hardly what you would consider a fanatic.

In truth if we figure the standard "prime" of the childhood fascination with baseball starts around age ten and extends to age sixteen or so, I have no greater street cred than to state that in those years, 1977 through 1983, the Mets lost, in order, ninety-eight, ninety-six, ninety-nine, ninety-five, sixty-two (in strike-shortened 1981, while only winning forty-one), ninety-seven, and ninety-four games. The only bandwagon visible at Shea during those alarmingly futile summers was the cool caps-on-the-carts that used to transport relief pitchers in from the bullpen (a practice that was mercifully repealed when people started wondering why relief pitchers, who sometimes work as little as a third of an inning per day, needed what amounted to light rail to commute to the pitcher's mound). What was worse, of course, was that those years coincided with the rise of the detestable Yankees, who in 1976 had begun to emerge from a twelve-year slumber to again reclaim their throne atop baseball. In those same years the Yankees won 100 games (and their twenty-first World Series), another 100 (after surviving a forever pennant chase with the Red Sox, then winning title number twenty-two); eighty-nine, 103 (and a division title), fifty-nine (and an American League title), seventy-nine, and ninety-one games. I'm awful at math, but even I can tell you that means the Yankees won 187 more games than the Mets in those six years, plus five more division titles, plus three more pennants, plus two more world championships. You want easy?

Then don't be a Mets fan.

But you want fun? Well root for the Mets and read this wonderful book and realize that you're part of a legacy that will live long after we suffer, linger, and die over West Coast games and four-game losing streaks and leaky bullpens. Enjoy. Because what else is life as a Mets fans but supremely, sublimely, enjoyable?

—Mike Vaccaro

Prefatory Note

This book began in the spring of 2006 when I wrote "Playing Catch with Terry Leach." At the time I entitled it simply "Baseball" and it belonged to a very different book, *The Bardo of Waking Life,* where it served as an account of two generations (my son's and mine) playing and following baseball. Along with "The Ultimate Game," which now closes this book, it interrogated the meaning and paradox of sports within pop culture and sacred landscapes. As the piece grew to seventy pages, however, it fell out of scale with the surrounding material.

Then I decide to allocate it among my earlier Mets writings. Its combination with accounts of the 1984 and 1986 seasons were enough for a small book, but I wanted to capture the whole sweep of Mets history, so I went through my old experimental-prose volumes and unpublished writings and located several fragments about the 1962, 1969, 1971, 1973, and 1975–1977 Mets. The bulk of these appear here as substantially intact extracts, making up the next-to-last eight "chapters" (up to "The Ultimate Game"). I retained the style of their time, including sentence fragments, nonparallel clauses, and the alternative spelling "thru." I also excerpted a few more fractional ones into other pieces.

In order to include something from the 1990s, I picked my only piece of writing from that decade that discussed the Mets and retitled it "Lost Baseball."

Finally I wrote a new piece, "Endy's Catch," to open the book and tie the other pieces together.

I edited and rewrote the entire collection in its new context, removing repetitions.

I closed with two pieces that are thematically connected but do not deal directly with the Mets. "The T'ai Chi Baseball Dance" (1974) comes from an early literary book, and "The Ultimate Game" (thirty-two years later) was "stolen," as mentioned, from *The Bardo of Waking Life.*

The narrative travels chronologically backward, from the general to the specific, from memory of the past to actual writing out of the past, and from a diachronic view to a synchronic view of some of the same events. When an episode is told more than once, it is rotated to show different faces at different scales.

Here is the lineage of literary baseball anthologies that I edited and co-edited:

Io #10, Baseball Issue, 1971, an old-fashioned collection done on a Selectric typewriter and published in Cape Elizabeth, Maine. [Oddly, novelist Stephen King first appears in print here with a poem about the Brooklyn Dodgers—he was a student at the University of Maine in Orono, and I was a faculty member on the Portland campus.]

Baseball I Gave You All the Best Years of My Life (with Kevin Kerrane), 1977, enlarged in 1978 and again in 1980, published in Oakland and Richmond, California. My colleague, who taught baseball literature at the University of Delaware at the time, culled most of the individual pieces for this anthology, which is generally regarded as initiating the "baseball literature" renaissance of the 1980s and 1990s.

Baseball Diamonds: Tales, Traces, Visions, and Voodoo from a Native American Rite (with Kevin Kerrane), 1980, published by Doubleday Anchor, Garden City, New York. This was meant to be a fourth, mainstream edition of *Baseball I Gave You . . . ,* but our editor at Doubleday, Tim McGinnis, appended his own new material while cutting more than a quarter of the original text to produce a more compact book.

The Temple of Baseball, 1985, published in Berkeley, California. This was an anthology of work compiled by me between *Baseball Diamonds* and the end of 1984. "Public and Private Baseball" appeared here in its original form.

The Dreamlife of Johnny Baseball, 1987, published in Berkeley, California. This was an anthology of pieces accrued over two years following the publication of *The Temple of Baseball.* "Mythology of the 1986 Playoffs and World Series" appeared here as "Notes on the 1986 Playoffs and World Series" and then in abridged form in *Into the Temple of Baseball.*

Into the Temple of Baseball (with Kevin Kerrane), 1990, published by Tenspeed Press, Berkeley, California. This anthology combined prominent work from the prior anthologies with new writing and was assembled by me, Kerrane, and Tenspeed editor Sal Glynn. Ironically, *Into the Temple . . .* includes mainly material from *Baseball I Gave You . . .* but is doubly "misnamed" because the Tenspeed crew preferred the more recent (if incorrect) title, yet didn't want to create confusion by giving it in unaltered from to a different book.

Baseball I Gave You All the Best Years of My Life (with Lisa Conrad), 1992, published in Berkeley, California. After the core of *Baseball I Gave You . . .* was transferred to *Into the Temple of Baseball,* North Atlantic editor Conrad and I gathered the best of the remnants with material submitted since 1990 to create a mostly different anthology under the cachet of the old name. "Lost Baseball" was written for this book under the title "Baseball Variants III."

"Qabalistic Sex Magick for Shortstops and Second Basemen" by Rob Brezsny, summarized in "Playing Catch with Terry Leach," appeared in the early editions of *Baseball I Gave You . . . ,* as well as *Baseball Diamonds* and *Into the Temple of Baseball.*

ROD
KANEHL
NEW YORK METS   INF-OF

Endy's Catch: Retrospective from the 2006 Playoffs

Year of Writing: 2007
Mets' Seasons Referenced: 1962–2006

When Endy Chavez leaped at the wall with the score tied at 1 in the sixth inning of Game Seven of the 2006 NLCS against St. Louis, in his own mind (he confessed later) he gave himself less than a ten percent chance of making the play. Then, at full upward extension, he reached down behind and pulled in Scott Rolen's bid for a home run, squeezing enough of the cowhide in that prosthetic extension of mind and spirit that is a baseball glove to conclude an act common to the game, bringing the spheroid back (as the rules dictate) in a "snow cone" to the field of play. Manager Willie Randolph in the Mets' dugout turned to bench-coach Jerry Manuel and exclaimed, "We're going to the Show!" It was *that* spectacular.

Endy's catch was a play rarely made. Usually a ball sails a millimeter, an inch, or half a foot beyond the outreach of a leaping player's glove, or it passes the plane of intersection a tantalizing hundredth or tenth of a second too soon, so the glove arrives at the ball's trajectory just after it has passed. If the ball is contacted, it is most often a tick of the webbing: the classic near-miss. Occasionally the ball is snatched but, because of the awkwardness of the angle, contact with the wall, or the yoga of transporting it across the entire arc from short-lived snag to valid catch, it is dropped.

In football by rule the ground cannot cause a fumble. In baseball it can. A player who plucks, falls, and then is separated from the ball by collision with the field, however acrobatic the enterprise to that point, also forfeits the catch.

I am sure that a number of such plays have been made in the history of the game, although I cannot offhand cite another. I doubt that one of this genre has occurred at such a crucial moment on such a big stage. Thus, all things considered, it may have been the greatest catch ever, though there could be legitimate dissent from spectators of Willie Mays' over-the-shoulder bucket grab of Vic Wertz' drive in the first game of the 1951 World Series, witnesses of Ron Swoboda's belly-flopping one-handed ninth-inning clutch that saved Game Four of the 1969 Series, and even, in principle, author of many of the finest outfield plays of our time, Jim Edmonds, running the bases blindly at Shea at that very moment.

Nonetheless, it was a catch for the ages, a catch that had a meaning transcending the game in which it occurred (even though it took its drama from the context and significance of that game). It is a play that will likely engender its own cult in years to come such that people may begin to think, like Randolph in his flare of exuberance, that the Mets actually won the game. (Chavez himself, back in his native Venezuela the following winter, was stopped repeatedly by people who wanted to hear firsthand about the feat and how he did it; his generic response: "I don't know; it just happened.")

At the time, Chavez had the presence of mind and competitive savvy not only to complete the out but heave the ball to the infield to double up a disbelieving Edmonds and end the inning.

My own thought then was not that the Mets were going to the World Series; it was closer to the opposite—and not quite that either. What I felt was that the ante had just shot through the roof.

Why? Because it was Endy, the innocent "prodigal son."

The play became the amulet of redemption, the sign that a myth cycle had completed itself—but I feared that the Mets *wouldn't* win and thus the iconographic perfection of the act would be shattered. I suspected that the catch had *become* the game and that the journey of the 2006 Mets had pulled out its last rabbit. I thought something like, There's the climax of the magic. Damn, it might have been too soon. These guys are probably going to lose.

And while Randolph may have enthused, "Series, here we come," I decided, regardless of the outcome, to salvage the event in another way: "I'm going to recover those Mets pieces I've written over the years and put them together in a book."

I responded personally and rhapsodically so that the play spoke for the entire history of the Mets, not just a particular situation nor the fate of the 2006 season. That way the hieratic aspect of Endy's service wouldn't, couldn't be lost.

My Mets legacy is one of epiphanies, hexes, talismans, diasporas, mercurial rises, and symbolic crossroads. Endy's catch melds with other iconic moments in the greater design: Tommy Agee's running basket grab in the 1969 World Series; Darryl Strawberry's monster shot, like a cosmic clock striking a single chime, off Ken Dayley in the eleventh inning to beat the Cardinals 1-0 in the first game of a must-sweep series at Busch, October 1, 1985; Mookie Wilson's squibber under Bill Buckner's glove in the 1986 Series (and, just as importantly, each of the three immaculate singles and the wild pitch that preceded it); Todd Pratt's lights-out bludgeon to dead center in the fourth game of the 1999 playoffs against the Diamondbacks; as well as a more obscure hit by Ron Hodges off Dave Giusti of the Pirates in September of 1973, Keith Hernandez' well-placed slice that finally dented Bruce Hurst in Game Seven of the 1986 World Series, Lenny Dykstra's come-from-behind walk-off launch in the third game of the '86 playoffs against the Astros, and Jay Payton's game-winning line drive against the San Francisco Giants in the second contest of the 2000 playoffs (after Armando Benitez, in character, squandered a hard-won lead to a chilling dinger by J.T. Snow the previous inning).

Other moments stand out equally, not because they were critical but because they were luminous: Jim Hickman's third homer in the same game against the Cardinals, September 1965; Steve Henderson's ninth-inning, come-from-behind walk-off blast that overcame the Giants at Shea in the early '80s; a dozen or more stinging ropes during Gregg Jefferies' hitting tear at the onset of his career in the late '80s; a three-strikeout inning by Julio Machado in the '90s; a pure double to the wall by Rod Kanehl during the Mets' second month of existence, 1962. I carry indelible images of at-bats by players as diverse as Elio Chacon, Dave Schneck, John Gibbons, Bruce Boisclair, Ryan Thompson, Mark Carreon, Robert Person, and Lute Barnes. I remember innings hurled by Al Jackson, Carlton Willey, Rob Gardner, Jack DiLauro, George Stone, Roy Lee Jackson, Dwight Gooden, Timothy Leary, Grant Roberts, Jae Seo, Aaron Heilman.

For me the Mets are measured in discrete games and at-bats—curses, synchronicities, and karmic chains—not in victories or pennants. I leave those to Yankees and Braves fans. Mere winning, in fact, loses its resonance and oomph after a while. When you have to cite strings of pennants and Series triumphs and (these days) taunt fans of other teams in their chatrooms, as supporters of the Celtics and Patriots, Spurs and Steelers do (an act known as "trolling"), then you have lost the spirit of your game (and your team) and are trapped in a rooting hell, without gentility, nostalgia, or even pleasure.

Gems occur apart from championships; wonderful plays, even in lost games or dreadful seasons, are not squandered. They create the context for championships. (Admittedly they mean more when you also win the game—they can be savored without regret. That is why I desperately pulled for the Mets to outlast the Cardinals that night. I wanted Endy's catch to be a shrine that could be visited in untroubled luxury. Instead I got a more karmic outcome.)

Endy Chavez was a Met at the beginning, traded to the Royals in 2001 after five fruitless years in the farm system, an inconsequential minor-league transaction. He was claimed back on waivers from the Tigers a year later, but grabbed from the Mets by the Expos a mere three weeks after that. From his minor-league stats it appeared then that Endy was one of those forever-anonymous Rule Five guys who just disappear, either without making it to the Majors or after a brief, lackluster career. If I remember correctly, he was deemed a speed-burner with outfield skills but not much else—more than Herb Washington but less than Marcus Lawton or Esix Snead. [Snead (rhymes with "speed") was a burner of whom his former team, the Cardinals, said, "He can't steal first base." After being picked up on waivers, he quickly (if illusorily) cast off punch-and-judy status in 2002 by smashing a towering three-run homer in the eleventh inning to beat the Expos in what I believe was his first official Met at-bat.]

When, as an Expo rookie, Endy began swinging for average and power, pummeling the National League and, in particular, the Mets with gap shots and even an occasional home run, while playing a spectacular centerfield, I realized that the Mets had lost a gem. They had Endy for five years the first time, three weeks the second, but others were scouting him too and, when it counted, the Mets let their prize slip away.

They got a third chance in 2005 after Endy's career puzzlingly tanked with the Phillies, and Omar Minaya (an ancillary party to previous Chavez transactions) signed him as a free agent. Thus, a series of hexes was reversed, and the Mets began the process of neutralizing a curse that went back to 2000 when they dealt away Melvin Mora and ripped the heart and soul out of their team—and here I am talking esoteric not real baseball. To me, Mora was the vital force of the 1999 Mets, the "Endy Chavez" of his time.

Mets officials (Minaya included) rationalize now that they had no idea Mora was that good. But how could I, a casual and remote observer by any standard, be so sure they had just traded the kind of impact player you cut your way through swamp grass to get onto your team, when those guys, sitting right there on the donkey, were clueless? The Mets lost not only an All-Star but the magic and mojo that synergized them almost to the World Series in 1999.

Mora was a late call-up in '99, and it was his fourth—or maybe fifth—major-league hit in the ninth inning of the 162nd game that sent the Mets into a one-game Wild Card playoff with the Reds the day after. He had been spotted, unappreciated, on the Astros by Minaya during his original go-around in the front office. One assumed the Mets had some clue who he was, as the Astros certainly didn't—but even the "good guys" underrated Mora. I mean, Steve Phillips was patting himself on the back that Mike Bordick, the shortstop he got in return, hit a home run in his first Mets at-bat—as did Bubba Trammell, acquired for farm-system blue chips Paul Wilson and Jason Tyner at roughly the same time. Listening to Phillips gloat, you'd think the cat had swallowed the canary. But did Bordick actually get another meaningful hit after that? Yes, he did, but those puppies were as scarce as Hungarian wirehaired vizslas among epidemics of pop-ups and ground balls.

I know the party line: they had no *bona fide* shortstop after Rey Ordoñez went down and they wouldn't have made the World Series without one. I don't believe it for a moment—and exactly what did they show for themselves in that Series against the Yankees except a team of poseurs that didn't belong there? Rather than quibble here about what might or might not have been, I will say simply that the Mets reached the 2000 Series against their fraternal New York foe in a zombie state—a squad that didn't belong. Mora might have provided a spark, might have made difference. Probably not, but at least he would have performed like a warrior. Instead the Metropolitans were represented by those smug, unctuous politicians, Al Leiter and John Franco, plus an uninspired motley crew of Rick White, Mike Hampton, Dennis Cook, and Kurt Abbott. In fact, the hex quickly played out when Timo Perez, auditioning as 2000's "Melvin Mora," failed to run out a line-drive by Todd Zeile in the opening round, assuming it was a homer, and was thrown out at home, divesting a momentum that the Bronx machine never gave back.

The Mets might have come up short anyway, and Melvin Mora as a middle infielder might have butchered away the season so that they never even made it to the show. But that's not how I read it. My interpretation—not on a concrete basis that can be demonstrated in terms of sabermetrics and precise plays but as a metaphysical event with nonlinear consequences—is that the trade of Mora to the Orioles sent the Mets plummeting for the next half-decade.

Mora hit only .161 in his brief September stint in 1999, but he went six for fourteen in the playoffs against the Braves and almost won, on more than one occasion, that tense extra-inning sixth game that proved decisive for Atlanta. Playing with the sort of samurai character that legends are made of, he was more clutch than the entire rest of the Met team and the sole player in the lineup that Braves manager Bobby Cox truly feared. Midway through 2000 Mora was hitting .260 with six home runs when the Mets dealt him. In the years since, he has gotten better like a good wine, maturing into a difficult "out" in the clutch with power, an annual batting-crown threat—as the 2006 Mets found out during interleague play. "Damn," wrote one fan to the nj.com chatroom as Mora launched a difficult pitch into the seats, "we never should have let that guy go." A colleague assented: "He'd look great on second base at Shea now."

Endy's catch simultaneously purged the trade of Melvin Mora and the exile of Endy himself, at least as much as those were purgeable by then, their voodoo reversible. Even before the catch Endy had left his mark on the 2006 Mets with sublime hits and brilliant defensive plays. He was the favorite player, publicly proclaimed, of not only the manager's daughter but the manager himself. How often does that happen?

I feel the same way about the trade of Hubie Brooks (in company with minor-league ace Floyd Youmans and catcher Mike Fitzgerald) to the Montreal Expos for Gary Carter in 1984. I stand with a minority who believe that it cost the Metropolitans the 1985, 1987, and 1988 championships at least—though an unsealing of the papyruses of those years has revealed that cocaine and burning the candle at both ends did much of the job on the field of play. [The wild, uncanny 1986 bunch was riddled with drug addicts, nascent addicts, sex fiends, and assorted miscreants and psychos. As engaging a player as Kevin Mitchell was, he was also (rumor has it) killing a cat with his bare hands to amuse teammates, while Gooden was of course partying with the lethal crowd in Tampa. That team is said to have wrecked the interior of more than one aircraft with horseplay and food fights, notably while celebrating at 35,000 feet after their scintillating playoff win in extra innings at Houston.]

I likewise feel no Mets dynasty arose out of the miracle year of 1969 because of trades of Amos Otis and Nolan Ryan to the Royals and Angels, for Joe Foy and Jim Fregosi, respectively, and then the unnecessary inclusion of Ken Singleton in a deal procuring Rusty Staub from Montreal—these stars of a lost dynasty cast off casually and gratuitously, the first two for wounded players with no time left.

A coterminous piece of magic and hex-reversal took place in the sixth inning at Shea in 2006. Oliver Perez started the seventh game of the series for the Mets and was still dealing when Endy saved the bacon. If you had asked Omar Minaya to do whatever he could to undo the curse of the bizarre Scott Kazmir-for-Victor Zambrano transaction that blackened 2004, he would have been hard-put to come up with anything except, perhaps, a malediction out of his control like Kazmir throwing out his arm—and that would have been mean-spirited to root for. (But don't think for a moment that people up and down the Mets hierarchy weren't supplicating various gods, just to get the monkey off their backs. I am sure that somewhere members of the front office and Wilpon family were whispering the equivalent of 'Let that SOB punk with the boombox and wise-ass mouth blow a rotator. Guys with his delivery are blowing out arms all the time. Why can't he?'

Or at least they were thinking it . . . while making asinine jokes about the deal, e.g., pretending to forget that Kazmir was even still in the bigs.)

But Omar did come up with something. Faced with having to reverse the dumb loss of the rarest of commodities, a desirable young lefty—perhaps the most desirable one in the game for a useless righthander and a seriously impaired one at that—he picked up a lefty whose credentials (speed, stuff, and control) rivaled or even surpassed those of Kazmir at the time of the original trade. And then, from a convergence of factors that even a science-fiction writer could not have dreamed, Oliver Perez, a mere surrogate on the post-season roster, passed five guys in the rotation to be on the mound for the Mets at the start of that crucial game. He was doing fine when he snapped off the pitch that Rolen whacked to left, the one that Endy pulled back. However, the fact that Perez just about gave up a backbreaking home run meant that Cinderella's night was over and there was going to be a pumpkin on the field soon enough. Endy almost reached into the fourth dimension and turned back the clock.

Oliver Perez had worn out his welcome in Pittsburgh, and his decline from the best young lefty in the game was the mirror inverse of Scott Kazmir's ascension. So Minaya made a magical move to break the hex, getting Perez as almost a throw-in, while dealing Xavier Nady for Roberto Hernandez to fill the spot of Duaner Sanchez who was injured by a Miami cabbie run amok—and it almost worked to perfection. Chavez and Perez: Mora and Kazmir. A lot of "z's" and one key capital "X." That should have been a tip-off to alphabet sorcery.

I imagine, during discussions with the Pirates, that Minaya slipped in Perez' name as quietly as possible and as late in the deliberations as he could, probably asking for a player he couldn't get and then backing off and pretending to take Perez as a concession, hoping to fly under the radar while he completed the ceremony without the Pirates catching on.

Twenty years earlier, in the sixth game of the 1986 World Series between the Mets and Red Sox, the New Yorkers came to bat in the bottom of the tenth trailing by two runs that the Bosox had scored in the top half; and then, after two outs, they strung together those three improbable soft but flawlessly placed singles (Carter, Mitchell, Knight) and a wild pitch to tie the universe.

In 2006 they didn't even wait for two outs to get their first two charmed singles (the second by Chavez, sadly one at-bat too late)—but the rally fizzled there.

If we want to keep talking voodoo baseball, I take it that Cardinal reliever Adam Wainwright (namesake of pretty-boy rock-star Rufus) had the trump card, as he was the surrogate for an injured Jason Isringhausen, Mets prince of Generation K, whom the same Phillips regime that dumped Mora and Chavez traded off for a patent washout (Billy Taylor) to former Met outfielder and A's GM Billy Beane. [Beane celebrated his heists from the Mets of that era in a best-selling book called *Moneyball*.] Wainwright had a knee-buckling curve that Isringhausen could only ponder, and neither Cliff Floyd nor Carlos Beltran were narrow-banding it sufficiently during their at-bats, though they should have been, and will the next time when it doesn't count for nearly as much.

And there was another magical factor in 2006: the season-long refusal to use Aaron Heilman as a starter despite his clear prior success (see below) in that role. Heilman's attention, rhythm, and constitution seem better suited to starting, and his recklessly obstinate miscasting as an eighth-inning maven leads to chronic lapses, including the poor location of a single catastrophic change among dozens of dazzling high-speed offerings, a meatball that Yadier Molina *didn't* miss, which set the Mets two runs down in the ninth. (As in the second game of the Series, the Cardinals refused to let themselves get into sudden death, putting up a crooked number and then letting Wainwright close it out.)

Still, Beltran should have gone up there in that final at-bat swinging at the first pitch because that was the only fastball he would see. Failing that, he should have eyed the backdoor curve like an owl on a hare. But we were in pumpkin territory by then and, though 1986 made every effort to shine through the murk, the genie wore a Cardinals uniform this time, and the clock would not turn back.

Do I believe any of this? Of course not. But it is the way I watch the game and, if you take that version of baseball away, you might as well, to quote Ricky Nelson's "Garden Party" euphemistically, drive a truck.

Fans of the Yankees boast a historic string of pennants and World Series. Fans of the Braves were delivered fourteen straight division flags, an absurd skein. (My son Robin remarked a couple of years ago, "When they put the Braves in the Mets' division, I thought it might be a while till the Mets won again. But I didn't think it would be forever.")

Met fans have something more unconventional and idiosyncratic: they have a string of bizarre games, player synchronicities, extra-inning marathons, and a dialectic between Casey Stengel's "Can't anyone here play this game?" crew and the Amazin's, or Miracle Mets, who emerged seven years later, then eleven years later, and now eighteen years after that.* Theirs is an algebra of buffoons (from Jimmy Piersall and Marv Throneberry to Lenny Randle to Vince Coleman to Armando Benitez) followed by unlikely heroes (from Al Weis to Wayne Garrett and Benny Agbayani) and redemptions so magical and ecstatic that they make up for it all.

Of course, all teams and their fandoms nurture mythologies. The Buffalo Bills and their followers have a doxology caught up in four straight Superbowl appearances (1991–1994), all losses, tethered to a 1991 blown field-goal attempt by Scott Norwood that is iconographic enough to have generated a prominent indie film, Vincent Gallo's *Buffalo '66*.

---

*Casey's name was such a signature sobriquet in my childhood that I never imagined just "a man with a surname Stengel, first-named Casey"; "Kayceestngull" was a god, Mr. Kronos of New York baseball.

The Red Sox have forged a literary genre out of their curse, with sermons from John Updike and Yale President A. Bartlett Giamatti, Stephen King and Ben Affleck. Along the way, they had a larger-than-life curmudgeon, professor of batting Ted Williams, a warrior who could unilaterally raise others' averages by twenty points with one lecture, plus Bill "Spaceman" Lee delivering baseball koans.

The Cubs had fan interference (e.g., divine intervention) take away perhaps their last chance to get to the World Series before the next millennium: Steve Bartman reaching in front of Moises Alou to grab a foul ball in Game Six against the Marlins in 2003—and Bartman was one of the Cubs' faithful. He ended up having to apologize at least a hundred times, and the Governor of Illinois spoke publicly on his behalf, as his life and limb were threatened. It wasn't even technically interference because the ball was in the stands.

At least twelve-year-old Jeffrey Maier committed a pro-Yankee act in 1996 when he reached out of the hometown crowd in right and turned a long fly by Derek Jeter into a home run. Do you think he went to the ballpark that night thinking he was going to end up in the box score? (Now he is a star outfielder for Wesleyan University, still unable to escape the identity of that one impulsive gesture.)

Even the callow Florida Marlins and Arizona Diamondbacks have mythical and synchronistic talismans. The Marlins have captured two unlikely World Series as a Wild Card without ever winning a Division (think 1997, the Cleveland Indians still seeking relief from Willie's 1954 catch and Dusty Rhodes' pinch home run; think Al Leiter, Edgar Renteria, Craig Counsell, Moises Alou, Livan Hernandez, Charles Johnson against Jim Thome, Orel Hershiser, Sandy Alomar, Manny Ramirez, José Mesa in seven, winding down immutably to the last at-bat). And how many impossible times did the Yankees come back in the ninth against submariner Byung-Hyun Kim and the Diamondbacks in 2001 before Luis Gonzalez beat Mariano Rivera with a squib over a drawn-in infield (hey, what's Craig Counsell doing on base again)? Even the Kansas City Royals (George Brett and the pine-tar incident, Willie

Aikens, Bret Saberhagen) and Tampa Bay Devil Rays (who got Scott Kazmir and Jason Tyner from the Mets) have their own esoteric sub-plots. It would be provincial to claim that the Mets' mythology is more special. All I can say is that the Mets seem to have been a weirdness magnet from the beginning, and they have been run as much by magic (good and bad) as any team.

With the benefit of being a Yankee fan first, I racked up eight pennants in ten years before the Mets were even formed and three more while I followed both teams before becoming solely a Mets fan. Six of those eleven pennants were converted into World Championships. I took on the Mets because the Yankees' situation had become rote and tedious to me—too many gilded championships, no other purpose in life. They were pretty much a set team for years, with changes in position occur-ring only as transitions of thrones: DiMaggio to Mantle to Murcer; Phil Rizzuto deeding shortstop ceremoniously to Tony Kubek, Kubek less happily to Tom Tresh; Joe Collins handing first base to Bill Skowron, not heir-apparent bonus-baby Frank Leja; Roger Maris receiving Hank Bauer's crown in right after the demise of 1959; Yogi Berra finally pass-ing the legacy of Bill Dickey to the first black man in a Yankee uniform, the distinguished Elston Howard. Yes, I rooted for Yankee royalty, and my favorite player was Gil McDougald, but my ongoing interest lay in the team's understudies and immigrants: submarining Ewell Black-well, elder-statesman Johnny Sain, rookie flash Bob Grim, Angel plum Tex Clevenger, Mantle-caddy Bobby Del Greco, draftee Bill Kunkel, undoubtable Irv Noren, Jack Reed (with his from-nowhere extra-inning blast against Detroit), brief Rip Coleman, incidental Art Schallock, wild Bob Wiesler, slugging Don Bollweg, Bill Renna (whose wife caught his home run), Tiger refugee Duke Maas, September call-up Jim Brideweser, Suitcase Simpson, albino Jerry Lumpe, Mr. Pinch Double Bob Cerv, walking Earl Torgeson, Elmer Walrus Valo, screwballing Luis Arroyo, Sheriff Marshall Bridges, baby-faced Roland Sheldon, journeyman Eli Grba, gaunt overthrowing Jim Coates, pinch slugger Johnny Blanchard, consecutive-homer king Dale Long, and the one my brother Jon and I called Hector Slopez. They were the essential minor chords to the more central theme of Allie Reynolds, Vic Raschi, Bobby Richardson, Mickey Mantle, Whitey Ford, and Al Downing. As much as I relished winning, I resented that Kal Segrist, Pedro Gonzalez, George Banks, and Bill Bethel never got honest chances with the parent club. I wanted to dig down through the archaeology of obscure rosters and see the totems that lay beneath. I wanted a team that matched my own emerging countercultural milieu; an Aquarian clan without a hoary prehistory of the Babe, Herb Pennock, Old Reliable Tommy Henrich, and the Clipper DiMaggio. I wanted a brotherhood whose creation I could see. The Mets provided that opportunity in spades.

The year of American League expansion, 1961, was exotic because suddenly for the first time in my life there were new franchises, two fresh realities and emblematic systems. The Los Angeles Angels and Washington Senators* were actually quite good at the start because, when the National League announced expansion a couple of years earlier, the American League decided to beat them to the punch competitively and sprang it on their existing teams a year ahead of the NL schedule. Franchises in the AL had no time to hide all their best players, so the new teams were stocked with stars and platinum prospects: Buck Rodgers, Ken McBride, Dick Donovan, Dean Chance, Joe Hicks, Tex Clevenger, Joe McClain. The Angels soon added Bo Belinsky and the TNT boys—George and LeRoy Thomas—from the Tigers and Yankees, respectively (the latter for Clevenger). They made a real run at the pennant.

The New York Mets and Houston Colt .45s were created after the rest of their National League brethren spent a year burying their top young players under any obscure rule they could find. There was almost no one left.

---

*The old Washington Senators moved to Minneapolis and became the Minnesota Twins.

By the time the New York Metropolitans arrived at their first spring training in 1962, I knew the team by heart. Using expansion-draft rosters plus free agents (and accounting on the spot for transactions), I played an imaginary season on a spinner toy all winter against their compatriots, the Houston Colt .45s. I kept scorecards of all 162 games, calculating batting averages and ERAs, counting home runs, ribbies, and pitcher's wins, and compiling tables of league leaders. During the same winter I learned the full Arthur Waite tarot—major and minor arcana, meanings and applications—and then laid out fortunes for friends and relatives.

There was an even deeper link between the systems. The blue scrolls on the lap of the High Priestess, the jewel-filled Seven of Cups, the water jugs of the yellow Star angel, and the merchants of the Ten of Pentacles were runes in the same nonlinear pantheon as Ray Daviault, Hobie Landrith, Roger Craig, and Bobby Gene Smith. Both rosters remain inside me to this day, sharing a faint mnemonic link, which makes the original Mets as profound and evocative for me as the symbols of the Waite deck.

Because I played the board game, I can still recite a smattering of original Colt .45s: Bobby Shantz, Don Buddin, Roman Mejias, Merritt Ranew, Dick Farrell, and Bob Aspromonte. They weren't my team, and they were defeated by the expansion Mets in my make-believe league (perhaps from psi projected through my fingers onto the spinner), but they were the far better squad in the 1962 National League, finishing in eighth place, ahead of not only their fellow babe but the venerable Chicago Cubs. They remained better than the Mets right up to the latter's unanticipated blossoming in 1969.

For those of us who were there at the beginning and stuck it out, the quality of those early Met totems endures, and our subsequent years are marked by successions of teams that scrolled seamlessly like a sacred chronicle from their kiva to the present. The first day of the exhibition season, there was a novel team called the "Mets" taking the field against the old familiar Cardinals. It was like history starting over again from the beginning. Don Zimmer, ex-Cardinal, ex-Cub walked to the plate to bat for the New York home team even though he wasn't good enough to make the Yankees, and a guy named Jay Hook with "Mets" across the front of his uniform was throwing curves. Back then, seventeen years old, I wrote: "As a new game on the old radio dial, it emerges fresh, out of dying loyalties."

The next day Bob Miller started. I remembered him as a young pitcher on the Cardinals with great stuff whose back injury was said to have cost his team the pennant. Suddenly he was "Bob Miller of the New York Mets." I loved the sound of that. Even though he was wild and gave up a bushel of runs, his mere appearance made the game enchanted.

The Mets of 1962 for me are figures of a pre-Western mythology, minor constellations that never change and without whom there could be no theogony: junk-balling Herb Moford; Felix "break the wrong way on ground balls" Mantilla; versatile .152 Sammy Drake; witless Choo Choo Coleman (Roger Craig said that Choo Choo used to give the sign and then look down to see what it was); unflappable Richie Ashburn (the Mets' best hitter for average that first year, spoiling yet another pitch); the brief and ineffective Larry Foss; Sammy Taylor who homered in both games of a doubleheader in July and did little else. None of these guys lasted past 1962, and many of them did not complete the season; yet they are markers of the chrysalis: failed potential, unrealized hope.

From the originals drafted off manipulated National League rosters, the few that contributed in significant ways were not those with the fanciest resumés. The first "stars" were Jay Hook, Elio Chacon, Craig Anderson, Al Jackson, and Jim Hickman rather than Gil Hodges, Charlie Neal, Duke Snyder, Gus Bell, and Don Zimmer. In that dawn season many additional players arrived with delusionally high hopes, and there was always something wrong with them. Cliff Cook, for instance, a supposed slugging third baseman from the Reds, batted .232 with two homers; he hit two more the next year at a buck-forty-two.

The player to whom I attached most strongly in the '62 season was Rod Kanehl. It was because he came from nowhere. He wasn't on any list of players for spring training—and Casey Stengel had well over a hundred wannabes in numbered uniforms there, according to the indices in the New York papers, which in those days included a *Daily Mirror, Journal American, Herald Tribune,* and *World Telegram and Sun.* (Published rosters also failed to list the enigmatic Morris Cigar who threw for scouts under a bridge in the early spring rain in Queens and then never showed in Florida.)

Rod Kanehl was an utter nonperson, even on a squad of has-beens and nobodies. In the second exhibition game (in which Bob Miller lost his control), Kanehl's Met career began, a player I had never heard of replacing Charlie Neal at second base. Even the announcers had no idea who he was. In the eighth inning this anonymous guy made an error, but later he got a single up the middle to ignite a game-tying rally.

Legend had it that, on the first or second day of camp, Casey recognized him from years earlier when, as a low-end Yankee farmhand, he leaped over a fence to catch a fly ball on the other side in full stride. Lacking real talent on the field but with an unerring ear for good promo, the Old Professor grabbed onto Kanehl as an amulet. He told the story of that catch to sportswriters so often that it seemed Aesop's only fable.

Throughout the Mets' spring training Kanehl became the master of 1-1—one at-bat, one hit. He was always hustling, throwing himself at balls, so Casey began to refer to him as "My Little Scavenger." Even an obdurate George Weiss couldn't keep him off the roster. Kanehl survived scores of more highly regarded recruits to make the trip north to the Polo Grounds. In the metropolis he rode the subways recreationally, so was nicknamed The Mole—and his was the icon on the first banner unfurled at Shea: Hot Rod Kanehl.

At the start of the season, Charlie Neal got hurt, so Kanehl replaced him at second base and garnered two and three hits a game—his batting average soaring over .400. Eventually he cooled off, but he became a super-sub, playing all the infield and outfield positions at one time or other; he also warmed up pitchers between innings and was the emergency catcher. He was never great, or a starter, except for brief tantalizing spells, but he invariably seemed to do something memorable. One night he took a pitch on his arm with the bases loaded. Casey had offered $50 to anyone for that feat of duplicity, and Kanehl was the only one to get paid; in fact, he circled the black-and-blue mark and inked "$50" above it, then rolled up his sleeve in front of the manager in the clubhouse. He lined a couple of singles off Sandy Koufax on a night when most everyone else was striking out, and he delivered dagger pinch hits with improbable regularity.

Kanehl played three years and hit a collective .241, but I remember him for his thrilling bingles when they were least expected. After all, he arrived as no one; he wasn't supposed to be there. He was a player from another solar system, so every at-bat was special and cherished.

As fate would have it, he got a rare start, his first in over a month, against the Giants the night of my senior prom. While I was getting dressed and chatting with my brother, we turned on the radio in time for pre-game lineups and were startled to hear: "Playing first base for New York and batting second, number ten, Rod Kanehl." It was an omen, both wonderful and terrible.

"I'll tell you what he does," Jon promised. I thought at first that would be okay, but the notion didn't last. I felt a profound tug of loyalty: this was a momentous night, leading back to Kanehl's first appearance in the exhibition season; my mind couldn't let go of it. So I did what I had to: I hid a portable radio in the white box with the orchid, a place where my parents, hopefully, wouldn't discover it.

This was all so embarrassing. At my all-boys' private school I hadn't dated much and didn't have anything remotely resembling a girlfriend but, rather than miss the big dance, I ended up asking the sister of a friend from summer camp. Brother and sister had both shown up at my father's hotel the previous Christmas, and we had hung out together as buddies. Sharon was sweet, beautiful, and sophisticated—plus the only person I could think of—and I had no idea why she said yes.

I was especially nervous because most people were attending with girls they had at least dated. Then my mother and stepfather got a hold of the occasion and made it a full nightmare. They rented a tuxedo, hired a limousine, and ordered an orchid. Dressed like a penguin and fussed over by people who had even less confidence in me than I had in myself, I was alienated from the event from the start, so when the lineups were announced I grabbed my baseball-replica radio and made my move.

On the limousine radio en route to Sharon's house in Queens, I heard Kanehl's first two at-bats: a bouncer to second and an infield pop. Then I was at her door: number ten, Rod or Richard or somebody, holding a box with a corsage, the radio in my jacket pocket; a tall dark girl, bright red lipstick, backless lowcut dress, coming out the door. What was I doing here?

At a swish hotel in downtown Manhattan, the prom was a zigzag of events that never got into sync—a procession of mixed intentions, missed opportunities, stolen chairs, and competitive small talk. The main guys I had hung out with for six years didn't go to things like a prom. In the attending group I was pretty much a nerd, and my "friends" of the night flirted heedlessly with my date. Even more heedless myself, I slipped away to the bathroom to hear what had happened in the game, a Dodger blowout. I was just in time: "Now here's Rod Kanehl, a rookie who's had himself quite an evening...." I felt a jolt of disbelief followed by pure elation: magic had struck; the Ace of Pentacles had been drawn. "... he has a single and his first major-league home run in four trips to the plate."* Clenching my fingers into brief fists, I mouthed a voiceless "Yes!"

---

*Two of Kanehl's 192 lifetime hits and one of his six home runs came on prom night.

I wanted to carry my euphoria back to the table, but it was inconsonant with the developing situation. Sharon was out on the floor, twisting with one of our legendary class wolves. Afloat still on cloud nine, I hastily brainstormed a plan: ducking out to the lobby, I found a vendor, scanned his limited merchandise, and bought the perkiest of the stuffed animals, a small dog. In presenting it to Sharon, I tried to explain the wonderful thing that had just happened. Baffled but agreeable, she ostentatiously cuddled the pet and declared, once she got the pronunciation straight, that its name would be Rod Kanehl.

I went in a group to Basie Street after the prom, a singer and a comedian. Afterwards we were all headed to a late party when, out of the blue, Sharon suggested I call the limousine driver. "I'm tired," she said. "I'm ready to go home." The evening had flown by, the game long over—and now I had only remorse.

My stepmother ran into her just a couple of years ago. "How strange!" you might think. How was my stepmother, a parent in a different household, to know that she had run into my date from a prom forty-plus years earlier? As she put it, "I met this woman who is totally stunning. Everyone wants to know her. She is magnificent-looking; she runs her own international investment company and is one of the most admired and sought-after ladies in New York. I was at a dinner with her, wishing I could get to talk to her, and she came right up to me and asked if I was your mother. I was delighted; I told her I was your stepmother, and she said she had gone to your prom with you. I was flabbergasted. Richard, you never told me."

"I didn't know what became of her. Did she say what happened that night?"

"No. But something wasn't quite right. Something about a game."

"If you see her again, apologize for me, okay?"

That fable establishes a moral with few exceptions: baseball and girls stand in absolute antipathy to each other.

Every minor change on the Mets those first few years held intricate ambiances that beguiled me. They were a hodgepodge of names, most of them previously unfamiliar or incidentally noted, as players arrived and exited with profligate regularity.

A few of the '62 gang stayed around and contributed bits of fool's gold for two or three or four thwarted years: Galen Cisco and Al Jackson hurled some masterpieces; Bob Miller went 0-12, albeit with some pretty dazzling stretches, before winning his last outing; Chris Cannizzaro was a fine defensive catcher; Craig Anderson rarely ever got a W, but he usually threw a heavy, dancing ball.

In a televised exhibition game during spring training of '63, my stepfather saw Al Moran and Larry Burright, two newcomers, turn a dazzling double-play and pronounced, "We might have something here." Moran hit .193 and Burright .220; both were shown the gate partway through 1964—yet they are as memorable to me now as the Yankees of the 1950s, and I can still see that pivot. It was the continuity of the Mets, year by year—the texture and depth of those summers and autumns when the guys mostly got defeated, often in ingenious and heartbreaking ways—that was hauntingly magical and compelling.

Others arrived later with more fanfare than the original bunch and lasted for parts of a year or occasionally longer, a good number of them faded stars that acting GM Weiss* thought would somehow restore their luster in New York (or at least fill seats): Frank Thomas; Vinegar Bend Mizell; Roy McMillan; Jim Marshall; and the first African American on the Red Sox, Pumpsie Green (hitting Beantown twelve long years after the debut of Jackie Robinson, Elijah Pumpsie came over with Tracy Stallard, casualty of Roger Maris' 61st home run two years earlier). Frank Thomas actually became the Mets' first slugger (thirty-four homers in '62 at the Polo Grounds), but he was a one-dimensional sideshow.

---

* The Yankees from whom he retired would never allow it to be official.

Then there were balk-prone lefty Don Rowe; Marvelous Marv Throneberry (an ex-Yankee bruiser who actually played pretty well but converted a handful of fielding errors and base-running gaffes into the folklore of a national dufus); George Altman (with only a few bullets left in his once-mighty gun); Wayne Graham (great infield arm but three for thirty-three lifetime); and Jesse Gonder whom I knew from my Yankee days when he was a supposed hitting machine in the farm system. Bill Stafford, a family friend and Yankee pitcher, two years earlier handed me a signed Richmond baseball and, pointing to Gonder's scrawl, joshed, "Don't you want the autograph of the greatest and fattest slugging catcher of all time?"—a prognosis typical of the failed promise of so many prospects the Mets pulled off the junk pile—from Cliff Cook to Duke Carmel to Tim Harkness—only to learn why they were on it in the first place. Gonder at least justified Stafford's faith, hitting .271 in almost 600 Met at-bats with a hefty slugging percentage.

Two pitchers who arrived with little fanfare actually had stellar if brief careers for bad Met teams: Rob Gardner (fifteen shutout innings at the end of 1965 in an eighteen-inning duel that ended 0-0) and Dennis Ribant (an 11-9 ace in 1966). Shortstop Bobby Klaus and second-baseman Ron Hunt briefly amounted to half of a decent infield (in fact, hard-nosed playmaker Hunt, drafted from the Braves, challenged Pete Rose for Rookie of the Year and, a remarkably tenacious batter in the Rose mold, was the first Met to earn his way onto the All-Star team).

In the late years of "Can't Anyone Here. . . ."—1965 to 1968—new vagabonds supplanted expended ones. Some of the more notable names in my memory are: Don Bosch (the first of many good-field, no-hit centerfielders who teased with flashes they couldn't sustain); Al Luplow (a supposed slugger from Cleveland who hit maybe two homers in "too little, too late" situations); Chuck Hiller (of San Francisco World Series grand-slam fame); Jerry Buchek (quick bat, hitch in his swing); Tommy Davis (cost the Mets *both* Ron Hunt and Jim Hickman in a trade with the Dodgers, and had enough left—.302-16-73—to bring back Tommy Agee and Al Weis a year later from the White

Sox); Johnny Lewis (a little bit of Clemente in him, just a little); Larry Stahl (never launched one of his epic clouts in a Met uniform, at least during official play); Phil Linz (he of the Yankee harmonica incident; beaten out by Tom Tresh all the way through the system, not much better as a Met); and Tom Parsons (one shutout and then used to procure Jerry Grote from Houston). Among the first virgin "star" prospects from the farm system were Bob Heise (actually hit nearly .300 over three years and then was used to entice the Giants to part with both Ray Sadecki and Dave Marshall); Dick Selma (opened 1968 at 6-0; selected off the Mets' roster by San Diego in the '69 expansion draft); and local St. Johns hurler Larry Bearnarth (a better pitching coach than a pitcher). None of these guys made it to the Miracle Mets. Like Moses they "died" in the desert in sight of the promised land.

The breakthrough 1969 team bore remnants from the last-place 1967 and 1968 teams, including successful retreads like Fat Jack Fisher, once a Baby Bird Oriole ace; dignified and graceful third baseman Ed Charles (from Kansas City); Cal Koonce and Don Cardwell, steady workhorses from the Cubs; Art Shamsky (Reds' backup, Mets' clutch avatar); Jerry Grote (Colt .45 third-string catcher, redneck stud for years on the Amazin's); and Tommy Agee (over from the White Sox with Al Weis). Then there were debutantes from the farm system: Ron Swoboda and Bud Harrelson (class of 1965); Cleon Jones (who arrived at an early tryout announcing "Break up the camp, Cleon is here!": class of '65 after a peek in '63); Tug McGraw (class of '65); supernatural Nolan Ryan (class of '66); and the leader of the pack, the man who would change everything, Hall of Fame starter Tom Seaver (class of '67) whom the Mets were lucky enough to pull out of a lottery after he was signed improperly by the Braves). Seaver might have been one of the five best starting pitchers of all-time, and he anchored the Mets' rotation for years.

Also reporting in '67 were rookie-of-the-year candidate Ken Boswell (who replaced Jerry Buchek at second and drove in the winning run in late September of '69, extra innings against the Expos, to put the

Mets in first place for the first time) and Jerry Koosman (discovered in Minnesota by an amateur scout via a Met usher). Jim McAndrew showed up in '68; he was almost always effective but got no hitting support, leading the team in both losses and shutouts more than once. The number-five guy in the Miracle Year, McAndrew actually had four straight winning starts in which he gave up a single run in total while the Mets scored all of twelve, six in one game.

Only a few arrived in '69, in time for the party: Gary Gentry (after thirteen W's his rookie year, he not only pitched but hit the Mets to victory in the third game of the World Series); Rod Gaspar (one big home run during the eleven-game winning streak, one big outfield assist down the stretch, and the signature quote of the Series with Baltimore, predicting a sweep and eliciting Frank Robinson's "Who the hell is Ron (*sic*) Gaspar?"); Jack Dilauro (in a minor trade with the Tigers, only one win on paper but a string of quality starts); and my favorite Huck Finn infielder, Wayne Garrett, drafted from the Braves the previous winter—a clutch gamer beyond his numbers.

While the '69 team was gestating in the really bad teams of the mid '60s, of course no one survived from all the way back in '62 (the snake shed its skin at least twice since then)... unless you count Ed Kranepool who logged a few at-bats as a Monroe High visitor to the team's inaugural season and appeared in some guise or other all the way to 1979. Kranepool was Mr. Met, pretty good at times, especially in the 1973 playoffs, never great—a longball threat, a dangerous pinch-hitter, but a bit of a klutz.

The collective of these guys synergized seemingly out of nowhere in 1969, forging a new mythology. The 1969 run was so improbable that, when North Vietnamese jailers told their American prisoners of war the outcome of the World Series that year, the GIs were sure the guards were lying to them as a way of messing with their minds.

A fact not usually interrogated: the Pirates were really the better team during the era that began in 1969 and ran through the 1970s, but the

Mets beat them out twice, first in 1969 by flying under the radar (while the Cubs, unintentionally, ran interference); then in 1973 when they crept up all the way from the basement and caught the Bucs by surprise in September. However, if Manny Sanguillen had had the restraint to take ball four from Buzz Capra instead of swinging at a pitch over his head with the bases loaded in mid-September, the Pirates would have taken that pivotal game and the Division.

The 1973 Mets who survived Capra's wildness were largely the 1969 Mets, but not entirely. Key players were banished in the interlude between pennants: Nolan Ryan, Ron Swoboda, Al Weis, Gary Gentry (who was sent to the Braves as damaged merchandise for the essential Felix Millan to displace Boswell at second base), Art Shamsky, Tommy Agee—all gone. Local (Mount Vernon) prospect, 1970 rookie Ken Singleton, an articulate Denzel Washington sort, was dealt before 1972 with two other promising players, Mike Jorgensen and Tim Crazy Horse Foli for Rusty Staub, a Met archon-to-be. (Foli was a number-one draft choice who played hard but fought with teammates—both he and Jorgensen would return to the dreadful Mets of the late '70s.) The Staub deal would have been admirable if someone other than Singleton had gone to Montreal, as he was a classy player and a leader, a star who hit for average, power, and in the clutch for over a decade, mostly in Baltimore. He was a long-term loss of incalculable proportions—and it was claimed at the time that allegedly racist owner M. Donald Grant wanted his ass out of town with that white wife of his.

Others replaced these guys: all-star slugger Staub, once the pride of the Colt .45s; Don Hahn (a light-hitting outfielder from the Expos in a trade for Swoboda—Hahn hit a big triple against the A's in the '73 World Series); Sadecki (a starter, reliever, and pinch-hitter); streaky Buzz Capra (who was bitten by Pedro Borbon in the brawl during the playoffs with the Reds, a mayhem triggered by Pete Rose's take-out slide of Bud Harrelson); George Stone (arriving in the Millan trade, carried the Mets through their surge at 12-3, the last eight in a row, and then was ignored by manager Yogi Berra in the World Series because he preferred Seaver and Matlack on short rest in Games Six and Seven in Oakland, something that probably cost the Mets the trophy*); Willie Mays (lumbering around the centerfield twilight in Oakland, of all people); and Bob Miller in an encore (this was the ex-Cardinal right-handed 0-12 Bob Miller and the better of the two of that name on the '62 team).

There were a few last gems delivered by a sold-out farm system: John Milner (dead-pull lefty, reliable except when dogging it); erratic, grumpy Bob Apodaca; hard-throwing stalwart Craig Swan; '72 Rookie of the Year Jon Matlack (who two-hit the Reds in the playoffs to get the Mets into the '73 Series); and the unlikely Ron Hodges (summoned from the low minors to fill in when Grote got hurt, only to deliver key hits down the stretch).† Curveball artist Harry Parker was picked up in a disastrous trade for a much sexier farmhand, fireballing Jim Bibby, sire of a basketball lineage, and Parker cost them the pivotal game of that Series in extra innings against the A's (see later in this piece).

No one could have foreseen that the success of the 1969–1973 contending teams would suddenly wither and that none of the holdover players would have long enough careers to compete for the post-season again on the Mets (unless one considers the briefly returning Tom Seaver). As the wheels came off and the situation deteriorated, many would stay around for termless futile campaigns: Bud Harrelson, Jerry Koosman, Tom Seaver, Ray Sadecki, Jon Milner, Harry Parker, George Stone (who injured a finger trying to dunk an imaginary basketball in an awning and was never the same), and Cleon—along with Apodaca, Hodges, and Swan, a trio who played most of their careers in the dias-

---

*From the mouth of A's manager Dick Williams, years later: "Pitching George Stone would give ace Tom Seaver an extra day of rest so that if there was a Game Seven, he'd probably be damn near unhittable. We figured the Mets had us whipped. Imagine my surprise, and my team's surprise, to discover that we had figured wrong. Yogi played right into our hands."

†Apodaca and Swan had mere cameos in '73.

pora. Swan was the ace for some pretty bad teams, leading the league in ERA in 1978, before blowing out his arm. For almost a decade the Mets were defined by a host of strange players, some of them very good, most of them marred or leaving their better years elsewhere or elsewhen.

It was a less charming situation than '62 because it wasn't the dawn of a franchise or cosmology—mediocre and choleric more than improvisational and endearing. Names from the period sound a dirge that can't find a tune: Benny Ayala (home run in his first at-bat, the absolute high point); Hank Webb (hard-throwing prospect, rushed to the bigs before he was ready); Del Unser (from the Phillies at the price of Tug McGraw; hit .300 for most of the '75 season and patrolled centerfield like a cannonball; both he and McGraw, as fate would have it, played huge roles in bringing the 1980 Championship to Philadelphia); Nino Espinosa (super Afro, passed for a Tiant-like ace on bad Met teams); Gene Clines (hit great against the Mets, lost his moxie when they got him); José Cardenal (traded to the Mets between games of a doubleheader, great before and after New York, zero while there); Roy Staiger (first-round pick, flashy at third, a slugger only at Triple A); Skip Lockwood (dorky-looking but an assortment of absurd hard stuff, probably as good a relief pitcher as the Mets ever had); Mickey Lolich (Rusty Staub was traded for this guy because of M. Donald Grant's pique at him, and all that the corpulent Tigers' World Series hero had left by then was that he knew how to win, hook or crook); mound philosopher Mike Marshall (seven ragged years after his Cy Young); John Pacella (one pitch: a straight fastball); Lenny Randle (great speed, big talent, equally big trouble; punched out his manager Frank Lucchesi in Texas, also tried to blow a bunted ball foul); Dave Kingman (tape-measure home runs, but a loser in the clutch and clubhouse); Mike Vail (a record start—23-game hitting streak—then nothing; a danger to himself in the field); control maestro Randy Jones (far too many arm burnouts removed from his Padre success); bozo grave-digging Pirate Richie Hebner (he hated being on the Mets and played like it); Tom

Hausman (cheap Met entry into the free-agent market while the Yankees inked Catfish Hunter, but he got traded up: to the Braves for Carlos Diaz in 1982, then a year later, Diaz and Bob Bailor to the Dodgers for Sid Fernandez); Elliott Maddox ("Best things about New York were playing for the Yankees and leaving the Mets"); Dwight Bernard (sunglasses and curveball); Juan Berenguer (the next Nolan Ryan, the next Camilo Pascual, but couldn't get his 100-mile-an-hour torpedo anywhere near the plate); Mike Jorgensen (back in town older and wiser); Roy Lee Jackson (one fourteen-strikeout game, one fourteen foul-ball at-bat); Mike Phillips (June 25, 1976: four hits including a homer versus the Cubs); Lee Mazzilli (a switch-hitting all-star, who was traded and returned in time for a key cameo in '86); Joel Youngblood (picked up from the Cardinals for Phillips; at times a solid player, at times a utility guy forced into a starting role); Bruce Boisclair (wide whiffle-ball stance, .571 pitch-hitting average in maybe 1977); and Mike Scott (a hard thrower out of the farm system who was always one pitch short, then learned the split-finger in Houston after being sent there for Danny Heep and, using it to perfection, almost singlehandedly kept the Mets out of the 1986 Series). Steve Henderson, Doug Flynn, Dan Norman, and Pat Zachry came over in 1977 for Tom Seaver when M. Donald had enough of his franchise pitcher's "insubordination." The decent but tarnished play of these four characterized the subsequent decline of the Mets, while Seaver went on to pitch the Reds to post-season glory, throwing one of those no-hitters that ace pitchers only managed before they got to the Mets or after they left town.

I find a dangling, undated Mets note among my unpublished writings from 1975 to 1977:

Pulling out of Northampton, Godfather Restaurant, into radio/Mets opening day. Highway 91 through spring, four feet of new snow in our front yard back in Vermont. In Connecticut: flowers in the luxury of a prowling sun. Kingman lofts out his first homer. The hills faintly green, glacial farms. The first game is a mystery and always will be. How each happening scores a fine line in clay. The perfect rhythm of baseball as irregular as my mind.

Torre singles in the winning run, bottom of the ninth, Connecticut Turnpike just outside Westchester. And we flow on a stream of cars and daily business, into the empire.

The year I moved to California, Steve Henderson and Lee Mazzilli were in the outfield, Willie Montañez at first, Doug Flynn at second, Tim Foli at short, Bobby Valentine everywhere, Kevin Kobel, Wayne Twitchell, Pat Zachry, Jackson Todd, and Mark Bomback on the mound. This was a full-fledged 60-win squad. Yet, as the obscure teams of the mid to late '70s gradually shed stars whose last triumph was 1973, the successful teams of the mid to late '80s were built out of the debris of the late '70s and early '80s. Soon thereafter we began to glimpse some of the players who would herald the revival but not really be part of it: Ellis Valentine (an imperfect five-tool giant whom the Expos dangled in order to steal relief ace Jeff Reardon when the Mets preferred Neil Allen out of the pen; luckily they traded Allen for Keith Hernandez a few years later); Greg Harris (baby face and jughandle curve); flashy, error-prone Frank Taveras; Mike Torrez (the old Mexican potato farmer who, as a Red Sox, served up Bucky Dent's killer home run, his career behind him but still a workhorse); gritty utility-guy Bob Bailor; New Yorker Pete Falcone (nasty stuff but always burst like a piñata at some point in a game); John Stearns (a sparkplug catcher who could steal bases but got injured right before the resurgence, making Gary Carter ultimately necessary); cerebral junkballer Ed Lynch; George Foster (Triple Crown threat with the Reds, turned lazy and sullen with the Mets, bitched his way out of town in favor of the returning Mazzilli in '86); José Oquendo (a spectacular shortstop who developed a bat after going to the rival Cardinals—the Mets gave up on this guy way too soon).

The 1984–1988 teams were woven out of Met legends-to-be: Darryl Strawberry (farm-system behemoth—fans urged GM Cashen to promote him before the apocalypse so they could at least see his Jovian swing); Ron Darling (a Yale product, along with Walt Terrell in the glittering trade with Rangers that exiled Lee Mazzilli); Dwight Gooden (shot through the farm system in one Hall of Fame season); Keith Hernandez (bringing a World Series resumé and first-base genius from Cardinals—like Seaver in '69 he was the missing link, the hub); Wally Backman (farm system); Mookie Wilson (farm system); Hubie Brooks (farm system); Jesse Orosco (minor-league prospect sent by the Twins in a trade for Jerry Koosman); Ron Gardenhire (farm system); Roger McDowell (cyborg of the farm system after arm surgery gave him a sinker); Howard Johnson (trade with Tigers for Walt Terrell); Bobby Ojeda (trade with Red Sox for Calvin Schiraldi, John Christiansen, and others); the returning Rusty Staub (no longer svelte, a sessile slugger and pinch-hitting machine).

Terrell was a horse of a pitcher, but he was the ultimate .500 guy; his pinnacle was hitting two home runs off Fergy Jenkins at Wrigley. Darling danced on a fine edge, unleashing his best stuff but losing control, taking it down a notch and getting bombed. Backman was an over-achiever, a hard-nosed second-baseman who switch-hit but really only made contact lefty. Mookie Wilson blended speed with a nip of power; only a hole or two in his swing and a weak arm kept him from being a five-tool maven. Until José Reyes, Mookie was the all-time Met who dashed around the bases most breathtakingly. A legendary Arizona State batter, Hubie Brooks was an all-around solid infielder whose bat got better and better. He started at third but moved over to short in 1985 when Rafael Santana went down late in the season. Almost impossible to retire with two outs or when he was on a streak, Hubie, sadly, had his best years in Montreal.

Orosco, after failing in his first stint in the show, became a dominant cross-firing lefty reliever with a sharp curveball and won three games in the 1986 playoffs. A spate of synchronicities: he was on the mound for the last pitch of the '86 World Series, tossing his glove in the air in a cameo for the ages, while the guy he was traded for, Jerry

Koosman, stood on the mound and stared at Cleon in left as he clutched last out in '69 and then bowed—a spontaneous gesture that was part gratitude to any Met-biased demigods, part demarcation between sacred and secular time. The Oriole who lofted that can of corn was Davey Johnson, the Mets' manager in '86.

Ron Gardenhire neither hit nor fielded much, but he was a capable sub and sometimes-starter till '86. Howard Johnson could turn on a fastball left-handed like no one in the game, but Met fans suffered through his struggles timing the curve, his difficulties batting right-handed, and his battles with ground balls, especially as a makeshift shortstop. In fact, Davey Johnson figured anyone could play the position when Sid Fernandez or Dwight Gooden were creating most of their team's outs in the air or via strikeouts so, in order to steal another bat, he put the Barrel Kevin Mitchell, at short too. Johnson's error at third with Rick Aguilera pitching the third game of that must-sweep series at St. Louis opened the floodgates and cost the Mets a chance at the 1985 Pennant. HoJo loved to cat-and-mouse it with Whitey Herzog, the Cardinals' manager—curve, curve, changeup; when was the damn heater coming?—and strangely he got much better as the Mets went downhill, so his glowing reputation doesn't line up with his contributions to pennant races.

Not everyone was there for the full illustrious run. Ron Gardenhire and Hubie Brooks were banished after '85, HoJo and Rafael Santana (a Yankee farmhand) more or less taking their places. Len Dykstra and Roger McDowell arrived in 1985; Gary Carter also came that year in the mega-trade for Hubie Brooks. Bobby Ojeda arrived in 1986 in a swap that sent Calvin Schiraldi to the Red Sox. A big strong Texas right-hander, Schiraldi coasted effortlessly through games and then suddenly seemed unable to get an out, an uncanny flaw that tolled a Mets jackpot in the sixth game of the '86 World Series. Tim Teufel arrived in '86 from the Twins as the right-handed platoon for Backman. (Interestingly in that deal, a rookie outfielder, future Oakland GM and Met larcener Billy Beane, went from the New Yorkers to Minnesota.)

Kevin Mitchell was a Mets farmhand who put in a decent year as a rookie in 1986, even, as noted, filling in at short, a position for which, as a thumping but marginal third baseman, he was ill-cast. After slumping late in the season, he lined one of the three antic singles that kept the Mets alive in the sixth game of the World Series. Then Mitchell was traded with several others to the Padres for Kevin McReynolds. No one could have foreseen his success with the Giants: 1989 MVP with forty-seven homers and 125 RBI. Few realized the degree to which this former San Diego gang member, while a Met, participated in the corruption of impressionable kids Strawberry and Gooden—but *someone* noticed and that's why he was vamoosed before the next season.

Kevin Elster, possibly the Mets' best all-around shortstop until José Reyes, sneaked onto the post-season roster in '86 but contributed nada; he was among the players whose influence extended mostly beyond the years of "meaningful games in September" into the late '80s and early '90s. Kevin McReynolds, who had an MVP run his first season in a Mets uniform in '88, was strangely irrelevant thereafter; he made the revealing comment during the playoffs that year that he'd be happy either way because if they won he'd be still playing ball and if they lost he'd be hunting in Arkansas. His at-bats against Orel Hershiser ensured the latter.

The following guys also oversaw the transition out of the Championship years into the also-ran phase: Jesus-freak Keith Miller, infielder-turned-outfielder (to crack the lineup), who threw himself at the game with kamikaze zeal and had some amazing spurts, crashing singles into doubles, doubles into triples; John Candelaria (as dazzling a hurler as there was in his Pirates heyday); slopballer John Mitchell (traded to the Mets with Bob Ojeda, just good enough to break your heart); the unappreciated Terry Leach (see the second chapter of this book); Dave Magadan (one-dimensional but relentless "go with the pitch" hitter, stuck with replacing Hernandez at first base—then a total adventure at third, like a cardboard cutout trying to be a real player); Randy Myers (intimidating fireball lefty reliever and Rambo imitator with his fatigues and Crocodile Dundee knives; gifted to the Reds in a bell-wether swap for the prima donna John Franco who went on to steal money from the Mets for over a decade; the Reds got better, the Mets worse); Barry Lyons (a bit of an oaf but a battling backstop with occasional power); self-made wonder-kid Greg Jefferies (a crybaby and liability despite his mirror-image right- and left-handed strokes, his martinet drills swinging a bat both ways underwater, his living up to his rep with an astonishing career-opening binge that carried the Mets in '88—but he couldn't handle it when he turned out to be ordinary); bedeviled hillbilly Mackey Sasser (a line-drive-slashing left-handed catcher who would double/triple pump and still not get the ball back to the pitcher); David Cone (bewildering that the Royals let a guy with such incredible stuff slip away—one of the Mets' best all-time starters, Cone was dealt to Toronto in '92 for supposed sexual-misconduct reasons; the two guys who came in return, Jeff Kent and Ryan Thompson, had far more disturbing issues than corporate Coney).

The period from 1989 into the mid '90s marked the abandonment of the philosophy of building from within and, insofar as the Mets approached the free-agent market with less than full zeal, looking for bargains and PR bites, they produced the so-called "Worst Team That Money Can Buy" in 1992. Their demise was typified by a crew of stellar whiners and overpaid quitters: Vince Coleman (picked up as a lauded "replacement" when Strawberry bolted for his hometown Dodgers, this guy who terrified the Mets on the base-paths while a Cardinal nearly a decade earlier turned out to be an Astroturf superman; his Met dossier included tossing firecrackers at a kid in the parking lot, decommissioning teammates with a golf club, and dissing Jackie Robinson—as one fan put it, "all that is wrong with baseball: gigantic ego, no understanding of the game, no respect for the fans, brain of a gerbil"; somehow got run down by the automatic tarpaulin in St. Louis, an injury which caused him to miss a post-season); John Franco (amazing how far this histrionic con artist got: 276 Met saves, on the single trick of getting guys to swing at sinkers out of the strike zone, while pretending to be Mr. New York; decided he was Acting GM too after a while); Frank Viola (for whom the Mets gave the Minnesota Twins half a pitching staff—David West, Kevin Tapani, and Rick Aguilera—enough to win the 1991 World Series; this arrogant, smug mercenary was the most irrelevant twenty-game winner in baseball history in 1990, complaining he couldn't do it all by himself: after lauding his hometown New York, walked for the Red Sox a year later); Eddie Murray (Mr. Surly, way past his prime, shell of an Oriole/Dodger slugger); Brett Saberhagen (picked up from KC for Gregg Jefferies, Kevin McReynolds, and Keith Miller, big-time starter in the '80s, anger-management candidate on the Mets; still could pop darts into the catcher's glove, put up decent numbers, but dumped bleach on a reporter with whom he had a beef); Jeff Kent (punk Southern Californian Texas rancher with a fake Southern drawl who hated New York but proved to be a hitter if not nearly as consistent a one as after he was traded to the Indians with Vizcaino in 1996 for Carlos Baerga; became National League MVP in 2000 with the Giants); Baerga (awesome difference-maker and charismatic leader with Cleveland, total bum with the Mets, one of the most absolute and inexplicable drop-offs in baseball history!); Juan Samuel (at the expense of both Dykstra and McDowell in '89, a bad second baseman with a hole in his swing whom Frank Cashen somehow thought could be converted into an impact centerfielder); and the captain of the *Titanic*, Bobby "You're Not Gonna Wipe That Smile Off My Face" Bonilla (a Pirate stud but a spoiled and bullying clubhouse lawyer in New York).

More honorable players also typified this era: Todd Hundley (team-record forty-one homers plus 112 RBI in 1996 for someone who started as a skinny weak-hitting catcher, learned on the job, and improved every year until his "Sleep-gate" run-in with manager Bobby Valentine; in '98 he was injured and replaced by Mike Piazza); Jeromy Burnitz (the ultimate pull hitter with the hole in his swing who did two spotty longball/strikeout toggles with the Mets); Darryl Boston (a five-tool player who wasn't); canny Blaine Beatty with a bum arm from Texas amateur ball; Tom O'Malley (better in Japan or singing karaoke); Pete Schourek (big curve, funky but effective batter); John Cangelosi (tiny fireplug who would charge the mound unpredictably); Chris Donnels (number-one pick, always in over his head); José Vizcaino (flashy clutch hitter, left town with Kent vowing revenge after being traded and got it with a game-winning hit for the Yankees in extra innings to open the 2000 World Series); Chuck Carr (in the Esix Snead mold, didn't like getting the take sign: "That's not Chuckie's game; Chuckie hacks on 2-0"); Wally Whitehurst (baffling curve but, as one fan put it, "couldn't get out of the Dublin pub or the bottom of the second"); Charlie "Soul Man" O'Brien (jiving cheap-shot artist whom pitchers loved to throw to); Alejandro Peña (Mr. Petro, pitching on fumes and a bad arm, could blow leads fast enough to defy space-time); Tommy Herr (the die-hard Cardinal who never wanted to wear Mets blue); Yorkis Perez (lefty set-up guy, lit up for an 8.31 ERA); Julio Machado (Iguana Man, nasty stuff, nasty personality, ended up in a Venezuelan jail on a murder charge after a traffic dispute); and Josias Manzanillo (the ageless one, bouncing off the mound like he still enjoyed it).

None of that crew was good enough at the right time or fit together with the others into a team. Anthony Young was the signature Met of that era. The guy was pitching so well early in 1992 that I actually thought he might win twenty—I starting counting and got to two when he began a record losing streak (an unbelievable twenty-five straight). He never pitched poorly enough for his fate—2-14 with a 4.17 ERA and then 1-16, 3.77 in '93—bad luck and loser's karma. Eventually his skills descended to his record, and he was packed off to the Cubs.

It only got worse in the late '90s, even after cleaning house of pretty much all of the above. There were some good players in the new mix of guys, and a few of them combined with later arrivals to carry the revived Mets to 1999 and 2000 Wild Cards and three out of four winning playoff series (Giants, Diamondbacks, and Cardinals, plus a wrenching loss in '99 to the Braves, e.g., Melvin Mora's last stand). This is a team that peaked with a cameo in the 2000 World Series; its cast of characters included the traumatized Pete Harnisch (five shutout innings, then bang, bang, bang, three guys who never go yard actually go yard); David Segui (good-field, seldom-hit); Turk Wendell (amped middle-inning specialist with a necklace of animal claws, a darting hook that humped over the zone and bit at its corners, and a manic victory dance on the mound); Bernard Gilkey (Triple Crown numbers—.317-30-117—in 1996, nothing after that); John Olerud (fluid, graceful athlete with a clockwork lefty bat, but he slid into and out of town without a trace); schizo switch-hitter Carl Everett (alleged child abuser, bible-toting ex-Yankee with all the tools, who for a week now and then was the best player in the game—off the charts, no one could get him out); pinch-hitter supreme Matt Franco (homer off Pedro Martinez to win 1-0; two-run walk-off single against Mariano Rivera in interleague play); Rico Brogna (ex-Tiger who opened his Met career shooting hits all over the arena with plenty of long balls; took Segui's spot, pissing him off—then his back went out); dignified lynchpin Edgardo Alfonso (arguably one of the all-time best and most clutch Mets, a reliable fielder at all the infield positions, a deadly two-strike hitter who went to the opposite field with the elegance of a swordmaster; drove a scintillating home run off Randy Johnson in the pivotal game of the '99 playoff series with the Diamondbacks); Al Leiter (who had many of his best years with the Mets and pitched them into the '99 post-season with his cutter, tossing a two-hit shutout at the Reds in the one-game playoff; a neocon ideologue who hated Bill Clinton, rumored to be the driving force behind Kazmir's exile—he didn't like the kid's music or refusal to ass-kiss); Joe McEwing (everyone's favorite teammate and the one guy who owned Randy Johnson in his prime, but didn't hit anyone else); Robin Ventura (a grand-slam machine who smacked a game-winning one in the fifteenth inning of the '99 playoffs against the Braves that became a single when Todd Pratt kept him from rounding the bases by lifting him in the air; had a riveting set of jaw affectations while batting): Bobby Jones (who was unhittable with his soft curves and pitching to spots about one out of every six or seven starts, luckily against the Giants to close the 2000 NLDS with a one-hitter); Dave Mlicki (compact curveballer who beat the Yankees with a singular gem in interleague play); Armando Reynoso (armed with a thousand and one pitches); Rick Reed (a replacement player who stuck and evolved into a control-artist mound ace); contortionist Hideo Nomo who seemed to take apart his body and put it back together magnificently in his wind-up (came to the Mets only after hitters stopped being bamboozled); the disappointing Alex Ochoa (it looked bad when, advertised as the five-tool guy secured in the trade-off of Bobby Bonilla, he couldn't track easy fly balls in right; chalk him up with Alex Escobar as superstar frauds); Butch Huskey (who didn't become the next Kevin Mitchell, a bear of a guy who never adjusted to the curve, never); the long-awaited Jay Payton (damaged goods, he was not quite as advertised but did hit for average and in the clutch); and of course Mike Piazza, the epitome of the millennial New York Mets, a huge numbers and power guy around whom nothing ever really jelled; a bogus catcher (he needed a position), he couldn't throw out base runners if his life depended on it. And joining these guys were the local avatars of failed hope, Generation K, all fragile arms: Bill Pulsipher, Paul Wilson (did Sosa's late-inning blast in 1996 kill his whole career?), and Jason Isringhausen.

Many of these players, as noted above, made it to the post-season with the false-spring Mets of 1999–2000: Ventura, McEwing, Leiter, Reed, Piazza, Olerud, Alfonso, joined by Orel Hersisher (eleven years after he knocked the Mets out of the 1988 playoffs and fifteen after Davey Johnson recommended fruitlessly that Frank Cashen draft him on Rule Five out of the Texas League); Todd Zeile (a replacement when Olerud walked, decent production for not great numbers, really a heartbeat from retirement and a cinema career); Derek Bell (hip-hop guy with a crack pipe, came over with Hampton, streaked for a month, slumped for a season); Timo Perez (Dominican who snuck in from

Japan, captivated in the 2000 playoffs, then returned to form); Armando Benitez (arrived along with Roger Cedeño for Todd Hundley in a three-team exchange, this macho, easily frustrated giant with a brittle ego and dominating stuff had the propensity to be overpowering for weeks, even months, and then inexplicably blow just those games that you couldn't afford to lose; he wrecked the 1999 and 2000 post-seasons and guaranteed there wouldn't be one in 2001; always vying with John Franco for who should be the closer—heat versus finesse: a plague on both their houses!); Melvin Mora (the exiled shaman warrior); spaced-out Hawaiian Benny Agbayani (an incredibly popular career minor leaguer who suddenly blossomed under manager Bobby Valentine, beat the Giants with a walk-off homer in the thirteenth inning of the 2000 NLDS, but also handed a ball to a kid in the stands, thinking it was three outs when it was only two, and had to get it back as the base-runners circled).

After 2000, it was back to the cellar, too many flaws, too many bad trades. Those years were characterized by some of baseball history's all-time slouches: Kevin Appier ($42 million for a blimp of a power pitcher turned finesse artist, a dead weight on the franchise); Moe Vaughn (a fraud; for the privilege of kicking the tires on him, Appier was sent to the Angels—but this 1995 AL MVP sure could turn on a pitch now and then and, for a lefty batter, was uniquely contemptuous of left-handed tosses); Roberto Alomar (the ultimate disappointment; somehow the Mets turned the best second baseman in the game and a guy on the brink of the Hall of Fame into a dull, whining bum); Pedro Astacio (great curve for a while, at least for an arm barely still attached to a body); Kaz Matsui (proof that Japanese baseball doesn't always match American, could hit home runs in his first at-bats each season and then whiff and wave thereafter at the plate and in the field); and Rey Ordoñez (hard to believe that Met fans tried to compare this over-swinging, hot-dogging brat to Derek Jeter because they came up at the same time; Ordoñez missed most of 2000 with an injury—costing Melvin Mora—but returned for two more ghastly years).

To this group, add an assorted bunch of unmatching pieces: Marco Scutaro (a hustling overachiever who delivered a surprising number of clutch hits and then went on to bigger things with the A's); Dicky Gonzalez (a nice run of quality starts in 2001 on an emergency recall from nowhere); Mike Stanton (really a Yankee-Brave: tended to walk the lead-off guy and let the inherited runner score); Tsuyoshi Shinjo (a Japanese pretty boy with one skill, he could turn on an occasional heater with remarkable adroitness); Tony Clark (very far down on his career, but looked for the fast ball and sometimes nailed it); Rey Sanchez (another supposed class player who turned classless and whose skills tanked with the Mets); Gary Matthews, Jr. (tools and flash, but it took him years to escape his father's shadow); Roger Cedeño (the second time around, an even more fragile swing and less sure in the outfield); Jaime Cerda (wildly inconsistent lefty); Brian Daubach (back from the grave of farm systems past, a tad psycho); Doug Mientkiewicz (as one fan said, "Polish for automatic out," a guy the Mets should have avoided like the plague when he made an issue of owning the ball from the last out of the Red Sox's 2004 Series win); Kaz Ishii (either unhittable or couldn't get anyone out); Jae Seo (signed as a kid out of Korea, came back from arm surgery and managed to turn into a precise and gritty craftsman); Pat Strange (jumped into his pitches, gave up eleven straight hits one night, named his son after tragic Mets farmhand Brian Coles who turned over his SUV leaving Spring Training in 2000*); Tyler Yates (one of those guys whom every team thinks has promise for a few months); John Thompson (this white-trash malcontent the sole value for Jay Payton?); Kris Benson (never a number-one starter as posited; finally his stripper wife stirred up so much unwelcome press that his undependability became a luxury).

---

*Probably nothing set the Mets back more in this period than the death of this promising and—by the way—compassionate centerfielder, a Kirby Puckett clone whom scouts rated a better prospect than Yankee Alfonso Soriano.

The Mets of this period did provide one of the great moments in baseball history when Korean relief pitcher Dae-Sung Koo, after not even standing inside the batter's box for his first Major League at-bat a week or so earlier, because of seeming terror, took his turn lefty against Randy Johnson, a career intimidator of the best left-handed hitters in the game, an at-bat that Tim McCarver promptly dubbed "the greatest mismatch in history." Then Koo whacked a pitch to the wall and ended up on second, stole third, and raced home with the daring of a burglar (was out but called safe). Met fans later recommended that the Red Sox pick him up to relieve and DH against The Big Unit.

That 2001–2005 team was the mulch of the phoenix 2006 squad that tied the Yankees for the best record in baseball. Minus its central figure, Mike Piazza—a crucial subtraction, both for credibility and a fresh look on reality*—the team that broke Atlanta's stranglehold on the Division had important carryovers: Tom Glavine (taking this fading ace off the hands of the Braves was hardly baggage the Mets needed, but he turned out to have a surprising number of tricks left); Steve Trachsel (an intelligent and erratic right-hander from Cubbietown who, though limited, at least won more often than he lost); Aaron Heilman (when the Mets tried to make him throw overhand, he was a 6.75 ERA guy, but after minor-league coach Al Jackson convinced the parent club to let him go back to his old Notre Dame motion, he became an effective hurler again); Cliff Floyd (smashed the bones in his arm while an Expo in a collision with Todd Hundley at first base, came back all the way to be a dangerous power hitter and intrepid outfielder); Roberto Hernandez (far past his prime but still bringing it, more or less); and of course the two who turned the carousel around, José Reyes (five tools, over-the-top speed, contagious Indian smile: once he got the kinks out of his wheels, a player for the ages) and

---

*He was a hard guy to see past, sucking all the energy without converting that charisma into championship-level leadership

David Wright (a Scott Rolen/Mike Schmidt type, probably even higher upside—but this son of a Norfolk policeman tanked big-time against the Cardinals in the playoffs the Cardinals in the playoffs and in general has shown a lack of power and strange cluelessness at the plate since overachieving in the 2006 All-Star Weekend "home run derby." (There seems a rule of thumb for these tournaments: if you weren't a prodigious home-run hitter like Ryan Howard before, then swatting a surreal cannonade of dingers during the contest, like Bobby Abreu, is going to have a persistent adverse effect afterward.)

Omar Minaya became the first Met GM in history to outbid other mega-teams for top free agents: Pedro Martinez (a real number-one starter with drop-dead changes of speeds); Carlos Delgado (a prime-time Puerto Rican slugger who, while a Blue Jay, ducked the National Anthem in protest over the Marines' shelling of Vieques Island), Chad Bradford (the ultimate middle reliever), and Billy Wagner (the ultimate hundred-mph closer, unfortunately sporting a bum finger). Minaya traded for Dodger middle-inning virtuoso Duaner Sanchez (using the lure of a starter, Jae Seo), out-of-favor but high-potential Oriole prospect John Maine (as garnish with Jorge Julio for Kris Benson), and Paul Lo Duca (prospects), the latter rather than signing a pricey free-agent catcher he didn't like as much. Add Endy Chavez, the returning Pedro Feliciano (a master as a spot lefty out of the pen), the unexpectedly rejuvenated John Valentin at second base, the ageless Cuban master El Duque (still pulling the most exotic fluttering trinkets out of his medicine bundle), Shawn Green (slowed to a crawl from his salad days, but still some pop), and Guillermo Mota (a one-time Met minor-league infielder who learned how to aim his darts from the mound; infamous for a beanball incident with Mike Piazza).

So that's the lineage, the Mets' quilt. I have not named all 799 players who wore the uniform through 2006, but my retrospective speaks for them. I don't root for an All-Star team gathered in the name of the Mets. I root for a combination of quirky players and events, some good, some bad, some inexplicable, that make up a team over time. Mostly new, often very young Met fans who bleat online in chatrooms about "make this deal, make that deal" seem hopelessly provincial in this regard. They have no sense of tradition or history. They simply want to dump all the best Triple-A prospects—Lastings Milledge, Mike Pelfry, Philip Humber—plus Aaron Heilman and either Carlos Gomez or Fernando Martinez to get a recognizable name on the roster; they propose Dontrelle Willis, Barry Zito, Vernon Wells, whatever the cost; they want to skim off the system for Danny Haren or Carlos Zambrano or anyone half-decent they've heard of. They don't seem to remember that everyone was once unknown and, with their attitude, there would have been no Tom Seaver and Jerry Koosman, no Cleon Jones and Tug McGraw, no Miracle Mets. Instead they would have gotten Chris Short, Johnny Callison, and Woody Fryman for them. They would have dealt off Dwight Gooden and Darryl Strawberry and thrown in Lenny Dykstra for Mark Gubicza. There would have been no ground ball by Mookie Wilson through Bill Buckner's legs. Mookie would have been on the Padres by then; the Mets would have gotten Eric Show and Kurt Bevacqua.

A squad of the best players procurable from other teams would not be interesting at all, even if it won the World Series in Mets' linen; it would have little resonance or meaning. The unique amalgam of the Mets is what makes them real, a river of totems and glyphs flowing seamlessly from era to era, all the way back to their expansion roster.

I was a faithful, even fundamentalist, baseball fan as a child and teenager: I ignored all the other sports. From age seven when I began to collect cards and swing a black Joe DiMaggio bat, I took up the artifacts of the sport as more of a calling than a game. The word "baseball" never meant to me "a game of bases and a ball"; it was more like two beats of a drum summoning a supernatural jurisdiction and, if I ever thought about the word, it hyphenated in my mind as something beyond ordinary categories: "baseb-all," a realm of mythology and fairy tales. I now understand that when my mother would say derisively, "He loves baseball," she was imagining a game whereas I was inside numerology and Dreamtime. The other sports *were* mere games; unlike baseball, they were secular and expendable. For that reason I saw no rationale in football and basketball, the jock pursuits of my era.

My early adolescent enjoyment of a three-dimensional board with tin hockey players and a marble puck led me to become a *nouveau* Ranger fan near the end of high school. There was no hockey on television in those days; radio itself had just begun. So when I went to my first game at Madison Square Garden, I was astonished that the goal was so small. It was out of scale with the giant net on the cardboard ice as well as with soccer goals in Central Park. I followed the New York Rangers of Andy Bathgate, Rod Gilbert, Vic Hadfield, and Jean Ratelle from Massachusetts, Michigan, and Maine. At some point around 1973, I don't remember when or why, I lost interest.

I find a note in an old book that captures virtually the last moment when I rooted for the Rangers, going out of my way to attend a game against the Kings in Los Angeles in early 1972 while on a West Coast reading tour:

> We drive to within a block of the hockey rink, run across the street, the big round building lit and spinning the people in like a cotton-candy machine. We buy our tickets and find our way to our seats *at the exact moment the lights go out* and the Rangers stand in blue a center ice; the National Anthem is played.
>
> Another city. The same imago ten years ago, like a coin that is struck to commemorate this occasion each time it happens, and is cast in a hologram flash of Hermes and the Rosicrucian brothers; the fans do not know, because the players are dressed in costumes most likely to conceal their occult significance.
>
> In New York the last time, with my brother and stepfather. The same players even: Gilbert, Ratelle. Their faces the faces of the old ones. To come to a holy center here at a critical moment of my life and be purged like rain. They are here also, in their league race. For

both of us, silent and not able to communicate to each other thank god (for statues do not talk), in the absolute astrology of our being, determining each other, it connects to memories while yet a new thing. Chills down my spine, I see an ancient and decorated totem in its perfect décor, standing before me, the ancestral order. Its blue and white are the blue and white of clouds and oceans, as the totem of the Earth hangs in a kodachrome shrine. I have come of my own free will, here in L.A., to one of those moments that is timeless and stands forever in the center of my life. I have allowed sports to do this. An assurance that I will never know or think I know. A glimpse of the eternity we are in. Then the game. . . .

I picked up the New York Jets in 1967 while a graduate student in Ann Arbor, as they were the only New York team regularly (via the separate AFL network) on TV there. Joe Namath, Matt Snell, Emerson Boozer, Don Maynard, Jim Turner, Bake Turner, and George Sauer were a captivating bunch to me. I grew to love these guys, beautiful underdogs, shaggy anti-heroes. They commuted my long anathema to a scrimmage associated with jerks in my childhood and frat dandies in college.

The opportunity to root for a renegade league also won me over. The Jets' "impossible" Superbowl win in 1969, the year in which the Mets would later make their miracle run, was perhaps—given its context of anti-league versus corporate superstructure—the greatest game of my career as a fan. Nineteen-point underdogs, the outsiders won handily.

In 1984 my son and I started a satellite-baseball club in our garage in Berkeley, California. Numerous fans, mostly of the Mets, chipped in to pay for the dish. Folks gathered nightly to watch the games and root for teams and players. When our membership disbanded for the winter, Robin and I would go out to the garage and search the heavens for raw feeds of games and other interesting events. That is where I found the New Jersey Nets, formerly the New York Nets, formerly the

New Jersey Americans (almost the New Jersey Freighters, as the Mets were almost the New York Burros). The obvious sister entity to the Mets and Jets, as banal as the logic of that rhyme may be (spread over only five letters of the alphabet from "j" to "n," to boot), the Nets were usually on some transponder, and they gave us a game-by-game plot to follow.

While all the rhyming New York teams were underdogs with hexes, the Nets had a particular cross to bear, as the Knicks imposed a harsh territorial tax that forced them to get rid of their superstar, Julius Erving, upon entering the NBA from the ABA in 1976. Champions of a dying league, they never got to play for its honor and the crown of the rival universe with a full roster, as the Jets did.

Buck Williams gave Robin and me a focal point. A beleaguered, tireless power forward, Williams was unrelenting in his rebounding, flawed in his shot, surrounded by a charming complement of Otis Birdsong, Darwin Cook, Michael Ray Richardson, Albert King, Darryl Dawkins, *et al.* Not good enough to win championships, they were still a likeable team.

In an off-the-cuff letter to the front office in 1985, I explained why they should not trade our favorite player, and it elicited—to my astonishment—a phone call from not even the publicity department (which would have been remarkable enough) but the General Manager, Harry Weltman. Intrigued by the idea of a fan in Berkeley, he began, if not quite a friendship, then an exchange of good will. In subsequent seasons he took my son and me to games in Oakland and Sacramento, and a couple of years after that we hired his daughter Amanda out of college to work for a few months in our publishing company.

While she was on our staff, Harry tried to get the team's ownership to back us in a funky Nets book, the journeyings of a vagabond franchise. I imagined valorizing who the Nets were instead of some fraudulent glory they never had (except perhaps winning that last ABA crown behind Dr. J). Harry loved the concept and I found a writer in Harlem, but the team had difficult owners, the notorious "Secaucus

Seven." The GM warned that they never agreed on anything. They didn't on this.

Why do I root for the Ottawa Senators enough to know the names of most of their players—Daniel Alfredsson, Jason Spezza, Dany Heatley, Patrick Eaves, Ray Emery, Andrej Meszaros, et al.—and to purchase the Center Ice package from DirecTV for one disappointing season in 2005–2006? I guess it is because, first of all, I am not attracted to any of the New York franchises. I don't like Madison Square Garden and its corporate Knicks and Rangers any more than I can tolerate the Yankees now, and I have no connection to the late-forming Islanders and Colorado-transplant Devils. For a while I rooted lightly for the World Hockey Association franchises that came into the NHL in 1979 when the WHA folded: the Quebec Nordiques, Edmonton Oilers, Winnipeg Jets, and Hartford Whalers. I liked the grass-roots revolt that took place when the artistocratic Montreal Canadians tried to keep them out of the league on principle—the fastest-acting embargo in history. The fans in Quebec, Winnipeg, and Edmonton stopped drinking Molson beer and ale (Molson Breweries owned the Canadians). That boycott required but a day to get the Canadians' vote changed. The Molson marketing people said, "What! We're telling our customers in three major cities that they can't have hockey anymore?" Someone at Molson spoke to the Montreal GM, and they called another expansion meeting. It was a temporary victory, however. The Stanley Cups won by the Quebec and Hartford franchises ended up in Colorado and North Carolina, respectively, and the Winnipeg Jets became the Phoenix Coyotes. —

When the NHL expanded again in 1992, I transferred my vague loyalties north because (secondly) Ottawa has enchanted me, though I have never been there, with people skating to work on canals and its citation in the song "Northern Boy" from Randy Newman's *Faust*. I like the word itself: "Ottawa," pure Algonquian from "otaawaa." I like the names Alexandre Daigle and Alexei Yashin, disappointing Russians whom the Senators drafted with their high picks from finishing last. I like the fact that they are *not* the San Jose Sharks, the local expansion team where I live; they are the anti-Sharks, denizens of "O Canada" and the cold north. I am also remotely honoring my old friends from Ann Arbor, Andy Lugg and Lynne Cohen, who moved to Ottawa after graduate school and lived there for decades.

Thirdly, there is a symmetry with the Mets: The expansion 1992 Senators were even worse at the beginning than Casey's 1962 "Amazin's," the only major-sports franchise to surpass their futility, winning ten and losing seventy-one, while finishing last their first four years. The Senators, like the Metropolitans, were the revival of vintage nineteenth-century teams. The Ottawa Senators won ten Stanley Cups between 1893 and 1934. The New York Metropolitans played originally in Brooklyn and Hoboken, New Jersey, and then the Polo Grounds from 1880 to 1887, winning the American Association 1884 pennant and losing to the Providence Grays of the National League in the World Series. The first Mets were the forerunners, more or less, of the Brooklyn Dodgers, while their rivals, the New York Gothams, were the forerunners of the New York Giants—and all these teams were collectively forerunners of the 1960 New York Met(ropolitan)s.

(By the way the Senators and Mets also now share Binghamton farm clubs.)

At some point, I recognized these assorted attributes, and they sealed into a bond and I began following the team in the newspapers. Then I began to look for their games on Canadian ANIK satellites.

The creation of the Mets marked a turning point for me. In 1962 I was a backward teenager. It was my last year of high school; I applied to colleges and got into Amherst. Then in the fall, with the games winding down, I left my mother's home for good and headed for Massachusetts.

I watched and listened to the Mets faithfully during 1963 and 1964 summers while a mail clerk at my father's hotel in the Catskills and then a reporter for the *Sullivan County Democrat*. Despite the team's lack of success (or because of it), I followed them all through college and graduate school, abandoning the Yankees.

By 1969, when the Mets unexpectedly came from last place and won their first Pennant and the World Series, I had been equally transformed. I was twenty-four and married to Lindy, my college girlfriend, and we had a newborn son. I had finished graduate work in Ann Arbor and was doing anthropology fieldwork with fishermen in Maine for my PhD. I had long hair and a beard, and my first book, *Solar Journal*, was about to be published by Black Sparrow Press in Los Angeles. Humans had walked on the Moon and people recently gathered in the mud of Bethel for the Woodstock Festival, a symbolic gateway to Aquarius. The Miracle Mets not only matched my own awakening but aligned with a radical and hopeful transition in the world at large.

During the failed pennant runs of 1970 and 1971, I was living in Cape Elizabeth and teaching introductory anthropology at the University of Maine in Portland. The Mets were on an FM station out of New Hampshire, and I sat with them at Crescent Beach much as my brother and I held court with the Yankees while dipping into the waves of Long Beach in our childhood.

In 1973, the Mets were back in the World Series, and I was in my second year teaching interdisciplinary subjects at Goddard College, a hippie school without courses or departments. Our daughter Miranda was about to be born. From the mountains of Vermont, I listened to radio broadcasts of Met games at night. It was the florescence of the counterculture amid mounting Watergate drama. Once again, the Mets were in harmony with the planets, briefly ascending with the other crescendos.

In 1977 the Mets were well into their decline, having shed both the charm of their early years and the magic of the 1969–1973 teams. The counterculture and the economy were unraveling, Goddard was disintegrating, oil was running out, eco-catastrophe was prophesized and, in abandonment of New Age Vermont, we headed out West in a U-Haul with two little kids and no jobs.

Between Chicago and the Iowa border I lost radio contact with the games as Ed Ott slid into Felix Millan. The Pirate catcher then threw the Mets' second baseman to the ground, ending his career and, during the subsequent brawl, the Mets faded into bluegrass and static. I was headed to Northern California and a new world. The team became results at the end of the local news broadcasts and box scores in morning sports pages.

During the years from 1977 to 1983 I earned a living by writing books on medicine, astronomy, and biology for various publishers, while gradually turning our own publishing company into a business and paying myself a small salary. The 1969 Mets accompanied me into parenthood, authorship, and the so-called real world outside school; the 1984 Mets marked the beginning of my real career and profession at age forty-two.

My son Robin discovered baseball in the late '70s and became a Mets fan in 1980. He was a high-school junior in 1986 when Keith Hernandez, Mookie Wilson, and crew outlasted the Red Sox. We watched the post-season games in our garage on the club dish.

In 1988, two years later, Robin was in college at UC Santa Cruz, and the satellite club had ended (though I had a different dish, bolted onto the publishing warehouse roof beside a new house that we shared with our growing company). Except when Robin was home from college or a former club member dropped by, I was watching games alone for the first time.

I was still following the Mets with rapt attention when a distracted Dwight Gooden issued a fatuous ninth-inning pass to John Shelby and then was inexplicably left in to face Mike Scioscia with Randy Myers warming up. After Scioscia poled one beyond Strawberry's gaze in right, Kirk Gibson supplied the death blow, courtesy of Roger McDowell, in the top of the twelfth.

I never really came back from that purgatory, especially once Terry Leach was booted out for a sack of oats the next spring. I watched more and more idly as the Mets declined. I stopped tracking the farm system. I was now in a mysterious valley, past my own childhood, past my children's childhood, past the prime of my own life, and I didn't know quite who I was anymore. I didn't know who the Mets were either, or what the games really meant to me.

By 1992 the team was mired back in mediocrity, we had no kids at home, and my wife and I hit our first major crisis after twenty-seven years together, so we lived apart for a year. I barely followed baseball. Things were too serious then. I sat a few nights a week at a Korean Zen center. I did ten sessions of Rebirthing, a form of guided breathwork and visualization. I expanded my martial-arts practice from t'ai chi to hsing-i and cheng hsin, apprenticing with a local master, Peter Ralston, and his disciple Ron Sieh. I trained in various manual medicines—Breema, Feldenkrais Technique, Polarity, and craniosacral therapy. For the first time in my life, writing wasn't the cutting edge. I was learning new techniques and practicing them. 1986 seemed a lifetime away.

After Lindy and I got back together in the spring of 1993, I wasn't that interested in the game or the team. I did watch games on the dish, but rarely live: I would set a timer and tape. I developed a fast-forwarding technique, eliminating space between pitches, ads between innings, and even whole at-bats of the opponent unless the Mets' pitcher interested me. If a game look unwinnable, I turned it off. I made no particular effort to orient my time around the Mets. The team had shifted from a frequency of my daily attention to a peripheral zone. The truth is: my new rituals were more necessary and compelling. Plus, Lindy and I were making our life together anew without kids.

In June of 1993 in celebration of our fresh beginning, we took our first trip ever out of North America, going to Holland, Germany, the Czech Republic, and France. When we got back a month later, I read the box scores in *Mets Inside Pitch* and discovered that the boys had lost just about every game while I was gone. This seemed oddly apropos, as if I were no longer keeping them afloat.

We moved into a new "empty nest/no publishing company" house in 1998; our kids were adults, our business had grown to a dozen employees with an office and a warehouse, and we were about to take a second trip abroad. When we got back from England, I saw Mike Piazza in the box scores, so I knew that a king's ransom must have been dispatched to the Marlins. I guessed that Preston Wilson would be gone and I was right.

Even before interminable prospects-for-star transactions, the Mets were becoming unrecognizable because baseball itself had changed—it had bred wealthy teams and also-rans and, while the Yankees soared to the top on their money machine, year after year, the Mets made half-hearted and futile attempts to join the ranks of the contenders. For the Yankees, Red Sox, and Braves, it was no longer a matter of natural cycles of good years and bad years: not to contend had become unthinkable, so the ownerships drove the salaries up, battling one another to sign players away from the poorer clubs.* The Mets toyed with that strategy, sort of and badly—they became the worst of both worlds: a rich team among bottom-feeders.

Now they are a mega-team too, and so are we, in a sense: our publishing employs twenty-five people and puts out eighty books a year. In 2006 Lindy and I went to our fortieth college reunions at Amherst and Smith and celebrated our fortieth anniversary. For the Mets, formed when I was a high-school senior, it was their forty-fifth year in the National League. Along parallel paths we had both come of age.

In truth, the Mets were probably never all that admirable an organization. Their mythology and charm have run on a different track from their corporate mentality. The early teams were the purest, the ones that made losing a redemptive proposition. But even these were the accidental result of the well-intentioned but clueless ownership of Joan Payson under the advice of Yankee emeritus GM George Weiss (who probably should have stayed in retirement because expansion in 1962

---

*I used to joke that, for all this extra money, the teams still finished at a collective .500.

wasn't like requisitioning Ralph Terry and Roger Maris). Weiss ended up pandering to nonexistent fans whom he imagined would come to the ballpark if they had lots of name players to cheer for, especially old Dodgers and Giants. The Colt .45s actually tried to build a team from the ground up. The Mets of those years were a combination of baseball and fairy tale, and the fairy tale was invented by their fans to transform the travesties of management into a lovable circus and work of early performance art.

Weiss lasted till 1966, and Johnny Murphy oversaw the Miracle Mets. By the time that the Mets won their first Series in 1969, M. Donald Grant, Ms. Payson's henchman, was effectively in charge. A closet fascist with the *modus operandi* of a plantation boss, he required subservience and made sure that players who ruffled his many feathers were railroaded out of town. He also believed in the meekest of checkbooks even as baseball was entering the free-agent era. In '69 he equated the championship group absurdly with our "boys in Vietnam" and at the victory celebration at Gracie Mansion referred to the assembled team members beside him as "real red-blooded American heroes, everything those scruffy hippies aren't." Guess what! The Mets of Ron Swoboda, Tom Seaver, and Wayne Garrett *were* the hippies of baseball. Tug McGraw complained, "We're being used."

Bob Scheffing and Joe McDonald soon wrecked the team, overplaying their hand with the Amos Otis and Nolan Ryan deals. They were lucky to salvage a pennant in '73.

My favorite Met story (at least on a level of black humor) is the report of then-farm-director Whitey Herzog (later a New York nemesis as manager of the Cardinals) hunting in the woods—off-season, 1971—and getting a message from Joe McDonald at his lodge. I can more or less reconstruct Whitey's comments from memory: "He wanted Lee Stanton's phone number. I asked why, and they said, 'We traded him.' I asked, 'For who?' They said, 'Jim Fregosi.' I said, 'I wouldn't trade Lee Stanton for Jim Fregosi.' When I got back I found out we had thrown in Nolan Ryan and two other guys as well."

When original owner Joan Payson died in 1975, her daughter, Lorinda de Roulet, became president, but M. Donald was still calling the shots. His regime would destroy the remains of the Miracle Mets, in part from its amateur, impulsive decisions; in part by indulgent vendettas with players, and of course by their refusal to recognize the rising labor movement within baseball. They triggered the long dark age that was more medieval than the one from 1962 to 1969. From pretty much 1975 until 1984, the Mets were a bland and troubled franchise, always in crisis, often in open turmoil. The M. Donald Grant-Joe McDonald regime was not only cheap but petty—witness the public banishments of Tom Seaver, Dave Kingman, Tug McGraw, and Rusty Staub. There were no doubt other indecencies behind closed doors.

When the team was sold to Fred Wilpon and Nelson Doubleday in 1980, I expected a lot from the new bosses, as most fans did. Wilpon was a business friend of my father's, while Doubleday was my publisher, having backed my book *Planet Medicine* in 1977 and then buying the first baseball anthology from our press, *Baseball I Gave You All the Best Years of My Life,* releasing it in a new version soon after the sale of the Mets. Wilpon-Doubleday quickly hired GM Frank Cashen, who had an illustrious Baltimore Oriole resumé. Cashen suffered from major blind spots and his own regal prejudices, making countless flubs, but he hired fine scouts and rebuilt the farm system. He presided over the Gooden-Strawberry-Mookie-Dykstra harvest, along the way dealing for Keith Hernandez, Sid Fernandez, Ron Darling, Gary Carter, Tim Teufel, Ray Knight, and Bobby Ojeda. He brought in Davey Johnson, an old Oriole crony, as his manager.

Then Cashen was just as adroit at dismantling his creation, making indefensible player moves from 1989 to 1998 that led to the third long Mets decline, before retiring a decade too late in 1991 and leaving his mantle to his aide-de-camp Al Harazin, an unprepared and haughty peacock, a money guy in way over his head. Harazin was followed by the right choice, scholarly Joe McIlvaine who quickly found that baseball had entered an era of full-scale moneyball in which, as a gentleman and classic scout, he had no interest. In 1997 he was succeeded by his assistant, Steve Phillips, a former minor-league washout and smug poseur who got taken by rival GMs, while expostulating as an expert. Grade Phillips by his trades for Moe Vaughn and Roberto Alomar: if it looks too good to be true, it probably is. Chalk up Mora-for-Bordick to him too.

At the same time, Billy Beane was becoming *the* superstar small-market GM, coining "moneyball," dazzling sabermetric and rotisserie fanatics as he reinvented player evaluation for the digital era, and establishing himself as a literary idol (at least in sports terms—and, in significant part, at Phillips' expense). Beane's overall game was so cool that Bostonians would have given him Fenway Park, Tom Brady, and the head of Ted Williams if he had left Oakland for the Red Sox.

Beane lost his favorite dupe (try Terence Long for madman and choke artist Kenny Rodgers) when Phillips was fired during the 2003 season, to be replaced briefly by interim Jim Duquette, another naïve meddler. Duquette somehow got it in his head that the Mets could make a run for the 2004 Division with a couple more pitchers, so he trafficked like a drunk at midnight. In the now-legendary Kazmir-for-Victor Zambrano fiasco, he dealt his blue-chip prospect for a guy who wasn't even that good with a healthy arm, something he no longer had, and then a few more prospects for Kris Benson, a declining ace about to be a free agent. In the former swap, Duquette was overmatched by a Tampa GM who was astonished that anyone would fall for his negotiating ploy as a serious offer: "I asked for Kazmir as a joke, and he said yes." Duquette is now distinguishing himself in Baltimore, while Phillips is professing baseball wisdom weekly as emeritus scholar on ESPN.

Meanwhile, Doubleday and Wilpon never got along, even in the best of times, each meddling in his own way. Both upper class, they came from opposite sides of the track. Doubleday was Protestant old money, Manhattan, the Hamptons; Wilpon was Jewish new money, Brooklyn, Queens. Wilpon was also a high-school teammate of Sandy

Koufax, something that gave him a false sense of omniscience that ruined him as a responsible owner. By contrast, Doubleday was a sporting man in the polo/yachting mold and he refused to be Wilpon's errand boy; he had his own causes, one of which turned out to be Mike Piazza. With the old professor, Frank Cashen, as their GM and referee, Doubleday and Wilpon had one great run from 1984 to 1988, though it netted only the 1986 Championship—and that one barely. After Cashen came junior GMs whom the owners each tried alternately to convince and browbeat. Plus, they both wanted to make the team on the cheap while pretending largesse—and their charade went on crosstown from George Steinbrenner's "Best Team That Money Can Buy."

Wilpon and Doubleday feuded publicly until they broke up in 2002, with the Wilpon family buying the team. Their version of the Mets was lampooned during the next three years in fan chatrooms for its haggling, its bullshit to media, and its skinflint policies, with visitors vilifying Wilpon by his unauthorized name: Freddie Coupon. He had retained the worst of the previous regime without Doubleday's flair for an occasional headliner. After all, Doubleday was generically a publisher, a media man, Wilpon a real-estate broker.

Not that I think Alex Rodriguez is the be-all and end-all—far from it—but after making a demonstrative show of going after him full-bore under the stewardship of Steve Phillips (and the Mets were apparently A-Rod's favorite team and first choice), they supplied no real offer and fed the world a line about wanting a team of twenty-five equals rather than a "one and twenty-four guy." A-Rod was spoiled and asking for the moon (he got it from Texas), but no one believed Phillips' sudden onset of morality was anything but posturing and money.

Elsewhere in this book I am even harder on the Wilpons, possibly unfairly so. My own interactions with Fred are detailed in separate stories, and you will see that he left something to be desired in the realm of creative imagination and basic goodwill. But I wrongly presumed that his son Jeff, heir apparent to the team, a man of my son's generation, was bringing much of the same preening, interfering, and camouflaged miserliness. In fact, I blamed him for the Scott Kazmir trade. I pictured Leiter and Franco intimidating him into making the deal, Duquette playing the fool. Actually I initially used to think, along with most of the angry and disappointed fans, that Rick Peterson, the cocky pitching coach, orchestrated it with the assurance that he could fix Victor Zambrano in fifteen minutes, a statement which led to a whole genre of Internet jokes vis-á-vis other players that he could fix or was trying to fix: "Hey, Pete, you wanna give Trachsel another fifteen minutes." However, I think Peterson probably just gave an honest answer to a loaded question and then was made the fall guy. But I no longer think Jeff Wilpon had his fingerprints all over this trade.

Having watched him in action in the media for the last year, I have reconsidered entirely. I think Jeff is probably the one who broke the team out from the Freddie Coupon MO of his dad. First of all, he apologized for the trade, wished Kazmir the best, and proposed that they could either continue to lament the guy or move on to improve the team. His pet project, the Brooklyn Cyclones in Keyspan Park, is a commitment to community and old-fashioned baseball in Brooklyn, and the Mets' Flushing Stadium on the drawing board is elegantly traditional and explicitly fan-friendly. The Esperanza microbanking program run by the Mets in the Dominican Republic to help the poor in the community, over and above their scouting for talent and developing young players, is a radical extension of a baseball team into an NGO. When the Mets lost their Triple-A affiliation with Norfolk in 2007 after thirty-eight years and were beaten to the desirable location at Scranton by the Yankees, they were stuck ("musical chairs") with the New Orleans Zephyrs, located in Metrarie where the ballpark had been a National Guard and FEMA base during Katrina. This raised concerns of player safety as well as proximity to the parent club, but management chose to look at the bright side, taking the opportunity to become a force in hurricane recovery and kicking off their participation with an immediate $20,000 donation for rebuilding damaged playgrounds. Plus Omar Minaya led an off-season 2006 delegation to Ghana, bearing bats, balls, gloves, and hope, and setting up a long-term connection between the Mets and West African youth. He even invited eager underprivileged Ghanian players back to Shea, boys who had no chance of cracking even minor-league baseball.

Ever since Minaya was brought back from Montreal/Washington at the end of 2004 and put in charge, the litany of dumb, stingy, and outright bizarre moves has been eliminated, and ever since Jeff Wilpon became the *de facto* face of the Mets, the team has developed character and substance, along with a mission of international service.

Though glib and parvenu in his own way, Minaya is probably about as resourceful a general manager as the Wilpons could have come up with—Hispanic, native New York, clever. Would that they had recognized that on his first go-round at Shea before they let him bolt to Montreal, while they held onto Steve Phillips. That vain charlatan continued wreaking his damage (sexual improprieties and crocodile tears on the side*), while Minaya was making the Expos a contender in the Mets' own division, even though starting with a lame-duck fran-

---

*The following contribution to the nj.mets chatroom (in response to Phillips' prediction that the team will finish third in 2007) testifies to the man's legacy: "Thought trading Melvin Mora for Mike Bordick, Izzy for Billy Taylor, Jason Bay for Steve Reed, and an eighteen-year-old David Wright for a washed-up José Cruz, Jr. were good ideas too (luckily Blue Jays GM J.P. Ricciardi turned down the Cruz deal; that was near the end of July 2002—check the papers from then). Also, let's review December 11, 2001. That was the fateful day the idiot failed to convince the Indians to take a Class A shortstop name of José Reyes as part of his already-brilliant transaction packaging Matt Lawton, Jerrod Riggan, and Billy Traber for Roberto Alomar. Cleveland insisted on Alex Escobar instead, so Phillips begrudgingly relented. Consider the source: if Phillips was a genius, why is he still looking for a job in baseball? We were unbelievably lucky; the guy could have liquidated the Mets. Also the skank secretary he was doing in Florida was ugly."

chise, a twenty-five percent handicap in the standings, and one-fifth the budget.

Like Beane, Minaya recognizes that baseball has changed inalterably, and he has proceeded along daring parameters. Keeping a youthful nucleus, he has recruited and traded for an all-star team of Latin Americans—notably Cuban, Puerto Rican, Venezuelan, and Dominican—because that's where the future of baseball lies, in the slums and sharecropping outback to our south where millions of legal and illegal aliens await their tryouts, their red carpets to Norte America.

Whereas I wouldn't have signed an aging Pedro Martinez or sent callow Mike Jacobs to Miami for Carlos Delgado, Minaya developed his plan and made it work. At least he didn't trade Lastings Milledge plus his two best pitching prospects to lying-there-in-the-weeds-pretending-not-to-be-interested Mr. Beane for Barry Zito in his walk year, as his forerunners would have by now, kidding themselves that they had stolen the bacon. At least he didn't sign Zito at $126 million and seven years. At least he didn't fall for Beane's likely suggestion of Milledge, Mike Pelfry, and Heilman for Dan Haren. He is going with Pelfrey, Phillip Humber, Jorge Sosa, Jason Vargas, Chan Ho Park, and maybe Aaron Sele, or Heilman liberated from the pen.

A member of the original class of Met fans, I will be a Met fan for the duration and, although I don't follow the Mets as closely anymore, they are a track that has been playing my whole adult life, a soap opera I watch from within my own. Disapprove of them though I have in recent years, I would miss them if they weren't there. You want to know the day's score before nodding off to sleep.

I am actually now more fond of the Nets, especially since the arrival of Jason Kidd. Not only is he a charismatic player who teaches the "team" concept and makes everyone around him better by giving life lessons within the game, he is a wry philosopher and a local Berkeley-Oakland schoolyard legend, so he brings my two polities together.

Through the first six years of the 2000s, the Nets were more appealing than the Mets—aesthetically, philosophically, and in terms of success, making the NBA finals twice and winning four Atlantic Divisions. Headed for *risorgimento* Brooklyn as a replacement for the Dodgers half a century later, they have had interesting players (Kenyon Martin, Richard Jefferson, Vince Carter) and a complex if controversial storyline (i.e., Kidd's single-handed transfiguration of a bad franchise and his domestic-violence problems and the razing of artists' lofts and low-income housing to make way for the team's poststructuralist Frank Gehry arena under eminent domain).

Age has something to do with my drift—I've seen so many cycles that I no longer have "beginner's mind" for baseball games, while hoops are relatively fresh for me. In addition, the transformation of baseball into a rigged affair in which teams with wildly disparate payrolls compete as if on a level field has contributed to a feeling that Pennants and World Series don't mean as much anymore; the contests are waged in inflated currency. While they can't be out-and-out bought, you do have to pay a certain amount of ransom to the Scott Borases of the world even to compete, so many teams are just sparring partners. Not so in the NBA.

Until Minaya remade them, the Mets of the post Gooden/Strawberry/ Carter/Hernandez era were exemplars of "The Worst Team Money Can Buy" philosophy. Not only were their rosters mostly empty of their own farm-system players—pure Mets—they were marked by a mishmash of unappealing imported "talent." Most of the unalloyed Mets—those who came up with the team or arrived early in their careers—were playing elsewhere. With those who should have been representing the franchise scattered all over the map, the Mets on the field were imposters.

If I liked a player, I could count on him soon being gone. Not all of my favorites were stars or even good, and not all of the trades dispatching them were ill-advised, but many of them were—usually the Mets got nothing back or a player they could have had anyway as a free agent if they had waited ten minutes. What these transactions did was not so much sabotage pennants as destroy any real semblance or esprit of a team. The Mets on the field were identity-less mercenaries, whereas the guys I liked had collective soul and an ineffable quality that made them, in my mind, vintage Mets.

Players with whom I resonated emotionally who were then traded or released included: Melvin Mora, Jay Payton, Jason Isringhausen, Preston Wilson, Jae Seo, Paul Byrd, Pat Mahomes, Brady Clark, Gary Matthews, Jr., Mike Remlinger, Grant Roberts, Robert Person, Luis Lopez, Jason Jacome, Dicky Gonzalez, Octavio Dotel, Jason Phillips, Desi Relaford, Mike Jacobs, and prospects Nelson Figueroa, Scott Kazmir, A. J. Burnett, and Terence Long.

What did I like about these guys?

Paul Byrd flat-out looked effective; he had an unorthodox sidearm delivery and punctuated rhythm that were aesthetically pleasing and hard for hitters to pick up; it was great that the Mets got him as an after-thought from the Indians—really the third player in the deal for Jeromy Burnitz (along with the targeted Dave Mlicki and Jerry Di Poto). Byrd, who turned out to be the best of the three, was swapped a year later for a decent fly-by-night reliever (Greg McMichael), while it looks as though the one no longer "in hand" will win a hundred games as a starter.

Robert Person was a converted infielder whom the Mets bartered from the Marlins; he pitched a bit in 1995 and all of 1996 and, at moments, looked like a prime-time starter (5-5, 4.07 all told). A bit of Doc Gooden in his manner and approach, he threw hard and for stretches was overpowering. He could still hit as well, though all his Met "homers" hooked foul. The Mets did get John Olerud for him, but Person went on to have his best years for the Phillies.

The Mets waited years for Jay Payton to get over his arm injuries and make the parent club. Yet then, when we finally had the pleasure of his fierce at-bats, line drives into the gaps, and speed on the bases as well as his intense, competitive mien, he was dealt off for a loudmouth, fake-macho pitcher who went 2-7 and whom the Mets didn't even ten-der at the end of the season.

Grant Roberts struggled with his stuff, control, and assorted per-sonal baggage, but I was rooting for this hippie playboy with his bong. He was dumped in 2004, a steroid felon. He never made it anywhere else, so I suppose it wasn't a great loss, nor was Jason Phillips, though his defensive prowess as a catcher and unexpected batting surge in 2003—.298-11-58—made him a rising star, while his goggles and irre-pressible personality anointed him as a free spirit and character. Traded for the disastrous Mr. Ishii, he lost his way after leaving town.

In 1999 Pat Mahomes came from an anonymous five years with the Twins and Red Sox to go 8-0, bat .313, and singlehandedly bail Al Leiter out in Game Six of the NLCS with the Braves. After the Mets' ace was stunned for a quick five-spot, Mahomes kept the Mets in the season with four-plus scoreless innings—allowing the team to come all the way back and take the lead—a game that Mel Mora almost won, that Benitez blew, that Kenny Rogers finally gave away for good. Mahomes was 13-3 in two seasons with the Mets, then bye-bye.

Jason Jacome looked viable in 1994 (4-3, 2.67) and, as one fan put it, "for a lousy team, they sure gave up on him quickly," but then he never pitched much anywhere else. It was hard not to like the pronun-ciation of his name, "Hakomi," and the fact that he taught grade school during the baseball strike—the kids dug having a Major Leaguer auto-graphing their homework.

Denny Gonzalez looked like a stalwart, pitching with guts and craft when he came up to fill a hole in the rotation; then it seemed that the Mets just gave him away (for the mercurial Scott Strickland who always got worse results than his pitches portended)—neither player had much of a career thereafter.

Yes, Octavio Dotel was used as the bait to get Mike Hampton, but Hampton was a certain free-agent-to-be, the kind of yokel who always bolts the Big Apple, and Dotel had the potential to be a junior Pedro Martinez. He looked so damn good, compact and explosive, slinging darts. Hampton was an ox; he brought the Mets the 2000 Pennant, then walked for the dough and school system in Denver. Until he hurt his arm, Dotel was an unhittable banshee out of the Astro pen.

Signed as a teenager from Kwanju, South Korea, Jae Weong Seo made it back from arm surgery. After losing his 90-95 heat, he pitched tough games. He carved the plate with immaculate craft and willed the ball to spots, sometimes with a leap and *kiai*. I loved to watch his starts because you could *see* his mind working and his pride flaring up, his desire to prove he could do it without the fastball, without anyone in management believing in him. He was always devalued, so he had to pitch for honor. The Mets kept dissing him, punishing him, then needing him again—and he delivered, most of the time. Send Seo to Norfolk; fly him back for an emergency start, and he throws a shutout—in fact strings together a whole line of shutout innings, Korean flags waving in the left-field stands—then dump him back in Virginia. Some guys just get treated worse: Terry Leach, Jae Seo, Aaron Heilman.

As one fan wrote in the ultimatemets.com website, "Only the Mets can trade away a pitcher who was 18-3 in the past two years and only the Mets can place a pitcher in the bullpen when the Mets were 15-3 in games he started. Aaron Heilman, meet Terry Leach."*

I felt that the moment Seo gave up even one run he was gone. He pitched as though that's what he thought too. They got a great reliever for him (Duaner Sanchez), but I was still sad to see him go; he was a Met to the core.

Long, Burnett, Figueroa, and Kazmir were farmhands, touted for

---

*Current (March 2007) gossip has it that Willie Randolph, having made a stand that Heilman is not a starter, is going to assert his authority by pigheadedly sticking to it. Despite enough relief pitchers to stock three or four rosters (and far too many to keep on the parent club) and a fragile rotation led by two pitchers over forty, Randolph is going to hold to his guns. This is a case where you need an owner with both diplomatic charm and moral resolve, even a Steinbrenner type, to sit down with Willie and discuss the matter rationally.

one reason or another, who never got to play for real on the parent club. Burnett didn't have numbers but threw with movement at over 100 miles an hour; Kazmir was signed by the Mets to a huge bonus as the top high-school pitcher in the country and was touted as a hard-dealing lefty for the ages. Figueroa was a Brandeis hurler with more pitches than the legendary Eddie Lopat and apparently the ability to change speeds and throw them all for strikes. Long was a power prospect with speed. The careers of all four speak for themselves—none of them unabashedly great—but they would have made interesting Mets, and together they were components of a team that never happened, a team that would have competed and played with heart.

Remlinger, Long, Lopez, Mora, Gonzalez, Matthews, Kazmir, Phillips, Payton, Figueroa, and Isringhausen went in horrid trades that brought little or nothing back. Relaford, Wilson, Seo, Byrd, Person, Burnett, and Dotel at least returned decent players, though in the case of Person it was a guy passing time (Olerud) and in the case of Dotel a carpetbagger.

Preston Wilson, the stepson of a Met legend, was packaged with others for a guy who was about to become a free agent anyway (Piazza). Burnett and Jacobs likewise went to the astute Marlins for Al Leiter and Carlos Delgado, players that the Mets should have been able to wheedle for less. Jacobs has a pure left-handed bat, a decent glove, and is eight years younger and about $16 million cheaper than Delgado. In 2005 he opened his Met career 7-13 with four homers, and in one hundred at-bats went .310-11-23. He may be one of those timeless hitters, and he was certainly a bargain.

Clark, Jacome, Roberts, and Mahomes are guys the Mets just let walk or waived.

Because of these transactions, there were moments when I quit following the team entirely, sometimes for a day, sometimes for a week—on two occasions longer. After the deadline-beating Payton and Kazmir trades (July 31, 2002 and July 30, 2004, respectively) I stopped watching games for the remainder of the season. I was flirting with apostasy.

Then the 2006 team took me by surprise. When players like Endy Chavez, Aaron Heilman, Duaner Sanchez, Ramon Castro, and John Maine began playing central roles on a team that also had a lineup of young indigenous stars, I reenlisted.

Months before the 2006 season began, Lindy and I agreed that we would take our third, long-postponed trip to Europe in the fall, and we set an itinerary of northern Italy, Slovenia, the Frankfurt Book Fair, and Iceland. We purchased our tickets even as it became clear that the Mets would be in the post-season. To give up a Mets playoff appearance, in part or whole, was a sacrifice, but an essential one. It was a demonstration to myself and my wife that games did not rule my life the way they once did. No radio at this prom . . . though that didn't mean I wouldn't sneak away for playoff scores now and then.

I found myself at the Frankfurt Book Fair as the '06 playoff series against the Dodgers began. Watching the Euro version of CNN was useless, as the ticker gave only three brief sports lines every few minutes. These were rarely updated and seldom American anyway or, if they were, they involved international sports like golf or tennis. Usual items included minutiae of soccer games and soccer gossip, Slovakian wrestling, European horse-racing, basketball in Singapore, etc. I would leave the TV on for a half hour while getting dressed and, amidst discouraging international news, the most I might see was an acknowledgment that the Yankees led the Tigers 1-0 in their series—day-old news.

My laptop having crashed in Slovenia, I was dependent on finding free machines or renting computer time. The combined exhibit of American publishers at Frankfurt provided a bank of computers for fifteen-minute stints (you could come back later, of course, after you gave others *their* fifteen minutes). Upon arriving those first two mornings, I kept an eye out for an open computer, and my first move was to see what the Mets did the previous day.

As soon as I got online, I went right to Yahoo! and held my breath. It was reminiscent of my childhood when the night games ended too late for me to hear the whole thing. Back then I got the final line score from the paper, all at once. By contrast, when you follow a game on radio or television or even pitch by pitch on a computer, you build through a plot to a conclusion. When you see the score first, it is like ice water to the face, and then you work backward to figure out what happened and try to pick up the narrative of the game. That splash is far more pleasurable in case of a win, as you get to ride through the details on the swell of the victory and relish reversals as well as runs scored and squelched opponent rallies, assured that it will come out okay in the end.

Both of our first two days in Frankfurt the Mets beat the Dodgers, not without setbacks in the process, none of which I suffered. I had only a happy storyline in my head and a shot of energy going into the Fair.

The last game took place on the day before we flew out of Frankfurt to Iceland, so we didn't attend the Fair. Instead we went on a Sunday walk with a German author in search of a much-praised fountain. After we visited the site and were headed back to the hotel, I told Lindy and our friend to go on ahead; I wanted to detour to an Internet point. After many luckless blocks I came upon a tiny storefront where, for a euro, I got a look at Yahoo! and a brief silent celebration, for the Mets had won the third game, sweeping their series. They would not play again until our last three days in Iceland, so they could be put out of mind.

A rainout delayed the start of the series with the Cardinals—the weather was even worse in Reykjavik, high winds and gusting rain. Earlier in the week, I had come up with a plan to follow the games in real time on Yahoo!'s MLB scoreboard. I would rent the hotel laptop computer for the last hour of the day for which it was available (22:00–23:00) and thus be able to keep it overnight without more than a one-hour charge. Setting it on the coffee table in our room October 12, I went to sleep at a normal hour with a suggestion to myself that I wake up around 1:00. I awoke a little bit after that, and the Mets were leading 2-0 on a Beltran homer. The game finished with the same score.

I was able to follow the flow without hovering pitch by pitch. I would watch a few at-bats, then write some emails, then go to the Mets' nj.com chatroom to read the comments, then write some more emails, then check out the game, etc. Occasionally I would linger through a developing situation, hitting the "Refresh" button when I got impatient.

Alternating activities was soothing; the game was kept in balance, and it ended happily and not too late.

On our last evening I rented the computer as soon as we got back to the hotel from a local thermal bath. With a late adventure and then packing up, I was awake when the play-by-play came alive at midnight, so tracked it from the beginning.

The Mets, who had won four straight post-season games to this point, jumped to a 3-0 lead on a first-inning home run by Carlos Delgado. The way information comes across the Internet on a site like Yahoo! is reminiscent of board games of my youth. There is no actual baseball landscape. In the 1950s facsimiles, you draw a card or spin a spinner, and you see the results of the play on a card or list—fly ball to right, double, strike three, etc. Yahoo! also replicates an old Yankees-Cubs World Series crossing the Midwest on telegraph keys. When the Mets had two men on base in the first and Delgado was at the plate, I thought (of course) "three-run homer." There was no action to watch or situation to develop, just a count logged in cartoon graphics, pitch by pitch, until a result. So when the screen said, "home run," I jumped and exclaimed out loud, as though I had landed the spinner on the fat 1 or drawn an ace.

The Cardinals came back. The Mets added a run for 4-2, were tied at four, then went up 6-4. Around 3:00 in the morning, tired, frustrated, and restless, I was stuck before the computer, going compulsively back and forth between Yahoo! and nj.com.

An outcome tended to show up first in the chatroom, although you didn't necessarily know what it was. "Sh*t!" was generally not good, nor were lines like "Mota, you a**hole!" (people wrote with asterisks to avoid site censors). "Yessss!" was great and would send me back to Yahoo! where the result would register in a few seconds, either a run by the Mets or, more often, getting the third out of a difficult Cardinals inning, which was pretty much every inning.

I thought the Mets were going to hold on. But with Mota on the mound in the seventh and Scott Spiezio at bat for St. Louis, Yahoo! froze for an unusually long time, a worrisome sign. Repeated compulsive toggles to nj.com showed fans still pulling for the pitcher to get out of his jam. Before anything showed on Yahoo!, a big "Nooooo!" was followed by a string of like comments: "Mota, you c*nt!" "My turtle can run faster than Shawn Green." Then: "They are one f*cking tenacious team!" I felt a pall, as I imagined that maybe Spiezio had hit a three-run homer. A quick jump to Yahoo! showed it "only" to be a game-tying triple. Back at nj.com, fans were complaining that Shawn Green was the worst outfielder they had ever seen, and they were arguing back and forth whether to blame him for not catching the ball or blame Mota for terrible pitch selection: "No way you throw that pitch. I blame Lo Duca," wrote one. When a fan commended Green for preventing a home run, another rebutted, "If you get to it, you catch it."

With the score tied 6-6 and Billy Wagner coming in to toss the ninth (the dawn fast approaching in Reykjavik), I needed to get some sleep.

An hour later, I was still tossing restlessly in bed and figured I might as well get up and look because thinking about the game was keeping me awake.

The damn thing never even went to extra innings; it had been over for an hour: 9-6 Cardinals. Wagner gave up a homer to the first batter he faced—and it went downhill from there.

I wished I had gone to bed at midnight.

The guy who was taping the third game of the series for me was also picking us up at the airport, and he was not, of course, supposed to divulge the score. He did. "Mets down two games to one. I wanted to save you the trouble of watching the tape because absolutely nothing good happens."

Then the Mets rebounded, but, yes, those Cardinals were one tenacious team.

That brings us to the seventh game and Endy's catch.

I believe in pivotal games. When the Mets lost Game Two of the 2006 playoffs against the Cardinals, they effectively lost the series, but of course we didn't know that at the time. The same game is not always pivotal, and the same situation does not always evolve. The Mets were blown out the first *two* games at home in the 1986 Series against the Red Sox and then came back to take two in Boston. Even a fifth-game victory was not pivotal for Boston, as the Mets took the last two.

If the Mets had held their lead against the Cardinals or won in extra innings that night, they probably would have won at least one in St. Louis and put a lock on the series. Note these two contrasting scenarios:

1969 World Series. Mets lose Game One in Baltimore, win the next four with the aid of Al Weis and Donn Clendenon homers, Gary Gentry and Jerry Koosman mound gems, and two amazing Tommy Agee running catches; it's a 4-1 rout. But the fourth game was pivotal. Swoboda's catch prevented the Orioles from beating Tom Seaver in the ninth, though they did tie the score on the play (sac fly). When the Mets won in the tenth, tallying on a Baltimore throwing error of a J.C. Martin bunt (though the runner may have been out of the baseline), they went up 3-1 and completed the "sweep" the next day.

1973 World Series. Mets lose Game One in Oakland, win the next one. The third game here was pivotal. Wayne Garrett homered to lead off the bottom of the first, and the Mets led 2-0 most of the game. The A's tied it with a run in the eighth and won on a single by Dagberto Campaneris off Harry Parker in the top of the eleventh. The Mets then took the next two at Shea and lost the last two in Oakland when George Stone was denied a start. If they had held their lead in the third game or scored first in extra innings, they might well have had a five-game victory identical to the one against Baltimore. Losing the third game meant that the Series went back to Oakland, where the Mets played two lack-luster, uninspired affairs behind tired pitchers and, as Roger Angell noted eloquently at the time, it was a wonderful season that was merely two games too long. The difference between a 4-1 series win and a 4-3 series loss was the result of a single game.

My Mets' affiliation began, in a sense, with an invisible catch, years before they were formed, by a young prospect vaulting over a fence at the old Yankee facility in St. Petersburg. Casey's glimpse became my first icon, and Endy's leap at the wall was its reflection across time, different in circumstance, meaning, and archive, but totemically the same act. The totemic Mets are what bind me, what join the high-school kid with expansion rosters and a spinner game to the father and son setting up a satellite-dish club in Berkeley to the guy in Reykjavik logging the plays over Yahoo!.

From outside a world age, an archaeologist or cultural historian looks back and says: "That was the Mud Turtle clan or Yellow Eel clan among the Osage; it had its ceremonies, its sacred objects, its lineages and moieties, its rites. Those are its relics and remnants: earth lodges, temple mounds, pipes, polychrome designs, and pottery motifs. You can trace the incised animals of the Southern Cult from Saskatchewan and Manitoba to Oklahoma and Louisiana, all the way to Rhode Island and Maine."

This book is a glimpse of something else entirely, not baseball as such, but a calendar and sacred alphabet, a chronicle that begins in the mountains of Eurasia and Sinai and ends up counting moons and carving rocks among the Penobscots of the north, Arawaks of Venezuela and Paraguay, Huichols of the Sierra Madre, Marquesans in Polynesia, Aranda of the Australian outback, Natchez of the Mississippi Valley. What is at stake are the lost and forever-returning tables of humankind. They appear faintly in box scores, speaking of forgotten clans and events that have made us who we are, events that no longer exist, things that we must but cannot know.

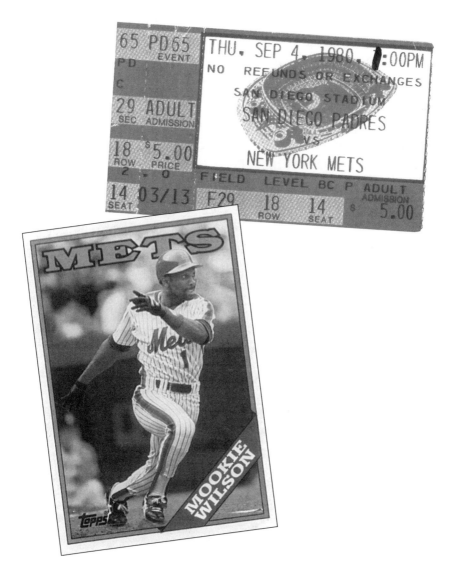

Playing Catch with Terry Leach:
Baseball as an Act of Transgression

Year of Writing: 2006
Mets Seasons Referenced: 1981–1989

My son Robin discovered baseball later in life than I did. He waited until eleven to be lured by packs of cards into the national game. The genie nabbed me around age seven: bubblegum dust on a yellow Gene Woodling Yankee amulet among blue and red Cubs and Cardinals. This initiated the key iconography of my childhood.

My landscape was New York City of the 1950s, an after-school program in Central Park called "Bill-Dave Group," and the Yanks. His was Richmond, California, of the 1980s, various neighborhood fields around Berkeley, and the Mets—my team from when they were formed prior to my senior year of high school.

We got into it together, a jungle that was soon overgrown in every quadrant. During the early weeks of his rooting, the Mets were a mysterious distant team that existed mainly in box scores. An occasional TV appearance was a gala event like a school holiday.

The baseball quotes from Terry Leach, David Cone, Paul Auster, Jonathan Lethem, and Bob Klapisch appear in *Things Happen for a Reason: The True Story of an Itinerant Life in Baseball* by Terry Leach with Tom Clark, with Introductions by Paul Auster and David Cone, published by Frog, Ltd., Berkeley, California, 2000.

The Giants' games with the Mets were broadcast on KNBR, so on six days a year we carried a portable radio, sometimes bearing the flame on odysseys around blocks to privatize the transmission. Players who had become magical in print sprang to life in the mantra of play-by-play. Frank Taveras dove and backhanded one in the hole; Willie Montanez lined a single to left—now coming in from the bullpen: Jeff Reardon.

The best, though, was the two times a year that the Mets played a series in San Francisco. We attended all six games, using comp tickets from the team via longstanding relationships between my family in the hotel business and Mets' executives. Arriving at the ballpark early enough to take in the warm-ups from our seats, we invariably found ourselves in a coterie of friends and relatives of Met players. We had surprisingly intimate conversations with these folks, at least intimate about baseball.

We subscribed to *Baseball America* and *Mets Inside Pitch*, which augmented our roster by more than a hundred names that we tracked through Met farm-system teams ranging from Single-A Columbia, South Carolina, and Lynchburg, Virginia, to Double-A Jackson, Mississippi, and Triple-A Norfolk. Of course, we did not know how good any of these guys really were, i.e., whether they were real prospects, fill-ins, or lemons who were topping out, but we built mythologies around their eponyms and stats and were rewarded as some of them made it to the majors. In fact, from a fortuity of the 1980 schedule, we saw the first games of three players we had been tracking—Hubie Brooks, Mookie Wilson, and Wally Backman—and then constructed a family trip so that we followed them down the coast to Los Angeles and San Diego, where we also took in beaches, zoos, and museums—the most memorable vacation of our son's and daughter's childhood.

In 1984 I devised another strategy for connecting to the Mets: press passes. A poet friend, Joel Oppenheimer, author of *The Wrong Season*, a book about the inadequate 1972 team, got the *Village Voice* to assign me an article on the team around the same theme (weren't they pretty much all "the wrong season"?). I used a *Voice* letterhead to request a certificate that let me onto the field at Candlestick as well as into the clubhouse both before and after each game. The billet was just for me, as Robin was officially a child as well as a civilian, so I let him debrief me on every interview I conducted, each conversational fragment I overheard.

Once I realized how fluid the situation was, I began brazenly slipping him past the guard and, though he never entered the actual sanctum of the clubhouse, he witnessed players outside in the tunnel.

The apotheosis of these events was the afternoon that Frank Cashen, the Mets' general manager, led both of us down the tunnel onto the field, and we sat in the visitors' bullpen before the game, talking over the farm system with him and pitching-coach Mel Stottlemyre. We ran down cherished names and got actual stories about players we had been following in our imaginations (plus correct pronunciations). We learned, sadly, that most of our favorites were not considered prospects; they were there to round out rosters, either too old, too slow, or lacking some other ineffable quality.

Though I submitted all of my accounts to the editor, the *Voice* never published any of them and, after a while, I took to getting my press pass more legitimately on the letterhead of our publishing company, North Atlantic Books. In the mid '80s I assembled my Mets observations and interviews from this period into a long narrative, "Public and Private Baseball." As it appears later in this book, I won't retell the anecdotes here. They belong to their era—pre-steroids, pre-9/11, when my children were still kids.

By now (2006) Robin is three years older than I was when he began rooting, almost thirty-seven, with a newborn son of his own. Baseball itself has mutated and does not merit the sort of loyalty we once gave it. Without a salary cap, it has become primarily moneyball, a mise-en-scène of gala if counterfeit superstars. With no level playing surface among foes, the payrolls of some teams approach ten times those of others, and players move around like freelance executives with their sorry-ass perks. Someone in our former shoes would get much less pleasure from the Mets farm system now, as most prospects are traded for expensive, usually over-the-hill veterans before they get a chance to make a local identity. A.J. Burnett, Jason Bay, and Scott Kazmir were all attractive Met farmhands, but none of them served an inning in a Met uniform. It is doubtful whether in today's environment Tug McGraw or Rick Aguilera would have survived to play in New York. They probably would have been traded for some overrated Brewer or Royal slugger.

So why even bother? All we root for anyway is laundry. We scorn a favored player when he is traded, even if he departs against his wishes, and we cheer a former despised foe as if he were the prodigal son the moment he puts on the orange and blue. This is the first law of baseball fandom. Yet if a team is bereft of indigenous players, its mystique evaporates, and even winning a Pennant or World Series is hollow and fake. The arbitrariness of a nondescript bunch of guys supersedes the epiphany of victory.

Real baseball for me lies back in the 1950s, '60s, and early '70s— from the great runs of the Mantle/Skowron/Whitey Ford Yankees through the Seaver/Garrett/Cleon "Miracle Mets" of '69 and the equally lyrical comeback team of '73 that won the Pennant with a September drive as blue as that year's Vermont sky. The 1980-decade Mets revived some nostalgic intensity because I shared those fierce, complicated pennant races against the Cubs and Cardinals with my son. The Mets' epic rumbles with Rick Sutcliffe, Ron Santo, Terry Pendleton, John Tudor, and Mike Scott were as rich and profound in different ways as Yankee-Indian pennant races and Yankee-Dodger World Series of the mid '50s.

Sometime during the early '90s the whole affair lost its tension and myth. Steroid-fueled home-run derbies and manipulated pennant races and playoffs (including imbalanced schedules with interleague games mid-season) seemed as staged and cartoonish as professional wrestling and as P.T. Barnum as the Ringling Brothers circus. Yes, baseball was always—quote—entertainment, but that's no excuse to forget that it is also the game of gloveless fielders and cricket-like batsmen on old fair-grounds, baseballers with roots in traveling squads of the mid-nine-teenth century when Troy and Newark were major-league towns, and Civil War soldiers laid out fields between battles. The original teams were neighborhoods that challenged other neighborhoods, and then the best ones went on tour. It was never meant to be a rigged carnival.

Of course, younger fans today don't see the demise because they don't know the old game. They didn't grow up inside the beauty of its fixed solar system, the planets in their primal orbits, a lone sixteen teams with homegrown players bound in kingdoms. Back then a trade was really a trade, as when the Yankees got Bob Turley, Don Larsen, and Billy Hunter from the Orioles in an eighteen-player potlatch that remade the zodiac. Nowadays trades have all the gravitas of a yard sale.

It is probably only a matter of time before the twenty-something demographic supporting computer athletes, X-games, and skateboard daredevils knock major-league baseball down to the level of indus-trial softball and professional curling.

One of the players Robin and I tracked during the '80s was a pitcher named Terry Leach. At first he was just a name and stat line. He appeared on the Jackson Mets as a league leader in *Baseball America* one issue fairly far into the 1980 season. Although we were close observers of the Met conveyor belt, we could not figure out where this guy had come from. We had no way of knowing that, having been released by the Atlanta Braves' Texas League farm team (whose name, Savannah, he later gave to his daughter), Leach was picked up by Jackson, in the same Texas League, with a 5-1 record and a 3.66 ERA already in the bank. He had been let go not because he wasn't doing well (clearly) but because the Braves needed to make room for some young prospects.

Lacking this information at the time, Robin and I invented expla-nations. We guessed that he had been on Jackson all season but did not log enough innings to qualify for the leaders previously, or perhaps he had come from an A-level Met club to AA and we had over-looked him among the shifting transactions in our two publications.

He curiously matched his Savannah 5-1 with Jackson, this time with a 1.50 ERA, making him one of the top pitchers in the league by season's end. In our mind he was a great prospect, though many players we cast in that role vanished or were released the way the Braves cut Terry Leach, as Frank Cashen was to demonstrate to us person-to-person a few years later.

We continued to keep close tabs on Leach. In 1981 he was 5-1, 1.71, at Jackson when the Mets promoted him to AAA Tidewater. There he went 5-2, 2.72—and suddenly one evening he was on the mound in Wrigley Field against the Cubs. We learned soon after that he was a submariner. He threw not over the top like most pitchers but at an angle somewhere between sidearm and underhand.

Beyond the numerology, Robin found this player's name evocative: he had left behind a friend, Rosemary Leach, in Vermont, and while she certainly wasn't a baseball person, she was a link to his small-town hippie childhood.

We learned the facts later: After the Braves released Mr. Leach, the Mets, figuring he had looked pretty good against them, signed him. Then, as he continued to impress, they moved him up the ladder despite the fact he was not deemed a prospect at any rung. When they needed a stopgap on the parent team, they summoned him for a brief tour without expectation that he'd stick or be anything more than a journeyman.

Leach yoyoed between the Mets and Tidewater over the next five years, though he continued to get hitters out consistently at both levels and, on the last day of the 1982 season, he threw what is still the Mets' best single-game outing, a ten-inning 1-0 one-hitter against the Phillies. I judge it the top pitching performance because the Mets have never had a no-hitter and all their other one-hitters went the regulation nine.

Leach did not breach the majors at all in '83 and was even traded from Tidewater in 1984, ending up briefly back in the Braves' organization before returning to the Tides. He threw half the '85 season for the Mets, the rest in Virginia, and then pitched very briefly for the '86 team that beat the Red Sox in the Series. At that point his cumulative Mets record, 72 appearances almost exclusively in relief, was 6-6.

Terry Leach wasn't always a bridesmaid or a submariner. He was a big prospect at Auburn University in the 1970s, going 9-0 with a 1.30 ERA one year, an overhand pitcher who regularly hit the mid 90s but, after he injured his arm, his fastball lost much of its bite. Out of Auburn he played in Louisiana in an independent league before the Braves signed him in 1977, and he bounced around their farm system until they released him from Savannah in 1980.

During these junkets Terry was developing his underhand delivery with the acumen of a chess master, learning from various coaches, experimenting with pitches at different speeds and arm angles, getting the ball to dart, often in unfamiliar ways. Conventional wisdom was that the small fraternity of sidearm and submarine pitchers couldn't master hitters who swung from the side of the plate opposite to that from which they threw. As a right-hander, Terry's arm angle was supposed to feed shark-bait to left-handers, but he developed unique pitches that victimized all comers. In fact, while no one was taking him too seriously, he became awfully damn good, his one-hitter finally proving that.

Yet, in the minds of scouts and executives, he remained damaged goods, too old, getting by with trick pitches. He was on the mound for the one-hitter, the last game of the 1982 season, only because the scheduled starter, mega-prospect Rick Ownbey, showed up with a blister, and someone had to be run out there. They probably thought they'd go through five or six bums among the September call-ups that afternoon in a meaningless game, then pack up their goods for the winter, but Terry threw the full nine—and an extra one—and was back in Tidewater the following April.

◆

I was very committed to developing my baseball skills during childhood. In fact up through freshman year of college I played hardball seriously. At Bill-Dave Group I hit and caught above the level of my peers and threw accurately—one of the better players, if not a star. Even though my favorite Yankee, Gil McDougald, was an infielder, I chose the outfield because I was naturally good at flies but shy of ground balls.

As the competition grew stiffer, my flaws became more obvious. In junior high, I went out for hardball but didn't hit well enough to get into more than an occasional game. I was afraid of the ball at-bat too, especially as the pitches got faster and started to hook. I didn't *think* I was afraid but, as numerous coaches pointed out, I was unconsciously closing my eyes, pulling away, not consistently putting bat on ball. Robin, despite his delayed initiation, succeeded in advancing quite a bit further than me, helping start a varsity team in the late '80s at the University of California at Santa Cruz, the "slugging Banana Slugs," and hitting for a respectable average against the kinds of opponents that send players to the majors.

My one real skill was that I could track fly balls. I could, in fact, do it better than anyone else, judging them flawlessly and running them down. One high-school coach would test me, shooting them all over the field, and I would grab fifteen, twenty, twenty-five in a row: shots in front of me, to either side, directly over my head. He was amazed I could do a thing like that but wasn't more of a player, especially since a lot of his contact hitters and sluggers flubbed easy flies that sometimes cost games.

This virtuoso ability was the grace of my childhood, my calling card in life. I didn't get to express it nearly as much in real contests as in freelance sessions, the baseball equivalent to music jams, a few of us taking turns shagging each other's flies (or tosses) in shifting dances of speed and timing. As a child, I recruited adults to throw or bat to me;

later I hit fungos with friends or my brother Jon. I did this on probably well over a hundred fields through my youth. I loved making two or more unlikely catches in sequence, finding a rhythm as if performing contact improvisation on summons of the ball—diving to my right for a backhand; bounding far to my left and plucking a rising liner in the webbing at the last possible minute; then, totally out of breath, racing under a blooper on the infield. Enough! I would hunch over in an altered state, huffing and puffing, taking my anonymous bow before the platonic gods of the diamond.

I lived for a certain kind of miracle catch that was more than a mere great play. The dime-a-dozen kind involved running down a ball hit beyond me and backhanding it over my head or tearing in for a shoe-string, tumbling as I picked it off the grass. But there were also the shots that I knew I couldn't catch yet I still gave my heart and soul, dashing to the spot closest to where they might be and lunging at the last moment, sometimes nabbing the ball at the tip of the webbing, usually crashing to the ground and rolling over afterward.

I missed far more of those than I caught, but I caught enough of them to be a legend, even in my thirties when it was softball and I was a faculty member at Goddard College in Vermont, joining student pickup games after the worst of mud season on a make-shift field out along Route 2 (now planted with corn, the school having sold off most of its property to stay in business through the '80s, years after we cut loose for California).

Although I never made my team at Horace Mann, a private school in New York City, I indefatigably went out for it year after year, taking batting practice, shagging flies, every now and then playing an actual inning against another school, rarely with an at-bat. It meant many lonely afternoons on the subway, wending home long after classes had ended. Staring out at the remote universe of neighborhoods from the el, I felt the mysteriousness of being an outsider everywhere. Wordsworth's "Ode on Intimations of Immortality" echoed in my mind: *"There was a time when meadow, grove, and stream,/The earth, and every common sight,/To me did seem/Apparell'd in celestial light....*" Even then, I wondered, *"Whither is fled the visionary gleam?"* I was lost in baseball, yet, with each scrumptious breeze, maples sent samaras spiraling across the wonder of existence and forsythia blazed with an ancient yellow of unknown worlds. I intuited something else that made baseball seem like a desert I had to cross, a desert with no boundaries. I was a stranger in a stranger land, but at least I could catch.

In summer camp I fared better because the skill level varied willy-nilly and everyone got to bat and field. I hit line drives and made some adept plays that kept the dream of "being good" alive.

My last real hardball experience was going out for the freshman team at Amherst College. During my first New England autumn the coaches held drills on an indoor diamond in a greenhouse, sawdust on the ground. Baseball finally became monotonous and boring, though of course, just as our classroom teachers were professing in their own disciplines, these sports masters imagined they were teaching the pro game. They barked at us and made the sessions as repetitive and military as they could. *"Where is it now, the glory and the dream?"*

I was not the worst player, but close to it. Since they were lobbing in pitches at the beginning, I hit okay—and I did run down my fly balls—but the afternoons were vacuous, the mood demoralizing. I began to discern the trap in which baseball had caught me. I saw how much fun my friends were having at softball and then hockey and, during the heavy snows of winter (when the greenhouse was particularly melancholy and cloying), I swallowed my lifelong hardball pride and bailed for intramurals.

While I never admired softball, religiously opposing its fat pellet for the way it slowed down the game and took the edge out of batting and fielding, I played it all through the rest of Amherst, then in pickup games in Ann Arbor while a graduate student there, and again a couple of years later on a student-faculty team at the University of Maine in Portland where I taught anthropology. I was a regular for Sunday slow-pitch at Goddard and on Berkeley fields through the entirety of the '70s and into the '80s.

All along I continued hardball jam sessions separately—hitting and chasing flies for an hour or more at a time—with friends in Michigan, Vermont, and California. I salute those fungo partners I still remember: Jerry MacDonald, Bob McKinley, David Wilk, Rob Brezsny, Sheppard Ogden, Will Lashley, Chuck Stein, Paul Auster, Dave Bullen, and finally Robin once he was old enough, and his friend Tad.

My great catches were essentially confined to these improvs. The few I made in games were meaningless—one at Camp Wakonda in Pottersville, New York, in 1959 when we were losing to another camp by fifteen runs; two at Goddard in matches that were more street theater than baseball; and one in California in a pickup game in 1981 after an opposing team in our Oakland league didn't produce enough members to play an official match. These were *all* with the mulligan softball.

I made only one in a game that counted, sometime around 1989—and I am startled to realize now that it is the last play of my competitive career. I was almost forty-five years old. A San Francisco literary magazine, *Zyzzyva*, recruited me for a softball encounter with a rival Berkeley magazine, *Threepenny Review*. I had no allegiance to *Zyzzyva* beyond having published a piece in it years earlier (which was their justification to *Threepenny* for allowing me on the squad). On site we were still short one player, so Robin, who by then was a centerfielder for Santa Cruz, was added to our roster. I don't believe I had played in an actual baseball game for about eight years prior. It is also the only time I recall Robin and me playing in the same contest, let alone for the same team.

I remember nothing about prior innings, just that we were leading by a run in the bottom of the seventh (the last inning) and they had the bases loaded with two out. I was the centerfielder and, by then, kind of antsy to get it over with. After a lapse of the better part of a decade, the interminable standing around—waiting to bat, waiting to get a play in the field—seemed foolish and retro, interspersed as it was with these guys' faux enthusiasm and the nuanced rah-rah between literary cabals. Their fashion was to show that they didn't care by a parody of partisanship and rooting, when each actually wanted bragging rights badly. "I feel like barfing," I whispered to Robin, and he mutely seconded. They were into it, but they didn't know how to claim that without appearing uncool.

Then the batter smashed a solid liner toward center. I left my reverie and instantly calculated. It was too far in front of me to catch, but there was no point in waiting for it to bounce because we would lose once it hit the ground—so I figured to make a pretense of it, running in and diving in facsimile of an impossible catch. And I caught it. I landed so hard that I got up seeing stars.

◆

Terry Leach was born in Selma, Alabama; his father, a cotton buyer, had played football at Auburn, and Terry was more inclined to the pigskin than the horsehide, except that his dad didn't want him risking injury. Growing up playing on youth-league teams, he pitched a little but preferred third base and caught some too. He was at the hot corner when he got to Auburn, but they needed pitchers, so they converted him full-time. During summer leagues, however, he went back to third, once hitting two home runs in a game and another time (1975) stroking a walk-off dinger against the legendary Mark Fidrych.

Terry's 9-0, 1.30 in his sophomore year was one of the best records in Auburn history, but even then he wasn't primarily a starter because, relatively new to the mound, he was being worked into the rotation. He would hit ninety-four, ninety-five miles per hour consistently, so that's all he did, try to beat hitters *mano a mano*. Years later he recalled: "Man, that fastball would just explode on people. I'd launch it and it would just take off." He experimented with a couple of curves per game, but they usually evaded the zone.

Those were partying and fun years, and Terry was putting on weight. Heedless about conditioning or good mechanics, on the mound he just kept firing as long and as hard as he could. A scout using a radar gun during the night end of a doubleheader against LSU (to clinch the Southwest Conference 1976 Championship) said Leach was throwing as fast as anyone in the country. He needed two catchers because the first one's hand swelled up—the second found he had the same malady the next day. All this time a hidden strain on Terry's elbow was building up.

His subsequent mound appearance was against Mercer University, a charity contest. As it got around the sixth or seventh inning, Terry was inexplicably losing velocity. A batter on the opposing team yelled, "Hey, Stud, who stole your smoke?" That got him angry, and he tried to pop one real hard. He could feel it snap; his arm went dead with the pain, the ball dribbling away. He had torn the collateral ligament in his right elbow. The catcher heard it and called time before the pitch even hit the ground.

After a period of rest, the elbow more or less healed, but Terry lost enough zip on his only real pitch that he was a mediocre hurler after that. When he tried to go more overhand to take strain off his elbow, he injured something in his shoulder. For years he searched for a delivery point between two pains.

From imagining himself a huge prospect and likely draft pick, after graduation he adjusted to merely wanting to keep playing *somewhere.* He figured Double-A was the max he could accomplish under any circumstances, but even that seemed out of the question, as no one wanted to sign a pitcher with a bum arm, especially at 215, thirty pounds over ideal playing weight. By his own admission, "I wasn't looking that good to the scouts."

A friend who was also undrafted convinced him that they should go together to the independent Gulf States League and sign with the Baton Rouge Cougars, a team looking for warm bodies. The level was considered Single A, but the Cougars had no major league affiliation. Three hundred and fifty dollars a month looked pretty good then.

By the time he hit Baton Rouge, Terry was up to 225. "I could still run," he remembers. "It would surprise people how quick I could move. But boy, was I a fat pig. . . . I had the ugliest Fu Manchu goatee deal you ever saw in your life. I figured if I was going to be fat I might as well be ugly to go along with it."

This low-expectation squad did well, in fact was in first place when the principals ran out of money. Abandoned near the Tex-Mex border, the guys refused to take the field for their game in Corpus Christi unless they were paid, so they were threatened with lifetime bans from pro ball. Instead of complying they headed back to Louisiana in their team kiddie vans, "drove all across East Texas like a bunch of bank robbers on the run and made the trip in one long nasty day."

During the Baton Rouge stint Terry was rehabilitating his arm, still trying to find a viable release point. That fall, after getting in some credits at Auburn, he headed home to Selma where he joined two softball teams, a church one and a commercial-league one. He was on the roster of a third team for occasional tournaments, so was playing a minimum of four or five games a week, sometimes an extra tournament during the weekend. He was getting his body in shape, shedding pounds until he was down under 200.

Before Baton Rouge, he had gone to a Cincinnati Reds tryout and was throwing pretty well there despite his lame arm. In fact he struck most guys out, but they sent him packing anyway. They admitted they weren't really looking for anyone that day. He was brash enough to inquire why they held the camp in the first place. That got a dirty look that said "Don't knock on our door again." Now, through a scout friend of his father's, he got a legitimate invitation to an Atlanta Braves camp.

Knowing he didn't have a fastball anymore, he decided to get creative: "You don't have anything to lose. You make up pitches as you need them. You do what you have to do to survive."

Actually he opened his performance with fastballs but could only reach eighty-eight, eighty-nine, and he knew that wouldn't get it done—so he tried a hard curve at eighty-five, eighty-six, and it looked enough like a slider that the scouts declared it one. He then threw a sloppy, half-hearted changeup to a big left-handed hitter and got him to screw himself into the ground trying to clobber it. The next time the guy came up, he dug to clobber the junk, so Terry threw it as hard as he could and hit him in the neck, not his intention, but he acted as though it was, real cool—scouts like a mean streak. The Braves offered him a contract for five hundred dollars a month to pitch for Class A Greenwood.

It was at Greenwood that pitching coach Kenny Rowe suggested Terry drop down and adopt a sidearm whipping motion. That had not been in the cards previously, as he was mainly trying to build his overhand strength back to Auburn level, toying with a poor man's slider because he couldn't master a curve. At most, he had goofed around with a sidearm delivery, but it was nothing he ever used with intent.

From the moment he went down under, Terry became an artist. He discovered amazing movement on all his pitches. Recognizing a "things happen for a reason" moment, he stayed with that release point, gradually working out a submarine repertoire on the sidelines. When he finally got into real games, twenty of them, he posted a 2.55 ERA, sixty-seven innings, a K per inning.

Even when he had bombed away at ninety-five overhand, trying to blow people out with his mustard, he was not a strikeout pitcher. Now, flinging sidearm in the low- to mid-80s and relying on finesse and movement, he was making guys miss by a foot and a half. It was a fundamental change in philosophy—guile and motion rather than sonic booms.

The initial commitment took guts because coming in slow and sidearm made him feel at batters' mercy. They had time to adjust and put good wood on the ball. Yet he kept delivering that way and getting results. The irony was, if he had come overhand at eighty-two or less it would have been like batting practice. Conversely, when he had tried to throw hard at eighty-eight, he had a very juicy fastball and a junk slider. Inhabiting the middle ground was his only way back to the kingdom of baseball. He could no longer throw the fastball so had to replace it with its shadow, do with yin what he had done earlier by yang.

Soon, pitches from down under came to him like disciples. He had a little Laredo slider, a quality strikeout pitch. Playing around off that, he found a nice sharp sinker waiting to be appropriated.

Because he was born with small hands, Terry always had the uncanny ability to feel subtle differences in the size and weight of a baseball. At Auburn they used donated American and National League balls, and he was the only one who could tell which one with his eyes closed. Coaches checked him five times in a row, each one blindfolded, and he named the league of the ball five times. They were sure he was cheating because no one else could feel it; no matter how many seams and signatures they fondled, they couldn't find a betrayal.

This subtle touch became a blessing once Terry slowed down and dropped to sidearm, because in essence he now assayed every pitch as if it were river gold. He was measuring instead of pounding. He discovered little movements and breaks, shifts of gravity that skidded into and out of the edges of the strike zone. It translated into a mastery he never had with a fastball. Plus, as he got stronger, he gained velocity back and could put mustard on and take a little off. Single-A hitters were so badly fooled that they were routinely striking out on three pitches.

The next season, 1978, Terry went to spring training with the parent Braves at West Palm Beach; from there he got farmed out to AA Savannah. Half a dozen years older than most of the players, he became a kind of father figure/den mother, packing coolers, making sandwiches, listening to love tales and sorrows, giving advice, organizing social events, leading Elvis singalongs on rattling buses.

He bounced around the Braves system in that role until midway through 1980, briefly showing his wares at AAA Richmond in '79. He pitched exceptionally everywhere, almost entirely in relief, but he never earned a reliable spot on any roster or made real professional progress. Used solely to fill temporary vacancies, he was demoted whenever so-called prospects came along. There was no sense that he would ever pitch in the show, so despite a sub-2.00 ERA at Richmond and a solid record at Savannah, he found himself back in Single-A when too many phenoms came up the ladder at once. The Braves had no investment in him or commitment to his career: he hadn't been drafted, he was past his prime, he was neither a starter nor a reliever, and he had a bad arm, so was getting by on horseshit pitches that any major-league hitter would deposit in the next county. If you weren't being groomed as either a starter or a reliever at Double-A, you might as well be nonexistent as far as real promotion went.

Years later he heard from the Atlanta scout who signed him at the tryout camp that the only reason he didn't move right up to the majors was that no one ever took the possibility seriously. He started out so low on the totem pole—a funky, marginal submariner—that they looked right through him.

In the middle of the 1980 season the Braves signed three number-one picks at the same time—Ken Dayley, Jim Acker, and Craig McMurtry. They wanted to start them at AA where they already had another number one plus the talented, hard-throwing Steve Bedrosian. Terry had also just confided to pitching coach Bob Veale that his arm hurt a bit. That was probably all the encouragement they needed in the front office. Someone had to be the odd man out, and it was "Mr. Bad Arm, Damaged Goods, Too Old"—forget the 5-1 record and dominance on the mound. He was a once and future mop-up guy.

He asked his manager Eddie Haas then if he had any hope of making the majors. The answer: "No, I don't think you can make it. Your fastball's not good enough. Your slider's too flat. I just don't think that stuff will ever cut it in the major leagues. I don't think you've got a chance."

That was about a year before he was standing on the mound in Wrigley.

There was little more than a month left in the 1980 season when Terry signed with Jackson, and they had just advanced a starter to Tidewater, so there was an opening. Plus, the Mets thought enough of him that they had tried to trade for him a few months earlier—the Braves had turned them down. After he was on Jackson, Braves general manager Henry Aaron called the Mets to ask if they were still "interested in that guy Leach." They told him that Terry was already pitching for them.

With Jackson, there was no more mopping up and spot-starting. He threw five winning games in a row as a starter, two of them shutouts, his first since college. He was pitching exactly the same for Jackson as he had for Savannah, but he was now a valued member of the rotation. Eddie Haas told him he'd never make it, but his manager at Jackson the next season, Davey Johnson, said, "Absolutely you can. . . . You can be a major league pitcher."

Terry had started '81 spring training as the prospective closer for Tidewater but didn't make the team because the skipper there didn't hanker the sidearm style. However, in June, Johnson pulled Leach out of a zero-zero tie after nine innings in Tulsa because he was going back up to Tidewater. Terry wanted to finish the shutout but, when he heard the news, he let his skipper win that argument.

At AAA he shifted between starting and relieving and had a 5-2 record when he was summoned to Wrigley. He went through a weird version of the legendary big-league gauntlet: the cab from the airport got a flat tire, and Terry had to help the driver change it, so he arrived late, covered with dirt, and the usher wouldn't let him in the visitors' locker room. When he did finally get situated, he was domiciled next to a grumpy Dave Kingman who answered with intimidating silence when Terry tried a cheerful "Hi Kong, howya doing?" It wasn't an auspicious debut on the field either—as soon as he came on in the eighth to protect a one-run lead, he gave up a two-run gopher to pinch-hitter Mike Lum—but the Mets won the game.

His maiden start was at Shea Stadium against Philly and he still recalls, prior to the first pitch, standing on the mound thinking, "Man, I'm in *way* over my head. I've got no idea what's going on! I'm supposed to be in the major leagues now, starting a game—whoa, it's pretty scary." Pete Rose was the leadoff hitter, and he strode in with a hard stare plus the hint of a smirk. "And Pete's got it right: I'm just this little fat kid from Alabama, who's got no idea what he's doing there."

But Terry's sidearm stuff was special. Coming from down under, some pitches rose a little bit, while others sank. Rose did a bit of a double-take. Then he lunged and grounded out to second. (Two years later he listed Terry Leach in *Sports Illustrated* as one of his toughest five pitchers; at that point he had struck out four times in six at-bats against him.)

In the bullpen while warming up, Terry had visualized facing Mike Schmidt, the Phillies' slugger. He spotted him an imaginary 1-2 count and put a nasty slider right on the black, right-hand corner. It was 1-2 again in the game, so he threw the same pitch, and Schmidt swung and missed and then walked back to the dugout with his bat on his shoulder, a sign of respect.

The sky was threatening in the fifth of a 1-1 game (the Phils' run was unearned), and the Mets had a guy on third, so they pinch-hit for Terry just in case that was the last inning. Ultimately the team won in nine, but it was a no-decision for him.

A few weeks later, back in the bullpen, he was brought in to face George Foster in a tie game late, bases loaded, two out. Foster was a monster at that point. Terry went to 3-2, then tried a fastball that the RBI king just missed, fouling it back. So he threw him a slider, breaking it over the corner for a called strike; Foster stood there "frozen stiff like a piece of ice sculpture." Terry gave himself a pat on the back, "Man, you've got guts."

He pitched thirty-five innings in that first stint in the majors, and all his stats were good: at 2.57 he was a point off leading the team in ERA, and he gave up only twenty-six hits. But at 1982 spring training, a host of young pitchers were in competition for slots: Rick Ownbey, Ron Darling, Tim Leary, Jeff Bittiger, Doug Sisk, Scott Holman, plus the Mets had an infielder they wanted to trade and couldn't, so the team started the season with only nine hurlers and the odd man out, Terry, went back to the Tides.

Davey Johnson had moved up to manage AAA and used his work-horse in relief where he had a 2.96 ERA and five saves in forty-nine innings before going up to a very bad Mets team for which he pitched poorly himself. In twenty-one games that summer he had an ERA over five and a half.

On the last day of the season, Rick Ownbey was supposed to show the brass his stuff: goofy Rick Ownbey who had three or four or maybe even five great pitches but couldn't get the ball over the plate; who was always far ahead of Terry Leach on the depth chart because he was drafted, young, and talented (until he was traded with Neil Allen for Keith Hernandez a year later); who was a better Frisbee player than pitcher (and could achieve a perfect arc from his toes); who, coming out of the movie *Rocky* one day beside Leach said to him, "I'm the eye of a tiger with the control of a newt." Rick may have been a tad hungover that October day; he didn't feel much like throwing and had a blister to prove it.

Terry had not gone over four innings in a game all year. There was no pressure; the Mets were eight games in the cellar, and everyone was heading home that evening. But, after making an adjustment in his follow-through early in the game, he found his best stuff and then got even better. Sticking with a sidearm sinker and a slider that was a rising upshoot, he was unhittable. He felt he could put the ball wherever he wanted. In fact, he got so picky he walked six, but struck out seven. Gary Maddox, Pete Rose, Gary Matthews, and Mike Schmidt went a combined 0-17 against him. No one got a hit except Luis Aguayo, a backup second baseman, who bounced a triple between the outfielders and was stranded on third.

In one at-bat, Leach threw a slider that was so radical it virtually slipped out of his hands, started behind Ozzie Virgil, came back between his legs like through a wicket, and ended up in the catcher's glove.

Trouble was: John Denny, hurling for the Phils, had a one-hit shutout too. They put someone else out in the tenth, and the Mets scratched a run. In the bottom half, Terry was about ready to collapse, bending to rest on his knees between pitches, hardly able to breathe. He walked Aguayo to start the inning, and the bullpen rose, but he got the next three.

"I well remember his ten-inning one-hit performance against the Phillies back in 1982," a fan wrote in to the Ultimate Mets website twenty years later. "It seemed that that evening the entire world was talking about it. New York was crazy with it. It was like no matter what TV or radio station you tuned into, they were talking about it. I wouldn't be surprised if some stations broke in with special reports. . . . A very special moment in Mets' history."

Another fan added, "One of the best-pitched games ever by a Met. It was one of the bright spots during some lean times."

A bunch of friends and ex-teammates back in Selma happened to be stopping by McDonald's for a cup of coffee the next morning, bought the paper, and looked at the box score: "A lot of zeroes and just one hit, no runs, ten innings—must be some kind of mistake here!" they admitted to Terry later. But it was what it was, a ten-inning one-hitter.

By the spring of '83 it was the same old story: a lot of young kids in whom too much money was invested. Terry was sent back to AAA, to be held there for insurance. It was, he admitted, "a pretty nice little team at Tidewater that year": Ron Gardenhire, John Gibbons, Wally Backman, Clint Hurdle, Rick Anderson, Gary Rajsich, Ronn Reynolds. They took the International League playoffs and then beat Portland, Oregon, to win the Triple-A World Series. Terry had a slack year, an ERA in the mid fours and a 5-7 record, but he distinguished himself in the championship round, including five perfect innings in relief in one outing. In the deciding game he faced Luis Aguayo in a key situation and fanned him. A week later the Mets traded him to the Cubs for two half-decent, indifferent hurlers who were topping out.

At spring training in Arizona, Terry quickly found out that new Chicago manager Jim Frey "didn't care for the way I pitched. . . . He got busy trying to change me around. . . . He wanted me to pitch all lefties the same way, on the outside of the plate." Frey was old-school in that regard, didn't think a sidearmer could beat lefties on the inside corner. Terry had a sophisticated post-graduate pitching routine, but Frey wanted kindergarten stuff; plus he asked him to change his release point to imitate Kansas City's Dan Quisenberry, the most renowned submariner at the time.

Terry was insubordinate: "He gets his effects his way, I get mine my way. I feel like I've been doing fine. If it's not broken, don't try to fix it." His previous game in the majors had been a ten-inning one-hit shutout, and his last two appearances had been near hitless relief in the Triple-A World Series; yet he was being treated like a pariah and a bum. During exhibition games the Cubs used him for three innings: "three punch-outs, three pop-ups, three weak little ground-balls . . . and one dinger in that light air," as Terry recalled it. Short-stop Larry Bowa on the bench leaned over and whispered, "I guess they aren't used to anyone doing that well." It could have been the epitaph for Terry's career.

Before opening day he was swapped to the Braves for a left-hander, and Atlanta sent him to Richmond where he was used situationally to face a hitter here and there—twelve games, fourteen innings, twenty-eight hits, a 9.20 ERA. Through the grapevine later Terry heard that Ted Turner, the owner, had just hired a money guy to save a few bucks. The pencil-sharpener looked at one box score, saw that Terry got lit up and was on the major league payroll, so told his boss that here was an easy forty thousand off the bottom line. Terry was informed of his release by manager Eddie Haas, the same guy who cut him at Savannah four years earlier.

So eight months after the Mets sent him to the Cubs, he was back at Tidewater, signed by the people running the Triple-A franchise, long-time admirers of his game. As Met general manager Frank Cashen put it a few years later, "Don't worry, Leachie. You'll always keep showing back up around here. You're like a bad penny."

First, however, the Tides wanted to ascertain that he didn't have a lame wing. They threw him into a lost game against the Cleveland affiliate at Old Orchard Beach, Maine, and he got pounded, but with virtually no spring training, he was seriously out of sync. Once he got his pitches going, he was fine. He spent the rest of the season at Tidewater and, even with that first outing factored in, went 10-2, 1.90, which earned him a trip back to the Mets' spring training in Florida. They had a bunch of new young arms: Roger McDowell, Randy Myers, Calvin Schiraldi, Sid Fernandez, and Dwight Gooden among them. Still, Terry was the last cut, at which time they asked him if he'd be willing to stay in camp and tutor minor leaguers. They no longer regarded him as a player but a coach in training. They figured at thirty-one years old, he wasn't going back to the show. But he wanted to pitch, so they figuratively shrugged and sent him back to Tidewater where he went 1-0 with a 1.45 ERA through half the season. Meanwhile the phenoms in New York were getting knocked around pretty good. Even then, Cashen ignored Leach and his record, advancing Doug Sisk over him from AA. Terry still hadn't pitched in the majors since his one-hitter.

A fan recalled this moment for the Ultimate Mets website: "One of the greatest wastes of talent in Mets' history. He had a rubber arm; he could be used in either relief or as a spot-starter. It still blows my mind that while we endured Doug 'Cardiac Kid' Sisk, Leach was toiling in Tidewater."

Finally, with the Mets playing well enough to be in a pennant race, the front office needed outs more than futures, so on June 21st they brought Terry up. During the Mets' chase of the Cardinals that came up just short, he went 3-4 with a 2.91 ERA, mostly in relief, with four rescue starts leading to all three of his wins. One was against the Giants at Shea when announced starter Sid Fernandez vomited right before the game. Terry was sitting in the clubhouse in long underwear, no shirt, doing a crossword when a coach told him he was going against Vida Blue, who was bringing it at about ninety-six miles per hour in those days. "'Sid's sick, you've got to go out and pitch the game. . . .' I put my shoe on my head, my shirt down on my foot—I didn't know what all. . . .'"

But what Terry tossed was the one-hitter all over again, maybe better: "That night those hitters were dropping like tin soldiers." They couldn't get anywhere near his pitches; it was as though they weren't even major leaguers they were missing by so much. Spinning a complete-game, three-hit shutout, he got a standing ovation when he laid down a bunt against a Giants relief pitcher in his last at-bat after six straight attempts and misses against Blue. Walking off the field with Terry, third-baseman Ray Knight pronounced, "That was the best game I've ever seen pitched."

During the winter Terry went to the Dominican Republic for his trademark 5-1, 1.93 and he expected to be on the Major League squad, but the '86 Mets were a big-time team, headed for gold. They had picked up Bobby Ojeda in the off-season and had no room for an aging journeyman. Terry went down to Tidewater, pitched decently, and then came back up when Ed Lynch tore some knee cartilage. He appeared six times out of the bullpen with a 2.70 ERA before management decided to pull Rick Aguilera from the rotation and put him in Terry's spot, bringing back Doug Sisk as well.

Remember, a couple of seasons earlier Sisk had been recalled from Jackson, leapfrogging better AAA pitchers. He didn't cut it either time, but he was young and threw a hard sinker, and the brass was enamored of him. Sisk was regulation, what teams went for. He wasn't about results; he was image, face, potential. And no one was topping the '86 Mets anyway with Gooden, Carter, Strawberry, *et al.*; they were running away with it. The tenth pitcher might as well be Dougie rather than a thirty-two-year-old guy without a future. Terry spent only five weeks in the majors that year before he went back to Norfolk as an insurance policy.

All that summer he followed the Mets on TV, taping the games so he could watch them after he got home from his own. As fate would have it, he started the next-to-last contest of the season for the Tides, one the team had to have in order to get into the playoffs. After setting down the first six batters, he came up for his first plate appearance of the year (the DH was used in parks of American League affiliates, the majority of International League members). He drew a walk, then tried to score from first when Stanley Jefferson hit the gap. The catcher had the ball waiting, but instinct kicked in and Terry went airborne, trying to dive over the guy in his equipment; he landed on his pitching shoulder. The x-ray showed he had dislocated *and* separated it. And he had been scheduled to join the Mets for the stretch run the next day. Instead he went home.

Over a vote of the players, management chose not to award Terry a World Championship ring that year. Ed Lynch who pitched only one inning got his, but Terry and Randy Myers, each with more appearances, were excluded. Almost ten years later Myers, with the Cubs by then, decided that, if the Mets re-opened the mold, he would contribute toward rings for himself and Terry. They did and, embarrassed by the offer, even chipped in the basic fee.

Terry had a bump the size of a walnut on his right collarbone and couldn't pick up a ball all winter, let alone throw. Yet he worked out at the Mets facility in St. Petersburg on his own money and time, wearing "the toe clean off a baseball shoe." By spring training, his shoulder was more or less healed, and he tossed five scoreless innings of two-hit ball during the exhibition season before he got told he was being sent out again. "Oh, I was hot. I cursed my way out of Davey's office. After all those years of hearing about the numbers game, I was tired of it. I did some venting. 'Some day it's got to be *my* number!' Slammed the door behind me.... I had watched too many guys step over me, for too many years.... I was having my best spring and it didn't seem to matter." Then he ran into Frank Cashen who hit him with the "bad penny" line.

◆

Baseball for me has always been about transgression. I don't quite know why, but its "crime" has recurred in innumerable forms throughout my life, enacted both as spectator and athlete, as myth-maker and outfielder. Soon after the Gene Woodling card of 1951, I embraced the magic of the little round orb; playing its game was the first thing that I was able to do well. The adults were amazed, as I was otherwise a daydreaming, withdrawn child; yet there I was, seven years old, running down balls in the outfield and hitting line drives. It was as though I had been initiated secretly by a guardian spirit of the Wolf Clan, taught its tricks of the trade. I didn't actually see when or how it happened. In order to be counted as alive on Earth, I must have decided to wake up.

The adults always presumed that I was going to play *their* game, the lionized one of Babe Ruth, Joe DiMaggio, and their youth on the Lower East Side. They had no inkling that I was about to start a renegade cult, a pagan church. The warning signs were there early. When I was seven my stepfather bought me and my brother Yankee uniforms, and I wore my pinstripes to Bill-Dave Group through the first snows of autumn. Well into November I carried my baseball glove and a hardball, more as talismans than useful articles since there was no one to throw to. I took them to the park and gym through February, hoping someone would have a catch with me instead of playing those other imposter games with lumpen leathery balls and stupid running around. The chain links of the basketball net in the gym seemed like dank medieval armor, and the roughneck clutter of football favored big kids, including my bellicose brother.

I loved the tiny compact pellet and the dance of pings that it orchestrated. I usually ended up tossing it in the air or bouncing it off a wall until the smooth white coat was grated. In fact, I don't remember ever wooing a companion later than the World Series and prior to spring training. Even if someone had wanted to play illicit baseball then, it was just too weird. No one else was into delinquency. My classmates worshipped conformity without knowing it; in the '50s it was the State religion. "Don't be a dope. No one plays baseball in the snow."

But a dope I was. I refused to condone other sports, an obstinacy I regretted years later because I would love to have dished the basketball to an open teammate or reached for a touchdown pass over a defender. Yet I was engaged in a ritual far more ancient and serious than baseball, and I got something untellable by defying the authorities and showing up with a glove when no one else was playing, by not allowing my body and mind to be impressed into their bouts. I was cutting an ugly, impossible shape, one I had to have.

Way in the future beyond that childhood, I feel I should have been able to relent and join the other guys; I long for the skills and moves, the minuets of football and basketball that I forfeited. But sometimes I glimpse again the truth—that before my identity was assured, I had to fight a life-and-death struggle for every particle of it, within an oppressive society, in a cruel family, against a regime of corrupting seductive images, in fascist schools and camps. I protected my psyche by the strictness of my intent, by my obsession and loyalty.

Until I had an identity, I needed to be pure, even if the purity was random and misplaced. It was never about fun back then; it was about survival. The hand-sized pearly amulet with its taut zipper of red stitches and shiny leather coat was a touchstone, a medallion, and a secret heraldry that opened the door to another realm, one that was kinder, happier, and more vivid to me. Baseball was my alias, a jealous master with its teams and cards and rules and plays. It was a password in the great dark when there was no other, a voice from somewhere else that never stopped talking to me and requiting my devotion.

I carried around a huge Philco radio for Yankee games, listening to them quietly at night in camp after Taps because the world was hollow, even dangerous, without such a vigil, without Mel Allen to remind me who I was and where all this was happening. The broadcast was a signal from the homeland to the boy in exile. I didn't dare look at what else was going on around me, dare risk seeing my place in it or making a stand, pro or con. My sanctuary was pretending I wasn't there.

At Camp Chipinaw where I spent most of the summers of my childhood, the rules set off a couple of hours after lunch and nap each weekday called "Optional Period" when we could pick anything we wanted but were permitted no more than three consecutive days of any one activity. Choices ranged from swimming and archery to theater, arts and crafts, and nature (a euphemism for kid biology), but, after tiring of lariat-making, imprisoning salamanders, and slapping a volleyball, I began filling out my morning's card for baseball every time. They kept telling me that that was against the rules, but I defied them and got away with it because they couldn't figure out how to stop me. Even when my counselor didn't allow "baseball" to be written beside the date, I showed up there anyway. And the guy in charge always included me in the game.

The odd thing was: I didn't like playing baseball that much. I secretly craved the relief of the other activities, the respite from competition. But baseball was home, and without it I felt blank and lost.

I had to be both special and in peril to be anything at all and, though baseball wasn't really dangerous, my involvement in it through a glass darkly reflected the world's jeopardy, especially as I used my outlaw version of the game to violate serious rules and make a commitment of faith and heart to a symbolic realm that few felt or understood.

Baseball was my cover; baseball was the name; but at the heart of it was something that had nothing to do with "base ball": it was a baptism for my body and prayer beads for my mind. It was a child's glimpse of the Dreamtime, figures in another dimension.

The beauty of the situation was that baseball's gestures were so commonplace and ordinary in 1950s America that I could do my own caper within them and still be impenetrably disguised—to the authorities and enforcers, to my tormentors, even to myself. By appearances I was a normal kid absorbed in our great National Pastime—not that much of a player and perhaps too rabid a fan for his own good . . . so who cared? Patriotism for kitsch Americana was to be rewarded. In reality, though, I was a reckless romantic and rebel, a sorcerer and radical artist in training, subverting the numerology of baseball into my own totemism and dreamscape. My compliance was mutiny, my devotion blasphemy. Once the counterculture came, my ruse was clear.

My particular fanaticism was (to the elders ultimately) a parody of their own lukewarm commitment to *everything* they espoused, baseball included. It was a statement that the era itself was lethal, much more so than atom bombs and leukemias portended. It was dangerous precisely because of its recreational meaninglessness. Everything was a joke or a contest: nothing counted; divine riddles were ignored. Until I could recognize sacraments in other forms, baseball was my compass—and even after I discovered alchemy and tarot, baseball was in my blood too deeply to abandon. With its daily gematria and aserial harmonies, it kept the anxious part of my mind occupied and provided a mantra against the threat of too much obsessive thought itself.

Though baseball wasn't truly special enough to warrant such devotion, I hitched it to my intimation of immortality and then my star to it. I was both in my milieu and not; in apple-pie America, yet in the cosmos from whence not only the ultimate totems and effigies (and broadcasts) came but to which many of those metaphysical rock 'n' roll songs referred when they spoke of everlasting love and somewhere beyond the sea.

My mother mocked and taunted me then by saying I "loved" baseball, implying that I loved it more than girls, hence was some kind of nebbish. But it wasn't that at all. Baseball was a hieroglyph through which love itself was transformed to outside her grasp. *It* wasn't special; it was irksome even as it was riveting. But as a practice beyond pleasure, it got me through the era like a magical cloak—and even preserved an innocence of love.

My friend Rob Brezsny confessed years later in his "Qabalistic Sex Magic for Shortstops and Second Basemen"* how he "discovered the sacred world of the ancestors at a game between the Tigers and the Boston Red Sox on June 23, 1956.... I was looking at the field through

---

*Published in Baseball *I Gave You All the Best Years of My Life*, edited by Kevin Kerrane and Richard Grossinger, Richmond, California: North Atlantic Books, 1978, pp. 381–390.

a concrete doorway opening onto the grandstand. As we stepped across the threshold I was stricken with the overpowering sense of HOLY. A dome of gauzy vibration surrounded the field and bound it in a deeper, denser dimension. Inside, the pristine emerald green . . . emanated an ethereal violet haze. The players themselves were dressed in the purest white. I could see shimmering shrouds of light around their bodies. . . . They were standing in sacred space."

Later, he is to realize that "the baseball field is a near-perfect analogy of the Tree of Life. . . . To be indoctrinated by the Great American Game was the perfect subterfuge. . . . My mother never would have allowed the revolutionary teachings of the Qabalah to reach me had they been offered in weird occult tongues of Angels and Archangels. [Yet] if astral structures are to become potent talismans, they must be nourished with the stuff of personal emotional associations. . . . Baseball is the model for the guerrilla meditation techniques of modern American Qabalistic Magick."

A few years younger than me and a true child of the counterculture, Rob was reconciling baseball with sex and magic. He would create the androgynous, hermaphroditic figure of the shortstop/extraterrestrial visitor from Sirius, Bowie-Bowa,* who would then initiate him into the "Great Magic Baseball Body" of rock 'n' roll, sex, astrology, and the Dionysian mysteries. His teams were not the nascent Mets and Colt .45s but the Tibetan Guerrillas and Neptune Egg Demons. His players included centerfielder Berq Qalqas, leftfielder Reptile Rodeo Man, second baseman Aqua Bilge de Ma Grotesque, and Shortstop Nemesis Pimpdragon. His pitching match-up was Violet Cloaca Protein against Ark-Brute Witch Whorl.

I was far too shy and abashed for that. When I was in high school, Bill Stafford, a towering, straight-backed Yankee pitcher whom I knew from my family's hotel, told me that I should be paying less attention to his stats and more to those of girls ("which is what I would do," he

---

*David Bowie/Larry Bowa

added, "if I weren't married to Janice"). That was confusing to me because Janice was pretty cute, and the gulf between baseball and girls held an enigma that troubled me. In the same conversation I was astonished that Billy couldn't name most of the players in the American League—only one on Kansas City, a guy who happened to be a former Yankee. Conversely he was amazed that I knew them all and cared so much, given that he was the one playing.

Stafford as baseball player and Stafford as man were two different items, an antithesis that I didn't much want to probe. After all, he was being a jerk, but he was one of my favorite players.

Maybe both of us suspected that the true mystique of baseball had nothing to do with the actual game, though neither he nor I could have intuited Brezsny's Tiger-Crocodile Body within the Baseball Diamond—to say nothing of his Winged, Mercurial Salamander at short or Naked Red-haired Priestess of Isis at second. Billy's goal then, like mine, was to keep girls and baseball separate, for each broke the other's spell. We were practicing an erotic ritual without understanding its archetypal sources. We shared that guise with a great many American males until Brezsny blew my cover.

At my all-boys' private school I was the only "scholar" who showed up for after-school hardball practice year after year, a strain on my homework regimen and quest for an A- average. In college, when I finally bolted Amherst's freshman team for intramural hockey, the coach berated me publicly. He insisted on having me announce to the assembled corps, "I'm quitting" before he would sign my transfer form.

That was okay. He made a ceremony out of something that was in fact a ceremony. I did quit. I said it out loud to the other players. I quit competitive hardball, but I didn't quit baseball. I played softball on manicured Amherst fields and meadows of Ann Arbor. I continued playing through intramural leagues in Portland, Maine, and then the hippie street-fair version at Goddard before I put in six or seven years of competitive matches in Berkeley.

During some of those games, I brought a hardball along and would throw on the side with anyone willing. Much of the time it was Robin, as this became part of the rite of his accompanying me for long days at the field. Like my old Yankee uniform, hardball was a statement of difference. I'd be running down flies or pitching to my son off to the side, keeping an eye out for my turn at bat or our return to the field. I was both the child I once was and the adult with the magical child.

In Berkeley I was committed to a Sunday pickup game at Codornices Park, though I also periodically got involved in night adult leagues on teams that included other writers and affiliated literati. The skills learned at Bill-Dave and Chipinaw found their decisive expression and match against talented Berkeley and Oakland players, most of them at least ten years younger than me, who had matriculated on sandlots from Oklahoma to Washington and in tough Southern California all-year leagues, where baseball was a native crop. The kid from Central Park finally got to play from November through March and put his game on the line, to test what he had after all the years of training.

These were solemn encounters; one's moves on the diamond counted. The team that lost at Codornices had to relinquish the field so that the next ten players on the sign-up sheet under the tree could take their places against the winning team. The losers went to the bottom of the list, so the goal, if you were going to play, was to hold the field all day or at least a substantial portion of it. I can remember a few successful afternoons, winning four or five in a row, still in leftfield in the haze of evening, watching the moon dissolve into a violet sky.

Some big-time athletes were regulars at Codornices, including former Oriole first baseman Jim Gentile's two prodigious sons, Steve and Scott. They made their living at it on industrial teams the rest of the time (much as Terry did in Selma after his stint at Baton Rouge), on the company payroll in some capacity so they would be eligible to wear the logo. On weekends they considered it a point of honor to hold the diamond for whatever team their lordships graced. Their charisma kept the play serious.

It was slow-pitch so, when my timing was on, a rip over the third baseman's head was my best ploy. I couldn't go the other way too well, so did a lot of popping out to short and left. There were certainly better outfielders than me, but chasing flies remained my forte, and I was often entrusted with the left-field line or short center, an honor given the company, though never center—I wasn't fast enough and didn't have the arm.

Not only was I a loyal and serviceable player, but my pieces about the games were published in anthologies I coedited. Once the habitués caught on, just about everyone wanted to be in my stories, even the Gentile brothers, so I did a brisk business on the side, discounting editions that carried episodes from the previous year, a somewhat uncomfortable mercantile role for one of only two Jewish guys from New York who showed up as regulars. But then, as I said, baseball was about transgression, about breaking rules, defying clichés. It was certainly never about being cool.

The city-league games were even more strife-ridden than those at Codornices, as guys continually turned on their teammates for errors or out of unprobed constitutional irritation. When I played on Creative Arts Printing—a bunch put together by novelist Barry Gifford for the shop where he had his office—I was at constant odds with a press operator. Perhaps because his father was some sort of executive for the Rochester, New York team, this guy picked on me the way bullies once did in grade school, even though we were both in our forties. I remember his name: Donald Waful, though I always thought it should be "Awful."

On the day that the opposition forfeited and I made my running backhand catch crossing the rightfield line, Awful tried to give away my position to some guy from our opponent for the pickup game that we chose afterward, and, when I refused to budge, he cursed and then took a swing at me. I shoved him back, and Barry had to step between us.

Robin, who watched most of my games during his preadolescent years, remembers that exchange as the only time he saw his father in a physical altercation. The sport caused some players to regress to the quarrelsome baseballers we were as children.

Meanwhile Robin played in the Berkeley equivalent of Little League—his manager the esteemed poet Bob Hass, who recruited a team mostly of friends' and writers' children along with his own son Luke. They were in a tough division and didn't win a single game. Lindy and I cheered him from the stands every game, our little guy with his helmet at the plate, a late starter at baseball, but still able to catch up enough that he would line a single against Stanford on the Sunken Diamond in a real college game, by then towering over his parents' heights.

I occasionally played for another team called The Best Minds of our Generation, managed by Jack Shoemaker, a bookseller turned elite publisher, whose son was also on Hass' team. I tend to forget how combative they were because they were so smart and hip at their charade, far more radical at jive than the middle-brow *Zyzzyva* crew. I was never formally on their team but occasionally filled in when they were short a player.

One Sunday I went to practice with them, and afterwards they went out looking for a pickup game. On a nearby field they found a group that included one guy with a wooden leg and some girls who couldn't play a lick. We were winning something like 20-0 when, on a thrown-away grounder to second, two of our guys came barreling around third together just ahead of the retrieved ball and Jack was standing by home plate as if it were the major leagues, his face contorted, waving his arms up and down, screaming, "Slide, dammit, slide!" The ball went through anyway, 22-0.

That team also had a major malevolent presence, an art critic by the name of Snow. In the late '70s, I'd occasionally get recruited so that they could field a team, but Snow would try to find a way to keep me out of the lineup, usually because there was another recruit he preferred. For some reason, like Awful, he had it in for me, making me feel as if it were Bill-Dave Group all over again and I were standing in my Yankee uniform in the snow. I didn't have to be eight years old or shy and vulnerable for my sullen trespass to be communicated, for me to arouse the bully and regulator in a certain kind of person. Those who wanted to defend their own coolness invariably turned against me.

Eventually I decided I wasn't going to play for the Minds anymore, but one day they got particularly desperate. I was busy at work under a deadline, plus I was taking care of both kids that afternoon and didn't want to think about baseball, let alone drag my ass into a game. My book-designer buddy on the Minds, Dave Bullen, heard me out: *Planet Medicine,* children at home—this was when Robin was still too young to be a fan. . . . But he still pleaded on the phone for my attendance. I finally said I didn't want to show up just to have Ed Snow keep me out of the game. Dave gave me his word of honor that I'd play.

From where we lived then in Oakland it was six or seven miles out to the Richmond field. Sure enough, Snow had brought his own ringer, a former minor leaguer who was way better than I was. But I had two unhappy kids in tow and Dave's guarantee. He did speak up for me, but Snow ignored him and, turning to stare me down, snarled, "So what were you working on that's so important we've got to let you be on the Minds ahead of a better player?" Dave quickly offered a compromise: we'd each play half the game.

It's funny how baseball sometimes works out. This all-star guy had two at-bats and lined into two outs. I hit two bloop singles and scored twice in a game-winning rally as we batted around. Neither of us got a play in the outfield.

About the time that my playing career ended, I started the previously mentioned East Bay Baseball Satellite TV Club in the garage of our home in Berkeley. I recruited fellow revolutionaries at the annual April baseball reading at Cody's Bookstore on Telegraph Avenue and then a few more by word of mouth. Every member paid $100 and contributed monthly dues, as we paid off the dish and installation. We were the only guys (and women) in our circles able to follow their non-local teams, tuning in mostly raw feeds. We were breaking rules imposed by the networks, owners, and pro baseball itself.

Transgression by satellite dish meant that it was our game more than theirs because we cared more than they did and no one was paying us to watch or weave the venerable mythology. Like Hopi shamans praying the sun up each morn and then keeping its sacred calendar, we brought baseball to life each day by our devotion to real-time games and their box-score synopses.

An unpredictable group of fans, we would gather in our garage on game nights. Robin would bring his homework and do French sentences or math problems between innings. During the glory years (1984–1988), we were continually on the phone with Keith Hernandez' father John, south of San Francisco, talking over the game, us giving him the plays when the feed was on the one satellite he couldn't get on his dish because of a hill in his neighborhood.

I was issued my first press pass that same season and started visiting the Met clubhouse as a stealth reporter for the *Voice*. I talked to a number of players, briefly even to Darrell Strawberry and Dwight Gooden. They were used to answering questions from native New Yorkers who looked as though they should be teaching college instead of interviewing jocks. I created a stream of baseball hypertext (see the 1984 ethnography later in this book).

◆

After Terry went down to Tidewater in the spring of 1987, disaster struck the parent team, pitcher by pitcher. Gooden was placed on the disabled list because of substance abuse. Roger McDowell got a hernia. Rick Aguilera's elbow had to go under the knife. Sid Fernandez' arm hurt so much he couldn't lift it. Bobby Ojeda couldn't put any weight on his knee. Ron Darling tore his thumb. Before Terry threw a pitch for Norfolk, he was back in New York, helping to defend the title.

He didn't crack the starting rotation, however, until David Cone tried to bunt an Atlee Hammaker slider in San Francisco and got a finger in the way. In the words of Cone, "It was only then that Terry got his shot in the Mets' rotation. Little may have been expected of him, but everyone who knew the guy's heart and what he had inside him wasn't surprised. This so-called Triple-A pitcher promptly took us all on a ride rarely seen in baseball history."

The moment had come at last when the Mets, hard as they apparently kept trying, couldn't deny Mr. Leach. They had no one else. Terry had deserved it in '83, '84, '85, and, of course, '86, but no one spoke to those anomalies. I don't think the bosses or their finks even noticed them. I'm not sure, from ownership on down, they understood anything about Terry Leach—where he came from, who he was as a person or player, what their fatuous, knee-jerk dismissals said, not so much about him but about who they were and what baseball itself had become.

They may have feigned that it was about winning games, but it wasn't. It certainly wasn't about fairness or earning opportunity or honor even among thieves. I could say that it was about image and money, but I'm not sure that's the answer either—their dull choices cost games and pennants. In a sense, it was just plain bull-headed ignorance, refusing to acknowledge what they had, to grok Terry's deed because they hadn't orchestrated it by their inane protocols. They were like politicians whose main goal is to prove themselves right, especially when they are hang-em-out-to-dry wrong, all consequences be damned. Once they ditched Terry injudiciously, they were stuck defending that blunder for years, covering their asses rather than opening their minds. They couldn't validate the guy because his success was itself subversive, a critique of their own precious ideologies and covenants. So his actual achievements never registered above the pitching coach's unexamined criteria or the GM's Tory bias.

"Leachie," Wally Backman confided to him one night after he had just extended his scoreless-inning streak, "we're going to have to throw you out there to start one time. Every time we put you out there in the middle of the game you throw a gem. We've got to get you out there at the beginning." But it wasn't Wally's call.

The next stop after Cone's flubbed bunt was L.A., and Davey Johnson had only one choice for starter. The opponent was Fernando Valenzuela, one of the game's best pitchers at the time, almost unbeatable at home. Leach's performance that night comprised six innings, four hits, no earned runs, and the win. Then it was back to the bullpen because, without much of a rotation left, that was where he and Jesse Orosco were most needed, one or the other or both of them almost every day in fact. Hernandez took to calling him "Jack" for Jack-of-all-trades. Far from being a pitcher with a bad arm, Terry was the man with the bionic arm who could throw five days a week without decline in effectiveness.

After a skein of relief appearances, he got a second start in Montreal. With Tim Raines batting leadoff, the Expos were fast, and Terry wanted to "keep those guys off the bases. Okay, I went right after them, no walks, shut them out through eight innings. Got eleven guys on groundballs because I had that old sidewinding sinker of mine working fine. Down the home stretch of that game I retired seventeen batters in a row before they finally scored a couple of runs off me in the ninth. . . . I really wanted that shutout. I was getting hungry. . . ."

He was now in the rotation until further notice. He won his sixth in a row in Philadelphia in late June and then, next time out on July 2, pitched his best game of the season against the Reds in Cincinnati. The ball was moving all over the place; he felt he could make it change speeds and positions at will. He had become as unhittable as a pitcher gets, dealing his assortment with concentration and control, inventing new versions of upshoots and dippers, pushing the edge further and further, because no one (to present knowledge) had thrown those pitches or attacked batters in that motif before.

"The trouble was," recalled a correspondent to the Ultimate Mets website, "even though [Terry] always did well as a starter they refused to let him keep starting because he was a right-handed sidearmer and it was thought that he couldn't avoid tough lefties. . . ." Baseball being old guard, its prevailing wisdom sided with Jim Frey, that a right-handed submariner couldn't go inside against left-handed hitters.

But it was exactly by busting them inside that Terry kept lefties from leaning over the plate and whacking his outside deliveries. With them fearing the unpredictable inside ball, he could get plenty of groundouts from weak swings across the outside black: "I neither knew nor cared who was hitting against me. I didn't *like* knowing. I didn't want to be paying attention to that. I wanted those hitters to be attending to *me.*" Eric Davis, Dave Parker, and company offered meek resistance. Terry got the shutout, a complete game two-hitter. In the sixth, as the visitors were trotting off the field, Keith Hernandez called out, "Boy, am I glad I'm not hitting against you!"

The moment in the sun wasn't over, but its light was beginning to fade. Some loose cartilage in Terry's right knee hurt like hell, though he nabbed number eight in Atlanta, barely able to push off on the mound. He had to lift his leg up with his hands to transport it in and out of his car. Velocity was down to seventy-seven miles an hour, and he was in constant jeopardy of hanging an outside pitch to a right-handed hitter. Just before the all-star break Terry went on the fifteen-day disabled list, so wasn't eligible for the game. He came back right afterwards, but he didn't have his edge anymore. He beat the Expos twice on wile and guts to take the skein to 10-0 before finally losing at Chicago on the 15th of August.

His line at end of the campaign read 11-1, 3.22. The Mets came in second, three games behind the Cardinals. After the season was over, Terry had his knee operated on, and they picked out a career's worth of torn-up cartilage.

"Has anyone ever thought that maybe Terry Leach should have been the NL Cy Young Award winner in 1987?" asked Jeff in Florida of readers of the Ultimate Mets site. "The winner was Steve Bedrosian. I think Terry had a better year, 11-1. If I remember correctly, he would have been 13-1 had it not been for a young Randy Myers blowing a couple of his games."

Johnmn55 agreed, "If he hadn't hurt his knee on the hard mound in the Astrodome in about his tenth straight win, who knows what kind of stats he might have ended up with? He never could get any respect and it was frustrating that his good appearances in the early '80s couldn't win him a regular job even with a bad team."

DannyBoy added, "In a year of tight voting and no clearcut winner, Terry not receiving at least one vote or finishing in the top ten is a tragedy. He kept the Mets in the pennant race throughout the summer...."

◆

I met Terry in 1987, late in the streak when he was already out of the rotation because of his bum knee. He was by himself in the visitors' clubhouse, sitting on a stationary bike, pumping away, reading a mass-market mystery. He had a moustache plus a bit of a goatee and a sweet face, soft eyes and a ready smile belying the pugnacious rhino on the mound. He looked like lots of guys I had been friendly with in college. This was the first time I had encountered him at Candlestick and he seemed approachable, so I walked right up and introduced myself.

He said that he was doing a lot of clubhouse biking these days instead of throwing, trying to get his knee stronger. In fact, by Davey Johnson's edict, he was not warming up any more unless he was going into the game. His southern accent resonated heart, the King James Bible, and Shakespeare's England more than the Selma of Barry Maguire's "Eve of Destruction."

Robin and I had been following Terry Leach over the years, minors and majors. We knew almost every public nuance of his career, and we were luxuriating in his present success. We did not have the Satellite Club when he pitched his one-hitter but, like his friends in Alabama, were shocked to read the next morning's paper. I remember exclaiming to Robin, "What a great box score!" I repeated that to Terry, and he recalled his buddies at McDonald's. Then I mentioned Luis Aguayo coming up in the AAA World Series. His eyes lit up and he grinned—I had proven myself a true aficionado. "Yeah, I recognized him. I thought, 'Wait a second, I know that guy. . . .' Then I punched him out on four pitches."

I had quite a cache of news to bring back to Robin: We hadn't realized that Terry's knee injury was so severe and that it, rather than the hitters finally figuring him out, was causing his present decline. It was during our stationary-bike conversation that I found out he hadn't always been a submariner. He related how he had been released by the Braves before being signed at Jackson (somehow Robin and I still hadn't figured out that transaction). I learned too that he had never been considered a prospect "by anyone but you and your son who didn't know any better," and that was why he went up and down between the Mets and Tides, second fiddle to the Doug Sisks and Rick Ownbeys who couldn't touch his work any more than Leroy Niemann could carry Pablo Picasso's brush.

Over the course of our rambling discussion, Terry described how he and a bunch of his teammates at Tidewater ran around high-fiving one another in the clubhouse in 1986 on the day they heard that Rick Anderson, a career minor leaguer and everyone's pal, got called up to make an emergency start for the Mets during their pennant drive. He betrayed not a hint of regret or jealousy that it was Anderson and not him for that game.

He was such an effortless, compelling storyteller that I realized he could spin a whole book there on the bike, and I made a rash offer. He replied affably: "I can't do a tell-all thing like Jim Bouton, but I could do a true-life baseball book if you're interested."

I was.

He thought about it for a moment and then offered, "How about you contact me after I retire in a few years." He wrote down his phone number and took mine.

Suddenly Mel Stottlemyre appeared with news, reprise of an old song: Sid Fernandez was too sick to pitch; could Terry start?

The stationary biker smiled and said, "Well, I guess I better get down off this horse and make myself ready. We'll continue this conversation at another time." On that short notice, he turned in a credible performance, though the Mets lost.

I offered my interview of Terry Leach to the *Voice* and, after they turned it down, *Mets Inside Pitch* accepted but never used it.

◆

Well, Terry had a longer career than either of us imagined at that time. He pitched six more seasons in the majors, only the first and change for the Mets. In 1988 he worked out of the bullpen because all five Met starters were healthy: Gooden, Darling, Cone, Ojeda, Fernandez. Randy Myers was the closer. After making an early-season adjustment and driving harder off his right leg, Terry went 7-2, 2.52, with three saves in fifty-two games for a team that ran away with its division.

In the playoffs the Mets ran into a hot Dodger team led by Orel Hershiser just off a record scoreless-innings streak. Dwight Gooden, wasted on god-knows-what, carelessly hung that late pitch to Mike Scioscia at Shea, Game Three, to turn the series around. In the deciding seventh game Ron Darling was a lame if obvious choice. As a Met-fan friend said of the match-up, "It's not Hershiser who scares me; it's Darling." Who knows what might have happened if Davey Johnson had broken tradition and handed the ball to Terry Leach? Terry might have summoned up one of those performances from beyond. Maybe the Mets would have lost anyway because they got beat 6-0 that night, or maybe they'd still be playing.

When Darling couldn't find his way out of the second inning, Davey brought in Dwight Gooden on two days' rest. Gooden ordinarily never came out of the bullpen, partly because he needed above-average warm-up time. By the time he found a third out, the Dodgers had put five on the board, and that was the season. Terry pitched two scoreless innings in the game, five in the series, but his team came up short again.

An 18-3 record over two seasons usually garners raves, but Terry satisfied himself with a guaranteed contract and the assurance that he was in New York for a number of years to come—yet the 1989 season had barely begun when he was packed off to Kansas City for nothing (the Royals didn't want to make the mistake of a few years earlier when they gave away David Cone). "Frank Cashen, the man responsible for shipping me out of New York, got asked one time later on why he'd traded me away. 'Sometimes you do addition by subtraction,' was Frank's reply." 18-3? A guy who either started or threw relief, whatever you needed, whatever you asked of him—and did it well. "That's funny arithmetic to me."

Team buffs agreed. Here are three more entries from Terry's "fan memories" section on the Ultimate Mets database: "He was one of the most under-appreciated guys of all time. I can't remember him ever pitching poorly. I loved the guy."

"Terry Leach was a class act. Everyone is right when they say they never gave him a chance. He was and is one of my favorite all-time players."

"The 1987 season would have been totally lost without his performance both from the bullpen and as a starter. I lamented the decision the Mets made to trade him. I think it was probably one of the team's top ten mistakes."

Leach went from a year in Kansas City to the Twins, where he came out of the bullpen in 1990 and '91, pitching in the Series that year and earning a ring. His last full season, 1992 with the White Sox, was one of his best. Except for lacking a few innings pitched, he led the American League in ERA at 1.95. He had pretty decent results in '93 also, but was considered way too old by then. His arm was hurting and, though he could still get guys out, no one wanted a codger over forty with a bad wing, even one with a track record of rehabilitating and coming back strong. So Terry called me one April evening as the '94 season kicked off without him: "I'm retired. Now let's do that book."

Years later he heard from an ex-teammate still on the Mets how, after he left, the club tried to get another submarine hurler, Jeff Innis, who had a different game entirely, to replace Terry: "The guys would be all over him, telling him how Leachie used to do things. It was Leachie this, Leachie that. Leachie's way was the right way. Things haven't been the same since Leachie left. 'It was amazing,' the guy told me. '*Every* day your name came up in that Mets clubhouse some-where.' Finally Innis said to them, 'Well, *why* did you get rid of Leach anyway? Why don't you just get him back if you can't get along with-out him?'"

◆

Lots had changed since Terry's and my meeting at Candlestick: Robin was through college and working as a staff biologist at San Francisco Estuary Institute; our daughter Miranda was a student at Santa Cruz. I wanted to do the book with Terry but couldn't figure out how. He was busy running a baseball school in Largo, Florida, with ex-Royal teammate Tony Ferreira and Mets buddy David Cone (still active in the show though no longer a Met). He had zero plans to be in Califor-nia, while I had none to be in Florida. So the idea stayed dormant a couple of years. Then it got rescued by something unrelated.

I had been studying craniosacral therapy since 1989 as part of my long-term exploration of healing and medicine, and in January 1996 I was invited by John Upledger, an author of our press and founder of the system, to join an intensive in March at his institute in Palm Beach Gardens, Florida.

Craniosacral therapy (CST), a way of tapping into the body's many layers and matrices, involves using educated hands to sense and adjust subtle pressures of fluids and tensions of fascia and viscera, revitaliz-ing organs and restoring underlying rhythms toward their natural states. The March intensive was quite advanced, and I was a subject, not a practitioner. For two weeks a group of eight therapists worked with six of us.

In between these excursions by day, I took down Terry's story at night. He drove trans-Florida to meet Lindy and me and, for two whole evenings, sat with us in otherwise-empty corners of random motel lobbies, as I taped him, getting the details of his career phase by phase. While baseball was in complete contrast to craniosacral work, it was also a refreshing diversion, a balm and a catalyst for the act of healing.

When I met Terry on that bike in San Francisco nine years earlier, he was an active major leaguer. Now he was well on the nether side of a completed career. Though he was confident he could still get hitters out if summoned on the morrow from some hypothetical bullpen, that ability hadn't made any difference to the rulers of the sport in his salad days, and it certainly didn't matter now that he was older than just about all the players. In the Candlestick locker room he had looked harried and a bit gimpy on his injured knee. I didn't discern the athlete in him as much as the good old boy; he could have been a country-and-western singer or a genial guy at a bar. Here in Florida he was solid, trim, and sunburned, casually dressed in Bermudas and a crew shirt; he looked like a dapper coach or a golf pro, ready to go nine (or ten) innings, two sets, or thirty-six holes.

At dinner Terry questioned me. The first night he wanted to know about craniosacral therapy, and I did the best I could to put it into a context. I remembered that one-time Met pitcher Craig Swan practiced a related discipline, Rolfing. Terry knew Swan from his visits to major-league clubhouses, educating players on alternative training methods, so I based a description of my daily sessions on Swan's methods of manual therapy. CST was light and inductive, whereas Swanny's stuff was deep-tissue molding.

"Sounds about right," Terry mused. Still, he thought it sounded pretty weird, especially conversations with cells and past-life fugues. He was Christian in his upbringing and ethics, but I had a good tale from the day as vindication: one of five Hutterite-sect women accompanying two paralyzed men from Western Canada to the intensive remarked to the group during an evening discussion how she had feared coming to the Institute because "I wasn't sure this wasn't the work of the Devil. But after seeing *what you do here,* I know you are true servants of God. This is a place of healing and miracles that brings back the biblical times of our Lord."

When I reported that Hallmark moment, Terry "amened" it. It wasn't long before he stopped joking and wondered aloud if craniosacral work and his own submarine pitches didn't share a domain of subtlety, indirection, and bucking the establishment. He wished he had known about this kind of therapy back in his Auburn days when he kept re-damaging his arm but, even if we had instigated an unlikely cultural leap of faith, the Institute was a couple of years shy of inception then.

Over those two dinners Terry changed from a celebrity (whom Robin and I had tracked years earlier) to a compatriot. By the end of the second dinner Lindy, he, and I had set aside our differences of background and the circumscribed project that had brought us together and rambled on about families, childhood, pop culture, and metaphysics. The three of us shared some laughs about past lives (and life in general). Cosmic humor was one of Terry's gifts.

The tapes themselves, recorded after the meals, were thorough enough that I imagined we could finish a book by phone, but the project soon lapsed into dormancy. I did get an intern to transcribe the interviews, but the resulting manuscript was full of gaps and inconsistencies, and Terry and I never seemed able to make the time to address them. He was always at the school or traveling to out-of-town workshops. Finally he recorded two hours on his own, so I transcribed those cassettes and chronologically ordered them. The synthesis was still far shy of a book. As seasons passed and new players replaced Terry's last colleagues, the milieu of his story evaporated. I was losing confidence in the contemporariness of the story.

Like our kids' youths, Terry's career had become medieval history in the wink of an eye. Postmodern moneyball made the early '90s feel like 1955. After the latest strike and labor victory by the players in '94, after the banishment of Pete Rose with his 3,000+ hits, after the wink at doping and growth hormones in the locker rooms, after the disgrace of Gooden and Strawberry and the revelation that the '86 Mets had been among the all-time cocaine teams, after hundred-million-dollar contracts and preemptions by George Steinbrenner to steal every meaningful star and go to the Fall Classic by fiat, we had entered the era of the World Wrestling Federation and bionic Home Run Derbies.

One late summer day in 1999 local Berkeley poet Tom Clark phoned me. Tom was baseball's bard: a novelist, essayist, painter, and biographer, co-author of *No Big Deal*, the 1977 bio of ex-Detroit Tiger Mark Fidrych, the account (now out of print) of the career, in his own racy words, of one of the strangest major leaguers to come down the pike. Famous for talking to the ball on the mound, pure lower-class New England trailer trash, Fidrych strewed Deadhead rants and four-letter sound bites while posting a stellar record until he threw out his arm after little more than a season in the bigs.

During the '70s Tom painted a gallery of Warhol-quality baseball portraits, and we published *Fan Poems*, a collection of his Major League landscapes and player vignettes. He was very active in the literary scene then but had been a hermit and a misanthrope for over a decade, one of the few people in my world whose companionship exacted a mega-price in querulousness and abuse. I had stopped seeing him years earlier, though I knew through the grapevine that he had fallen on hard times.

By the time he said hello to me at the poetry reading of a mutual friend a few months prior to his phone call, his youthful Tom Cruise appearance had morphed into the tragic artist and executioner he actually was and I didn't recognize the surly "stranger" greeting me. I said, "Sorry, but who are you?" He retorted with more umbrage than comedy, "Jesse Orosco." Ringing me later, he more humbly stated the truth, "I'm sick and broke and need work." Moved and inspired, I at once began brainstorming what to pull together. The stalled Terry Leach project was on the short list that I offered him.

I ended up funding three books by Tom, none of them simple to collaborate on, all of them economic disasters. Finishing Terry's story was the opening foray and, despite the aggravation factor and cost, Tom was made for the job. He knew baseball inside-out, in fact still walked the streets like a hobo with a portable radio, tracking the Oakland A's, an act of defiant isolationism rather than communal fandom.

At the outset he either had never heard of Terry Leach or didn't remember him—he wasn't sure. One of his first questions, since all things had to be measured by Oaklandia, was whether Leach had played with present A's pitcher Tim Hudson's father at Auburn.

By conducting epic phone interviews with Terry, Tom soon mastered his narrative rhythms and language, taking down his story from the beginning again and filling in the holes. It required the better part of a year. If I were cynical, I would say that Tom dragged it out on purpose, extending the budget beyond even my worst prognosis.

Twenty years earlier Tom had picked a pet phrase of Fidrych's for the name of his autobiography, and he correspondingly chose to title Terry's book after one of the pitcher's favorite lines, *Things Happen for a Reason.* It was a cliché, but the right one.

Tom also used it as an axe to hit me over the head with when I objected to his cutting some of the better stories I had collected from Terry. I smelled competitiveness as well as recreational orneriness but kept my mouth shut as he snapped disingenuously: "There are two rules for everything in this book: 'things happen' and 'they happen for a reason.' Yours don't."

As *Things Happen . . .* headed for the printer, I worked on its credits. I got Tom's and my mutual friend, novelist Paul Auster, a lifelong Met fan living in Brooklyn, to write an introduction. It began: "I remember him well. A stocky right-hander with a sidearm delivery who wore number 26. Not much speed, but a tricky combination of sliders and sinkers that kept the hitters off balance: 'give them a little air to mash at.'"

Another mutual friend of Tom's and mine, science-fiction writer Jonathan Lethem, keynoted the back cover: "Without ostentation or nostalgia Tom Clark shows us how the Lardner-Runyon vernacular tradition still guilelessly lurks in the heart of American life. . . ."

I managed to track down senior Met columnist Bob Klapisch for another blurb: "In an age when baseball is dominated by scandal and dollar-lust, it's nice to know someone still loves the game for the most fundamental reasons." He called the book "a celebration of pure base-ball, tracking the career of a pitcher whose perspective is honest and touchingly innocent."

I had done the improbable. From that mysterious moment when Terry Leach's name first appeared as a stat line in *Baseball America*, I had ferreted out the inside story and then refined it and put it on full marquee. Though few fans realized it, Terry Leach had had a scintillat-ing, absurd career, vindicating the primeval hieroglyph of 1980. While making one of baseball's most ingenious all-time comebacks from injury, while posting preposterous, almost seditious stats in the bigs, he was routinely overlooked, insulted, exiled. But now his tale had become literature: with a bit of Valjean, Jude the Obscure, Billy Budd.

Terry Leach was the poster boy for Major League Baseball's myopia, its propensity to trivialize and even sabotage success that didn't fit a stereotype. Robbed of his fastball, Terry had invented a pitching style and repertoire so radical and unique, so zany and masterful, that new parameters were needed to scout and measure it. He demonstrated its effectiveness over and over on the field of play against red-blooded hitters of his time, right before everyone's eyes, and they just didn't see it, those so-called lords of baseball. His submarine pitching wasn't just theoretical—it disposed of hitters; it won games. If Frank Cashen had given Terry Leach the chance he earned in 1981, he could have logged a hundred, two hundred victories for the Mets before calling it a career. As it was, he was lucky to notch twenty. The only redemption left was telling it like it was—a transparent account. Not sour grapes or martyrdom, not whining and bitching, just the irreproachable tale of the journey itself.

For once, the imaginal and imaginary worlds evoked by baseball—its fantasy doppelgängers—had cloned their own genre. This was not some rotisserie-league ghost parasitic upon mere colophons generated by baseball; it went in the other direction, toward the human truth at baseball's heart. The wonder was that it sprouted in the same place as the make-believe and was fueled by the naive solipsism and wonder that fans everywhere nurture. As the pursuit of icons iconicized itself, imaginary and real fields of play merged. Publishing was a game too, after all.

The Terry Leach story had become the payoff for a lifetime of following guys from Gene Woodling and Gil McDougald to Rod Kanehl and Wayne Garrett, blindly through symbols, no matter who they really were. Had Robin and I, by some unintentional intuition or divination, found in the enigma of a few vagrant numbers a rare pitcher whose perspective was honest and innocent?

Terry supplied the final touch: David Cone's email address along with his offer to write a preface. What a lineup we were assembling, better than any fantasy league: Auster, Lethem, Clark, Cone, Klapisch, plus a signed photograph by Gary Carter for the frontispiece, a shot of the Kid embracing Terry after one of those 1987 games: "It's been an absolute pleasure catching you during your streak and always."

Cone gave it his best shot but, by his own admission, "I shouldn't give up my day job, right?" He and I went back and forth about a dozen times before we had our preface. I wrote more than he did, but there was nothing that didn't have roots in something he supplied or that he didn't rewrite back into the text. I joked with Robin that it was quite fun waking up in the morning and checking my email to see one or two from David Cone.

Our best conceit was an Elvis conflation saluting Terry's favorite singer, a blend of Cone and Grossinger, proving fan and player could jam:

They once said of Brooks Robinson that he played like a guy who came down from a higher league. Well, Terry didn't have Brooks' kind of raw talent, but he sure came from somewhere none of us had ever heard of before. It was as astonishing as if an unknown Elvis had just taken the mound and tossed "Hound Dog" and "Heartbreak Hotel" in succession right out of his hat impromptu, no warning. Then followed it up with "Jailhouse Rock" and "Don't be Cruel." And still wasn't halfway done. No way, Terry.

What followed is pure Cone:

Ten straight victories from the Southern gentleman out of Selma, Alabama. Ten pretty-much monster games. Ten masterpieces worthy of a crafty vet. . . .

To a man, our clubhouse was filled with admiration and hope as Terry carried the pitching staff—in fact, the entire team—through the dog days of summer back into the pennant race.

It wasn't just Terry's pitching success but rather the manner in which he carried himself both on and off the field. He was a friend and example to everyone around him, equally in adversity and success.

Then, a bit later, Mr. Cone spoke it all:

He was a colleague and a buddy, a man whose actions were as true as his words. At the same time that he was teaching a master class on the mound, he was a cut-up of the highest order, truly a funny guy. . . . Quite simply Terry is one of the best teammates I've ever been around.

During the years I was helping put the book together, Terry and I chatted now and again on the phone, and it was as if, through the book, he and I had become teammates. He treated me munificently, our project aside, almost like one of his old minor-league charges.

I didn't like being on airplanes, so had trouble going anywhere far. Yet Terry had flown all over the country during his career. I recalled his frequent travels to him, seeking transference of courage, good old-fashioned faith and confidence. What was his nostrum, I wondered, on those requisite flights to Atlanta and L.A.?

Gracious as usual, he recalled stuff I had been through already and out-and-out promised I'd be okay: "You got through the hard part of life; the rest is a snap." Some years later I recounted the exchanges between us in an essay called "A Phenomenology of Panic."* Here is a reconsidered version:

> As we became friendly, Terry took it upon himself to encourage and reassure me, even calling at times to check in. When my wife and I were flying to England and I was anxious about the long airtime, he reminded me to have a beer for him on the plane. He had had plenty of them during bumpy flights in his Met days, as he spent hours playing 'Name that Tune' and other goofy games between cities. He took down my departure and arrival times and told me he'd be thinking about me and sending me good wishes during those hours. Somehow he knew the right thing to say.
>
> When I was freaking out once about a marital argument, he sighed and said, 'Oh man, I get like that too. My wife would like me to disappear. I just have to go somewhere else, a ball-field, maybe catch a few innings, any game, just a park down the street. Wow, some days it just seems like I can't do life.'
>
> His pep talks were so real and heartfelt, so artlessly empathic and cheerful, that they had the amazing effect of snapping me out of whatever funk I was in, connecting me back to the world and making it normal again.

---

*Published in *Panic: Origins, Insight, and Treatment,* edited by Leonard J. Schmidt, MD, and Brooke Warner, North Atlantic Books, 2002, pp 95–163.

Although Terry is ten years younger than me, I am the eternal kid and he is the major leaguer. No one can enable a child to be here the way a parent can but, through our lives, many people get to ' play that role. We know instinctively who they are and recognize their authenticity. Likewise, they know who they are and, as best as they can, they nurture. We take care of each other.

Some of us do it better than others, and Terry had been doing it well since his days as an older player on buses to small towns in Georgia and Texas. Later he was supremely generous with guys on the Mets, Twins, and White Sox, Cone bearing witness ("Terry supported us. We knew that, and we rooted for him too. . . ."). As much as he wanted to get ahead in the game, there was not a jealous bone in his body, even when other guys succeeded at his expense on the depth chart. He was always ready with a handshake and kudos. To this day Doug Sisk, the guy who kept taking Terry's place on the major-league roster, remains one of his closest friends.

When he was pitching for the Royals and living in Kansas, Terry actually got off the interstate after midnight in rainy high winds after saving a game and helped a guy who had skidded off the highway onto the median to free his pregnant wife from their car, vehicles hydroplaning across the road in all directions, even past them onto the other side as they pulled and coaxed. He called it "getting two saves in one night." But he wasn't taking credit, just finding the cosmic humor, giving the universe its due.

You have to wonder about a business that won't give a guy like this a chance. A bad penny? Addition by subtraction? What did Cashen mean? The man was kind enough to sit with a dad and his kid in the bullpen and discuss Single-A players with respect, despite the fact they knew nothing and he knew everything. Was the game so corrupt that the elders couldn't tell the good eggs from the bad ones anymore? Was it, as Klapisch decried, no longer baseball, but scandal and dollar-lust?

Who were the Mets anyway? Once Fred Wilpon became involved with the team, they stood for less and less. It wasn't just a matter of being cheap with World Series rings. It was goodbye to dozens of players who represented Shea Stadium with pride and integrity: Hubie Brooks, Randy Myers, Terry Leach, David West, Paul Byrd, Melvin Mora, Jay Payton, Jae Seo. Forget Seo's 7-2 record. Forget the retinues of Korean fans who came out to cheer every time he pitched. Forget any team identity or loyalty or continuity. Just bring in another mercenary.

What was it? A mixture of vanity and ignorance? Rube-at-the-carnival gullibility? New York provinciality? An endless wannabe mentality so that you always envied what others had and never valued your own?

Wilpon tried to help my father out with his failing resort, proposing at one point to build condos around his lake. They enjoyed each other, and I met Fred a few times in the early 1980s, sat at Shea with him. He was the source of my comp tickets. I wanted to like and respect him. He was a savior who bought the Mets, by his own acknowledgment, as a kind of public trust.

The first time I visited with Fred was when I went East to attend a book party for *Baseball Diamonds*, the Doubleday edition of my baseball anthology and, since the team and publishing company were partly co-owned, our editor took a few of us out to the company box at Shea Stadium afterwards. By the time we got there John Fulgham of the Cardinals was in complete control with a big lead and John Pacella, a rookie, was mopping up for the Mets, his cap falling off (Jim Bouton style) on every other pitch as he overthrew his fastball.

I found myself sitting next to "the man," and we talked about the Mets' prognosis. He was negative on Pacella and another touted fire-baller, Juan Berenguer, but he said it was a good day for the franchise: they had just signed their number-one draft pick, Darryl Strawberry.

The rock singer and baseball maniac George Thorogood,* a buddy of my co-editor and a longtime Mets fan who had never been to Shea before, came along with us and was rooting vocally for the Mets while intermittently trying to get Wilpon to sign his buddies Bernie Carbo and Jay Johnstone. When an usher asked Fred if he wanted him removed, the owner responded: "No, but find me five more like him." In complete Met uniform with cigar, peering around the corner of the dugout to talk to Claudell Washington and Joel Youngblood, George screamed for Pacella to throw the curve that Wilpon promised he didn't have.

By the time George was signing autographs for players and bitching about recent transactions, Wilpon sighed and wondered whether he shouldn't have taken the usher up on his offer. "Rock music and baseball don't mix," he added enigmatically, then a *non sequitur:* "Concerts ruin the field."

(Afterwards, looking back at the ballpark from the parking lot, George announced: "To hell with Yankee Stadium. This place is a shrine.")

Later that season our whole family was East, and Fred provided tickets for us in his personal box. It was a chivalrous gesture, but I couldn't sense anything from the man in the adjacent seat but prerogative and possessiveness, a soft-spoken but unexamined arrogance, an inflated pride in his own minimal achievements mixed with a kind of myopic conservatism, a mild version of what one encounters in religious fundamentalists. He was basically humorless, addicted to thinking inside the box. In the rambling course of conversations, he decried or denounced indigenous culture, experimental art, magic, myth, qabala, synchronicity—I know, I was a fool even to bring these things up. He mainly wanted to preach with a kind of faux humility and measured urbanity. After a while, we just sat there silently, two cats sunning.

---

*George put up the money to have a *bona fide* hardball stadium built for community use in his and Kerrane's hometown of Newark, Delaware.

In a role reversal, Wilpon was the redneck and moneychanger in the temple; Terry the mensch, the team rabbi.

When I sent a letter to Fred a few years later about the Satellite Baseball Club, thinking that he would at least be amused and say the right thing since he *was* a friend of my father, he wrote that he intended legal action against those who were stealing his signal and I should take heed of law-breaking.

The Yankees of George Steinbrenner, as much as I dislike them as a mercenary crew, were created boldly, thinking outside the box, and they have a heart and soul, with homegrown players like Bernie Williams, Andy Pettitte, Mariano Rivera, and Derek Jeter at their core. Do you think even bully George would have given a fuck about the pirating of his broadcasts? His attitude was always: the more Yankee fans the better.

The Mets of Fred Wilpon were and still are* a coward's imitation of the Yankees, no heart or soul, no loyalty to their employees, a mere pretense of a family shop. While I would like the owners to represent true multicultural, improvisational, big-hearted New York, they are a bunch of *nouveau riche* clerks from Long Island, writ large—menial, turf-conscious suburbanites. Long ago they ceded the city to the Yankees and went yuppie and naugahyde. They are sorry descendants of Ron Swoboda, Tommy Agee, Felix Millan, Tug McGraw.

At a certain point, even if you win the whole enchilada, who cares if it's not your team, if all your blood guys, your own children, have been shipped off to Egypt or Kansas City? If you take the heart and soul out of a team, then it's really just laundry left to root for—Tom Glavine in a Mets' uniform rather than with Brave tomahawks and dispatching the good guys effortlessly year after year; John Thompson; Derek Bell; Mike Hampton; Victor Zambrano; and before these stooges and mercenaries, the other Wilpon imports: the Vince Colemans, Carlos Baergas, Mel Rojases, Juan Samuels, Bobby Bonillas, dis-

---

*February, 2006.

asters all. Lenny Dykstra was a bonzo nutcase, but at least he was the Mets' homegrown nutcase, and he went off the charts in the 1993 World Series not for the Mets but the Phillies.

A few years later they preferred Mike Piazza to Mookie's son Preston. Yes, Piazza was good, but he wasn't a difference-maker; he was more noise and hoopla than clutch or bottom line—and they could have had him at season's end anyway as a free agent—but they so little believed in their own product that they felt they needed half a season to woo him.

They traded 1999 playoff hero Melvin Mora a few months later to the Orioles for Mike Bordick, a nondescript shortstop who returned to Baltimore right after the season. That is, they swapped the soul of their team for essentially another mercenary and clerk.

◆

The actual publication of *Things Happen for a Reason* in 2000 raised the possibility of an adventure. Lindy's oldest sister had met a retired military man in a travel group in Costa Rica, and now they were living half the year at his home in St. Petersburg. We figured we'd visit them around pub date and I could hand the first books to Terry in Largo in person.

Terry got into the occasion. He had jokingly been down on Lindy and me for not taking enough vacations or having fun times, so he ruled out our modest choice of lodgings and insisted on finding us a room at a swish resort. It was actually *too* garish and anyhow they didn't give us the suite that Terry had booked, so we moved to a bed and breakfast—but that did not diminish the generosity of his gesture. He showed up our first night out of Oakland, and we hung around another Florida lobby.

I joined him and his daughter Savannah on the beach a day later, too cold for swimming, the sky gray, a nasty wind whipping in. Neither of us was quite dressed for it, but we had planned on sitting there together and we did. The ocean always brings out the metaphysical in me, and I preached about life and death, eternity and time, terror and redemption. Terry indulged me. He had been to church enough; he knew appropriate rejoinders. Then he wanted to hear all about our trip to England and how I did on the plane.

We walked the boardwalk, then along a strip of nearby shops where our mood turned slaphappy. We guffawed about egregious, over-dressed tourists camped at florid restaurant patios, and then we sat in one that was a bit less noisy and had a few beers.

The books came by FedEx the next day, and I tossed Terry's carton in our rented car and set out for the school.

Getting to Largo involved a freeway labyrinth, and then finding the obscure Leach-Cone-Ferreira academy required four false trails before I pulled into a parking space on a residential street. What I still remember about the trip is a revved-up right-wing commentator waxing ecstatic about George Bush winning the upcoming election because he was the true candidate of the Internet. Unable to change the station, I listened with a mixture of denial and dread.

I brought along my glove even though I hadn't played for years. Imagining pupils all over a diamond, I figured I'd find some outfield space among them and shag flies.

In fact, the school was the backyard of co-owner Tony's house, and tutelage was private, one student at a time in a makeshift fabric cage. There wasn't a whole lot of roaming space. If a ball took off and rolled into the canal, forget it, Terry said, because there were alligators there. He had three lessons lined up for the rest of the day and, despite the fact that this should have been pub-celebration time, there was really nothing to do but hang and watch.

Terry was already engaged in a lesson when I arrived, showing a dull, chubby kid how to swing a bat and then going through a fielding and throwing drill with him. He paused to glance at the book, but he had to postpone any real perusal until the scheduled sessions were complete.

The mother soon arrived—a cute, surprisingly young blonde. Terry promptly handed her a book before even examining it himself. "Check it out!" he declared, emphasizing all three words with showy space between them, a mixture of off-handedness and majesty.

"Terry, this is you? I didn't know you played in the majors. Look at you, there on the cover!"

This was, in a sense, the epitome reaction to the publication of *Things Happen.* ... Hardly anyone knew who Terry was. Two other mothers came later that afternoon, and they each got the identical treatment from him, a bashful, brash flirtatiousness that elicited versions of "Wow, Terry!"

In the months that followed, he was to receive letters from across the country and even overseas, people discovering and rediscovering him. The book, unfortunately, would never break through, and less than a thousand readers found it.

I figured, after the sessions were complete, that Terry and I'd go through the pages and extol. I forgot that I had my glove—it had become superfluous. So I was surprised when, at a little past four, after packing off the last kid, Terry gestured to me to put it on. For a moment I didn't know what he was talking about, but soon it became clear that his read of our developing situation was that I was his next pupil—perhaps that was his unspoken gift to me in exchange for the book. Once I grokked it, I was open to that possibility, but it was also a tad strange considering that I had stopped playing competitive hardball thirty-eight years earlier and had stopped playing *anything* ten years ago. I hadn't even thrown a ball in three or four.

I faced him across the zone, and we zipped a few back and forth. "Come over the top more," he suggested. I tried that, but it was uncomfortable and I lapsed back to the slot that had been familiar for so long, trying to get loose.

He kept at it, correcting my delivery on just about every throw. I had never had a particularly good arm, and I wondered then if maybe poor mechanics were the reason. Whether valid or not, it was too late to correct. In a backyard in Largo I wanted only to enjoy a friendly catch with a *bona fide* player. I didn't care about instruction or how I threw. My focus was on making the basic catches, transferring the ball, and tossing decently back. Not having missed any in the first two dozen or so, I was pleased to be holding my own.

But Terry wasn't having any of it. He kept at my delivery with ever sharper criticism and demands, so finally I spoke up, "Hey Terry, I'm retired."

He acted as though I hadn't said anything. I was now one of his students, and he was going to stay in character—forceful, insistent, not wanting to brook truancy. I hadn't seen this side of Coach Leach.

"No," he said, almost irritated now. "Over the top." He demonstrated again.

I exaggerated the motion. It felt foolish, but I did get some pop. "I'm too old," I tried. "You're forty years after the fact."

That didn't even draw a smile. He was earnest. I guess he was going to make sure I got a real lesson.

Then a stray thought visited me. It wasn't quite a thunderbolt, yet it had the effect of one in that it changed the whole landscape. It was a remembrance, but not something that had been forgotten; it was something so obvious, so second-nature to me that I hadn't thought to mention it to Terry in any of our previous interactions. I doubt that I even told Robin. On Terry's next throw I caught the ball in the web, flipped it jauntily to my other hand and, with the grin of a consummate trickster, went submarine and brought a perfect strike into his glove. He didn't have to move to catch it. I could see the surprise on his face.

"You can do that?" he exclaimed.

Yes, I could. You see, I may not have known that Terry was a submariner when his stats among the Texas League leaders in 1980 first caught my eye but, once I learned it, it made everything else about him perfect. I was a submariner too, a member of the club, though I hadn't used my card for a long time. During a summer at Camp Chipinaw, probably 1956, age eleven and a half, during those optional periods that I signed up for against the rules, I decided one day that I was a pitcher. I had occasionally imitated Ewell Blackwell at Bill-Dave and while playing stickball in the city, and buddies at the time thought I did it well. It finally struck me to try it out for real with a hardball.

I wasn't previously any sort of a pitcher—I had no experience on the mound. Yet once I got into throwing from down under, I began running up a modest streak of scoreless innings. None of the older players could hit the thing. I was beside myself with delight. I had found a calling in the sense that only a child could consider winning a Monopoly match or throwing sidearm a career event.

My success lasted about a week. One afternoon Freddie Grossinger showed up as a visitor to my summer camp. He was a distant cousin, a young adult who sometimes hung out nearby at my father's resort hotel even though he was from a remote part of Pennsylvania. Years later he lived in Toluca Lake near L.A., his name changed to Fred Holliday, and he acted bit parts in movies and TV, once as one of the IM team in *Mission: Impossible!*, something that gained him everlasting admiration from my kids.

I forget why Freddie came by Chipinaw that day, but the moment I saw him I told him excitedly about my being a pitcher now. He came to watch me try to extend my scoreless-inning streak. I was enjoying whipping the ball in and watching the cute little hook that submarine pitches can get. Freddie was sitting alone on the bleachers, cheering me on, when I walked a guy and someone got a hit. A counselor who wasn't supposed to be playing in our games, a star on his college team, had wandered by and was sent up to pinch-hit. I didn't understand what was going on and simply threw. He hit it over the wire fence into the next camp, something none of us had ever seen. I don't remember why—whether it was my choice or the baseball counselor's—but that was the end of my pitching career. I didn't pitch at Chipinaw again.

Five years later, in my last summer of sleep-away camp, at a different establishment in Connecticut—where my brother and I were needled relentlessly as newcomers (or "ranked," in the language of the time)—I got to pitch once more.

I was actually only a semi-camper at Kenmont, hired as editor of the *Clarion* newspaper, but I was eligible for the league when it started up in late July. No one paid me much heed until I showed my submarine pitch in practice; then guys were intrigued. I suddenly had status. They selected me for a roster and put me in the rotation.

As I was warming up for my first start, the catcher snapped off his return throw, a common affectation then among cool baseballers. It fooled me and caught the middle finger on my right hand. It hurt too much to pitch, so I was taken into town for an x-ray. The finger was broken, and I got a cast. By the time it came off, there was only one game left. I was nominated to start but had no control. I hit my brother with a pitch and then somehow picked him off first without knowing what I was doing. I struck out a guy and walked two more. That was it. The captain took the ball, sent me to right field, and got out of the jam himself: two-thirds of an inning, two walks, one strikeout, one hit batsman (in the family)—my eternal stat line.

The only times thereafter I brought out my submarine ball were in stickball with Robin, mixing it in with other stuff.

But all through Terry's streak, I had an echo in my head of this older thing, my own fling with pitching when I was eleven. I knew from experience a tiny bit about the down-under pitch and, if you were its devotee, how good it could be. I didn't have a thimble of Terry's ability or resumé, but I knew.

"You can do *that?*" he called out again when I didn't answer.

"Uh huh," I deadpanned, throwing another, adopting the slightly insolent tone of the eleven-year-old whose pitch it was. Now *I* was teasing *him.*

So he went submarine on his return throw, for real too, the Major League stuff, and he continued that motif, changing speed and spin, one after another, a total transformation from the Little League coach he had been minutes earlier to Number 26 warming up in the Mets' bullpen. I was both the bullpen catcher and another pitcher warming up alongside of him, or maybe we were both getting loose during spring training. We were in the '80s now, back to the future. He was bringing it, like from the backstop camera on TV.

His pedantics were waived, and along with them, the overbearingness of the instructor; we were peers again, fellow submariners in the club, despite the talent disparity between us. His ball really began to dance and dive, and I wasn't catching all of them anymore. A few had to be chased across the road. He was continuing to talk, but now he was describing the different movements he was putting on the ball. "This is the upshoot," he said, and I had to leap and even then it went flying off the tip of my glove. I had never firsthand seen a ball spin or dart that much. Each time I came back with more or less my same pitch; it was all I knew.

"Here's the dip."

I adjusted and managed to catch it awkwardly while stumbling.

We threw for ten more minutes. I got to see what Terry's pitches actually looked like, perhaps to Pete Rose and George Foster back then. I was such an intellectual follower of baseball that sometimes the reality of it evaporated for me. Radio was as good as television; it was all stats and iconographies anyway, like a fantasy league. The actual physics of bat and ball, muscles and coordination, had become an artifact, less real than the narrative and the scoring. But here in Largo, my own game and a true pitcher's game converged in such a way that I could measure them together as things in the same universe. I could *see* what I had only imagined, only watched in the satellite TV room at a great distance of scale and meaning.

I could finally understand the real challenge I had set before myself in childhood when I stood in Central Park for the first time with a glove, waiting for a play: the dazzlingly concrete reality of life on Earth.

Afterwards Terry seemed again to forget that I was neither a prospect nor candidate. "You've really got something there," he crooned. "I know. I've coached a lot of kids. Their fathers ask me, 'Can my kid make it?' and sometimes I have to lie; I have to make it sound better than it is. But you've really got something. Those pitches have a little tail to them. You could develop . . ."

"Remember, Terry, I'm retired. I'm older than you."

"Well, *I* can still get hitters out. If someone would sign me. . . ." And then he trailed into a recital of the teams that could have used him the previous fall and perhaps gone on in the post-season.

"Well, I'm *really* too old. No one starts a career at fifty-five. The time I needed you was back in summer camp when I was eleven and they didn't tell me I had shit. All they wanted to do was beat me up and make me feel bad because for a moment there, like, I was happy."

"Tell me about it!"

Not that I really believed I could have had a career, but it would have been nice to have had a coach as kind and knowledgeable as Terry, on a shabby meadow like this, alligators and all. Maybe I could have pitched a game or two in high school and made that Amherst team. But I was satisfied . . . because this moment with the book in hand, us holding our gloves, the submarine pitch between us, baseball was about as good as it gets.

There isn't too much more to this story. As I said, *Things Happen . . .* didn't sell worth a damn, and Terry and I more or less dropped out of touch. He phoned at one point in 2003 to say that he was abandoning the school and moving over to West Palm Beach, near where we had done the tapes, to go into business moving luxury homes—furniture, artwork, and the like—with his wife's first husband. "I know—that usually causes a double take." He had called to thank me for the book. He said it had been a pleasure to meet so many people through it and to get to look back over his career. He had recently been invited to a number of card shows to sign copies. It kept the game alive for him. "I didn't know if I ever told you how much I appreciate what you did for me."

I said it was a pretty even trade, and I thanked him too.

We didn't speak to each other again for a few years. He had neglected to give me his new phone number, and I couldn't get a hold of him. I wanted to ship him some of the overstock books, but letters to both the school and his home got returned.

In fact, he had forgotten to give his new address and phone to anyone—his pastor, the school, the local bookstore where he did signings.

I was cleaning out my Rolodex one day and was about to toss his card when I noticed a tiny number with an unfamiliar area code scribbled in the corner. I had assumed that it was left over from a previous occupant of the card who had been whited out, but I figured it couldn't hurt to call and ask for Terry Leach.

Good idea. It was his ninety-year-old mother in Selma, and she gave me his cell.

Terry and I chatted a few times after that. He extolled the moving business. It wasn't unlike baseball in that there was a team, and you had to win; that is, you couldn't have any damages when you were handling irreplaceable, expensive stuff. Recently an old minor-league teammate had shown up as a UPS driver: "In this life, all they do is keep changing the uniforms." He described a number of dicey transports across state lines where whole Fortune 500 households were conveyed and restored intact. One mogul recently gave them a huge bonus.

Terry was still having a good time. He was amused that his stepson, drummer in a local band, now had access to his father and stepfather in the same office. "Off to St. Croix, a gig for a couple of weeks. Don't feel too sorry for him," Terry laughed. "Like I told him, maybe they could use another musician."

"Do you play anything?"

"I can always stand up there on stage and shake the tambourine."

We met again in March of '07, at a bar in Jupiter when I was back in Florida doing craniosacral work. As I entered, Terry stood up so that I could see him, and he pointed to his hair. "It turned white real quick. I didn't know as you'd recognize me." After I sat down, he added, "It was starting to go when I was still pitching, but I dyed it. Didn't need that working against me too."

Conversation ranged from global warming and the short-sightedness of fossil-fuel dependence (Terry was advocating hydrogen—"You can take it right out of the sea"); to his mother still playing cards and cooking meals with her friends back in the old Selma neighborhood ("she'd like to be around her boys, but you can't just take her away from relationships and habits she's developed over ninety years"); to my hopes for reviving the book on the twentieth anniversary of his 11-1 season, especially with the Mets breaking in a rookie submarine pitcher (Joe Smith), and people talking about Terry again ("I heard about that—they got a new sidearmer, learned it in college, a little like me"); to why he didn't get together with his Met team-mates more often: "At reunions we always say we're gonna see each other; we never do—yet when we're together, it's like we never left. Heck, Keith has a place right down here on the beach, but I never see him. I talk to Gary Carter a bit. When he was managing over to St. Lucie, I went there a number of times and sat in the stands. I enjoyed giving him a hard time."

After my catch with Terry in Largo, I didn't pick up a baseball for another three years until the spring of 2003. The occasion was that my friend Richard Firme, an organic farmer about Terry's age, always had his glove in the truck when he drove up from the Central Valley to sell at the Berkeley Farmers' Market on Saturdays. Richard and I had been buddies for several years, and we had gone into business together in the sense that our publishing company had bought land in Merced County to allow him to go back to independent farming, as he came from three generations of Filipino and Chicano farmers.

As a non-profit, we were looking for a worthy project, and Richard, who was one of the leading local agrarian advocates, was a perfect beneficiary—pro-sustainability, pro-biodiversity, as well as an educator of migrant workers on organics and a provider of veggies in food boxes for the Oakland and Berkeley poor.

For two months Lindy and I went hunting for land with him throughout the Central Valley from Patterson and Manteca to Firebaugh and Los Baños and, after just missing on a number of farms, placed a winning bid on a twenty-seven-acre sector being broken off a chicken ranch on Snyder Road in Gustine.

Richard turned out to be as good a teammate as Terry, a nurturer of youth and a force at the market. One day this good-natured charmer of the ladies and father figure to all charged in to break up a nasty-looking knife fight among the booths, disarming both combatants. "Show some respect for the people's market," he told them.

We had been talking about having a catch for maybe two years when we finally set a Sunday date and met at the communal house at which he stayed when he was in town. It was a funky neighborhood where people sold drugs on the street. I thought we'd drive, but he knew a field within walking distance, and the day was mellow, a crowd outside the church. I had brought a bat and five hardballs as well as my glove, and he had his, so we strolled.

Since there was a game already going on with kids in uniforms, we stood away from the field itself on the northeast corner of the lot and began gently tossing back and forth. As we increased the distance between us, he began the ritual of floating his returns a little bit away from me to create a challenge. In our rhythm, we barely noticed that we were being engulfed by a group of maybe eight or nine black kids, average age about eight, and before we could gauge the situation, one had grabbed the bat, two had collected the extra balls, and another was pulling at Richard's glove, and they were running. It was like hip-hop "Lord of the Flies."

"Wait a second now," Richard announced as we chased after them. "These things are ours!"

"Can we play? Can we play?" a few of them cried out in chorus, taking up each other's calls. The innocence of those requests belied any implicit threat.

"Yes," Richard said, "but we've got to get matters in order here."

Already they were throwing balls helter-skelter, only a few of them pitches, while simultaneously fighting over and swinging the bat wildly like thug swordsmen. Somehow one of the balls had already been fouled over the fence, and it landed with a juicy clunk on a parked car that had a woman seated in it. Richard shouted, "Sorry, ma'am," but two of the kids were already retrieving the stray missile without a qualm.

We finally commandeered our charges and took up pitching to them in turn, placing the rest in the field. They had no skills. They couldn't bat and they couldn't catch. It was sad; there was so much enthusiasm and energy, but no one had taught them anything. Every boy wielded the bat like an axe or cudgel, one hand around its middle. Those in the field waited till the ball was past them and then chased after it. No one caught anything, but a few got plunked and were unhappy to the point of tears.

Still the dance went on, not quite baseball but a relative. They were yelling out the names of the same two Giants players again and again: "Marquis Grissom! Barry Bonds!" Anyone who hit a ball, fair or foul, instead of running around a semblance of a diamond, sped all over the grass as if it were tag with a bunch of them chasing until we could regain decorum.

Richard and I stood by each batter, corrected their grips, got their hands together, leveled their swings, and swung with their arms to give them a sense of correct trajectory. Most of their energy, however, went into shouting "My turn, my turn" after each batter had finished, even if they had just batted and someone else hadn't had a chance.

Soon Richard was coaching at the plate and I was helping in the field. All of them thought it hilarious that our names were both Richard, so they took to calling me "Mr. Richard" and Firme "Coach." Their names were Demone, Demetrius, Charvain, Tylee, Deshawn, Titus, Reginald, and Jamal.

Suddenly they all began to charge in one direction, and we realized that the organized game was over, and its managers and players were packing up. "Let's go there!" was the collective clamor. "Let's play on that real field, mister."

We segued across the lot and stationed a batter by home plate. Richard pitched, and I stood in the field.

"You can't play here!" I suddenly heard. Looking over in surprise, I saw one of the adults approaching. "There's gonna be another game later today. We don't want the field ruined."

Ruin the field by what we were doing? It didn't make sense, so we continued defiantly.

Then another guy came and stationed himself in the way of our pitches, so we more or less had to stop. He was impatiently conciliatory as he tried to explain that this was a league and they had to have the field in mint condition. He produced a sheet of paper from the city, ceding the whole square block to his organization for the day.

We nodded and, while not giving in entirely, gradually moved toward the outfield, continuing to bat and pitch as we went. Then I noticed something: the departing kids in uniform were at most a little older than the ones we were organizing, except not a single one was black, nor were any of their managers; yet this was a black neighborhood.

A relic came flooding back, as when I was playing catch with Terry in Florida; only this one wasn't so diluvian. What triggered it was a sudden *déjà vu:* I knew this field in a different context.

Robin had played in a similar league almost twenty-five years ago. That league was white too. One of their games, in fact their last one the season when they didn't win any, was played right here on this diamond. As time's tides rolled through my mind, two geographies— one of memory, one present—oscillated . . . and fused. I saw the scene as it was then. Lindy and I had been among the parents in those very stands, daughter Miranda in tow. We were rooting for Robin and his teammates. However, several neighborhood kids, all black, five or six years old, invaded the bleachers and threw dirt bombs into our midst, getting dust all over us.

These forays were intermittent enough that none of the other parents reacted, but ignoring bad behavior was not Lindy's style. On their third orbit she stomped right up to the kids and told them they were being inappropriate. They acted as though she were speaking a foreign language or perhaps as if she weren't speaking at all. She grabbed angrily at their arms while I urged her to back off. They fled.

At the end of the game, however, as we were leaving the field and heading toward our car, rocks came crashing down around us. We were being chased by those kids, and they were hurling stones at us, big ones. I picked up Miranda, and we raced to the car without getting hit. As we tore out of the neighborhood, a missile bouncing off our hood, Robin said simply, "Mom, maybe next time you could be quiet."

As the memory filled itself in, the full irony hit me: I was on the other side now. We were the enemy then, the invaders, taking over their field, not sharing our equipment or figuring out how to get homies into the league. Is it any wonder that they launched dust rockets and chased us away with stones?

What was astonishing was that the scene hadn't changed. It was a different generation, but there was that same soccer-mom look; the league had some Chinese players and parents now (like the university up the hill). Yet the number of blacks was, as then, zero.

I motioned to Richard—I wanted to reclaim the batting cage.

"Let's do it," he said. We truculently set ourselves in the infield and continued to play our ragtag game while the managers and parents glared at us. We ignored them. As we changed places, batter and fielder, I reminded Richard of his line: "Show some respect for the people's market."

"Right on," he said.

We went at it for another half hour or so and were pretty exhausted by the time the kids, without explanation, began to peel away because one of them had a dollar bill and they were going to spend it. I don't know what timer went off that told them it was the moment to break that George Washington, but they were streaming off the field toward the street.

Richard and I followed behind. "Hey, guys," he called out. "How about a thank you . . . a hug . . . good-bye at least?" But they were hell-bent.

We reached the street. The woman was still in her car, and there were a lot of other women around her, all in their twenties—her radio was rapping; it was a scene. The ladies were actually riffing with one another but, as we passed, several of them addressed us: "Thanks, guys. Thanks for taking care of the kids—'preciate that." It was a recital, their legs keeping time.

"You're welcome," I replied. "We enjoyed them."

"They wore us out," Richard added. "You've got a lot of energy to handle there."

"Ain't it the truth!"

We continued to the corner where the grocery—meaning the liquor—store stood. There were about ten black guys milling around with beers and bottles in paper bags. At the wrong time, this could seem a pretty menacing situation to two white guys but, as I said, it was a mellow Sunday. One usually averts eyes when passing such a parley, but this time was different. The males didn't say anything and we didn't say anything. Like the women, however, one by one they responded. It was a nod from the closest, a bow of the head from the guy next to him. The next gave us the black-power salute, and another comically saluted us like the brass.

At our closest point of contact, Richard said, "Right on, guys." And then we crossed the street.

I now knew something else. These were likely some of the same men who chased us from that field with stones twenty-three years earlier. Redemption comes in strange forms, but it rarely comes any better.

FIELD BOX

GAME 59   D
            ENTER

21E   3

SEC   BOX/ROW   SEAT

CHICAGO
AUG 14, 1983
SUN   1:35   PM

SHEA STADIUM

ADMIT ONE Subject to the
conditions set forth on the
back hereof.
Exec. VP & GM

59     $8.00

GAME   TOTAL

RAINCHECK

METS

TERRY LEACH

Lost Baseball:
Subtext for the 1992 Mets
Year of Writing: 1991

In the two-plus decades from the Miracle Mets to now, Major League baseball has turned inside-out. If I go back another twenty years to when I began following the game in 1952, I arrive at yet a different landscape.

To a 1920s player like Dick Bartell, whose *Rowdy Richard* North Atlantic Books published in 1987, the change has in fact obliterated baseball as he knew it. The modern game, despite its superficial similarity in rules and league configuration to the one he played, is a decoy. The distortion is at the level of meaning and syntax, not apparent structure. Babe Ruth and Ty Cobb did not play this game; the records broken by Henry Aaron and Pete Rose were not theirs.

On the one occasion that Bartell happened to visit me when a Major League game was on the television, I was surprised by his utter lack of interest. I called attention to the teams involved. He glanced briefly, watched one pitch (resulting in a fly ball to left), then snickered as he turned away. What barbarism could he have witnessed during such a brief, negligible scrutiny?

He never looked back even once during the time of our meeting despite the frequent exaltation of hits, supposed great catches, and replays. It was of no more relevance to him than the fly buzzing around the room's light. Yet it was ostensibly the subject matter and justification of both his book and his career and the very reason why we were talking.

When I pressed him about this disinterest, he dignified the question only by muttering that it wasn't baseball anymore.

Not having played in an era of even livable salaries, Bartell found that he could make pocket money (at age eighty) by selling signed copies of his hardcover at country clubs and Rotary halls. In fact, the only time he and I "played" a game we both recognized was when he came by to get a fresh carton of his books. I pointed to it on the warehouse floor, and he and I both reached—me out of deference to his age and him to prove he could still carry the weight. Two thin sheets of plastic foam rested on top and, as our trajectories met, they flipped in the air. We smiled at each other and said simultaneously, "We blew the double play!"

My son Robin was born in 1969, so I have had the opportunity to "grow up" with baseball twice. Now he is twenty-two and able to look back nostalgically himself—to Mookie Wilson's first Major League game, Dwight Gooden's rookie strikeouts, the Championship run of '86.... Recently when he was home from college, we saw portions of a rebroadcast of the third game of the 1969 World Series between the Mets and Orioles—a match that is engraved permanently into the scripture of Mets fans, him included, despite the fact it was played the year he was born.

With rapt curiosity we watched a parade of players like Gary Gentry, Donn Clendenon, Paul Blair, Boog Powell, Clay Dalrymple, Rod Gaspar, Cleon Jones, Jim Palmer, Davey Johnson, etc. Frank Robinson batting against Nolan Ryan was an antecedent Hall of Fame match-up. Gentry, the pitcher whom the Mets refused to part with a few seasons later in a trade with the Angels (substituting Ryan instead), disappeared almost immediately (a sore arm), but Ryan (whose stamina the Mets questioned at the time of the deal) is still pitching All-Star-caliber baseball—a remarkable feat. I reminded Robin that the veteran strikeout master has represented only the Mets in the World Series—and we were watching that youthful appearance.

Robin noted how quiet the broadcast was—no preemptive urgency imposed on every play, no barrages of stats and extravagant claims, no replays from different angles, no promo music punctuating events, no dancing cartoon scoreboards, no so-called "breaks in the action" stuffed with thought-stultifying garbage—nothing in fact to distinguish the game from a routine match of sandlot teams.

Yet I remembered a profound aura of tension around that decisive game—an urgency to which the announcers seemed oblivious. Weren't they aware that this was the legendary 1969 World Series?

Robin confessed that initially it was disappointing to hear the plays called so blandly, but after a while the tone became momentous in its understatement. He found it strangely powerful to be drawn into stark pitch-by-pitch sequences without anyone supplying overlay or drama to remind him how important each was. "It shows," he remarked, "how addicted we are to the hype. Without it I actually felt something was missing; the game wasn't real."

No wonder Bartell merely glanced and then glanced away.

We have moved, version by version, rule by rule, garnishment by garnishment, away from actual (or at least original) baseball until what we have approaches an arcade game that Bill Lee foretold: synthetic space-age baseball, an ultimate video display of digitalized and prefabricated transactions—no sweetgrass, no natural sounds, no soft bounces, no repose between plays, no sky even, just a giant indoor shooting gallery in which the players are reduced to blips on a screen. Electronic pollution and artificial playing surfaces foreshadow the patina of this landscape; the designated hitter is its politics. Its subtext, as always, is on a deeper level—but coming on strong.

I am reminded of a game I attended at Yankee Stadium in 1961. It was the last regular-season contest, and Roger Maris hit his sixty-first home run that afternoon, surpassing Babe Ruth's single-season record.

Its most telling aspect, in retrospect, was the relative lack of fuss. There wasn't even close to a full house, as I recall, at Yankee Stadium that day. Oh, there may have been an unusual number of reporters and TV crews for the era (Maris certainly complained about them), but the occasion elicited nothing like the buildup and hoopla for Henry Aaron in Atlanta when he commuted an Al Downing offering into his 715th round-tripper that surpassed Ruth's career count, or Pete Rose when he bingled past Ty Cobb's lifetime mark of 4,189. Far more attention was lavished on even Cecil Fielder's prospective fiftieth home run in 1990.

Maris' clout should have been all the more dramatic because, whereas Aaron and Rose would eventually have achieved their goals, there was no guarantee that Ruth's unlikely usurper would measure out another home run in the few at-bats he had remaining on the last day of the season.

An internal re-imaging of my memory confirms Robin's insight. The trigger of Maris' swing, the arc of the ball leaving his bat, its eclipse into a dwindling spot of energy against the stands have an indelible authenticity. The shot transcends far more critical home runs of recent years. Yet the image is incongruous, primitive, mute.

By now every image is multi-color, stop-action, a digital seriograh in search of some eternal epitome it can never attain. The overlay on baseball is so thick that one cannot attend a game without being blasted by robotized technology—a high-definition electrical scoreboard, a stadium announcer and various audio channels piped into the park, even artificial standing waves and placards of fans. But most telling is the corruption in one's own mind: we supply false urgency, artificial heroism, facile legend, bluster.

From the time of Maris' home run to the present we have been witness to an ever-accelerating debasement of most features of our culture. Everywhere the real is being replaced by the synthetic. Nowadays people grow up unable to distinguish between reconstructions and the natural events on which they are based, between a game and the narrative bracketing it. It's a wonder the integrity of the season holds together; it seems only a matter of time before it too fractures into mini-playoffs and wild cards.

If we are to seek out sources of this deterioration, even assign blame, we will find no lack of eligible intruders. Technology, as diagnosed by Marshall McLuhan, has slowly replaced meaning (or message) with its structural reassemblage of reality. We have been assisted in that direction by a virtuoso array of refurbished mimicries and computer-regenerated forms that are more real (at least more evocative) than the so-called real. Artificial sounds of birds in a jungle, animals on a farm, or the pounding of surf, are more commercial than real sounds that get "white-noised" in nature. Ever more refined processing of recorded radiation has led to super-realistic videos and soundtracks, cartoons electronically tatted into reality. While hi-tech medicine reduces bodies to functioning or flawed machines, synthetic foods feed cellular robots. We have come, as a culture, to prefer packaging to experience, altered space to indigenous landscapes, illusory events and soap operas to actual life.

Crowds at the baseball game and personae and icons of the players likewise must be synthesized and regenerated to seem real. By the time that "virtual reality" and fantasy leagues are considered improvements on experience (or at least competitors to it), Bartell and his colleagues have been demoted to fossils.

Les Enfants du Paradis, even with its grainy black and white video, scratchy sound, and illegible subtitles, concerns something desperately real, whereas *When Harry Met Sally* and *White Palace,* to pick just two from scores of current films, are utter fabrications. In fact, they are worse; they are self-deceiving heartfelt renditions of the psychobabble reality that has already been repackaged from consensus "experience" and sold planetwide as a substitute for precisely the unconditional love of the 1940s French cinema.

They are, as the eponymous movie so aptly glosses our era: *sex, lies, and videotape,* which is why that movie seems so alive. It is true.

The choice is ours, at least apparently. We could leave technology in its place (to do our work) and still enjoy wild streams in mountains or a cumulus-filled sky; we could experience our own ineffable existence apart from the cultural packaging of the ego.

We make the other choice collectively every day.

It would appear that we will vote for synthesized political candidates over actual people and we will select the fake pastoral and its handmaiden: synthetic baseball. The greater danger is that we have already come to sanction *only* those feelings and emotions that are juiced electronically. Thus we have lost our bearings and do not know how to relocate ourselves among the passions and griefs of real life. We experience—or more likely only seek—a version of love and tragedy glorified by ad agencies and Hollywood scriptwriters. We expect TV versions of heavens and hells. Ghoul-mongers have stolen even death from whatever it really is. Our own mortality stares at us from a grid of impenetrable dots.

As long as life (and even life beyond death) is pictured as sequential videos and sound bites—plots squeezed into gaps—then the fact of our incarnation and our inherence in the universe is lost.

Major League Baseball has become a computer game. Whereas once rotisserie leagues were a minor adjunct to the season, they are now the cart leading the horse. General managers are privileged rotisserie players who get to engage in a real crapshoot, but all over the country their activities are mirrored by amateurs in endless fragmented and reconstructed versions. Occasionally they buy teams and play the big game. Sandy Alderson of the Oakland A's is a paradigmatic version of the successful crossover rotisserie GM; he deals a better hand than most baseball men, at least in part because the game is no longer baseball. Now even his reign has been undermined by the players themselves wanting to be the dealers as well as the chips.

No one could dispute the tyranny of the labor situation that confronted Bartell and his colleagues in the 1920s. However, in an epoch of global poverty and environmental deterioration, it is hard to see how it serves the validity or credibility of the game to have its players demand (and be paid on demand) sums of money that could change the infrastructure of whole nations—also to have those players almost never turn their excess assets into helping inner-city schools or rescuing doomed African-American communities on the Georgia Sea Islands. It is Las Vegas lottery madness, and it can only lead first to failure of franchises, second to the impoverishment of victory, and third to the end of the historical structure of the leagues.

We are now in a brief mirage before the ever-expanding salaries and transfer of the best players to the largest and richest markets utterly skew the game. It is hard to see how, for instance, the Pirates could ever compete again with the Mets, except by a fluke. The 1969 and 1984 Mets were notable for turning around losing situations through the traditional channels of baseball, which involved all the complex and ingenious variations of building teams: finding and losing players through scouting, small-town scavenger hunts, risky trades, and other idiosyncrasies. The 1992 Mets will be about as "real" as Arnold Schwarzenegger playing "The Terminator." If they don't win, they can only look ridiculous.

Even Little League, as Pirate shortstop Jay Bell so rightly noted, had become an imitation of the Majors: "We're not men playing a kids' game anymore; they're kids playing a men's game."

Far from being immortal, games come and go as cultures do. The Hall of Fame at Cooperstown will yet be a museum of curios about an activity no one remembers or understands. Eventually "Babe Ruth" may be the only baseball-related noun known to our descendants (Hank Aaron notwithstanding), and it will mean something else entirely, much as that single starlike smudge of Andromeda stands for a whole galaxy of billions of suns and planets.

The heat we feel in games vitiates into an already infinite universe, and it must be reclaimed on another octave to hold any substance. The authenticity was what drew us to commit our internal mythologies and emotions to baseball in the first place. Without that, it is just one more string of traffic lights or laser billboard, a celebrity tournament of chessmen on Astroturf.

Mythology of the 1986 Playoffs and World Series

Year of Writing: 1986
Mets Seasons Referenced: 1969, 1973, 1985, 1986

Jesse Orosco heaves his glove into the night sky and kneels on the mound in a jubilation that is also spontaneous prayer. He is burning an indelible moment onto thousands of highlight films that will proceed into the future, cloning one another until no one will remember how we got to it or feel any longer the situation of two embattled teams. Its future is to become stale newsreel iconography. But in the present it is a hot log crashing to the ground, releasing thousands of embers, flashbacks in baseball time.

The most recent is barely hours old: trailing 3-0, the Mets went down in the bottom of the fifth inning in their twenty-second unsuccessful shot at an insoluble Bruce Hurst.

"Is it for real this time, or are we being led on again?" I asked my friend Nick* with feigned optimism, meaning: 'Are we finally gonna get beaten like any normal team, or do we have one more portent left?'

"I am *sure* we are being led on," he consoled.

At that moment I had little hope; it seemed the Mets' outrageous sixth-game comeback had merely postponed an inevitable Boston victory (predestined perhaps by Dave Henderson's fateful home run in the

---

*Nick Setka, manager of Cody's Bookstore

fifth game of the American League playoffs). Henderson certainly thought so, as he showboated the night before, after sending the Sox ahead in the tenth.

Then suddenly, sparked for the second straight night by a Lee Mazzilli pinch single, New York rallied to tie the score; an inning later they took the lead. The bottom of the sixth began a charge to the end of the season reminiscent, among "sudden-death games," of the back-and-forth reversals of the Yankees-Pirates finale in 1960 and the Phillies-Astros cliffhanger twenty years later. For a brief span the Mets and the Red Sox each seemed to have enough momentum to overcome whatever the other did.

Against Roger McDowell, who mowed them down an inning before, the Sox rallied for two runs on three hits in the top of the eighth and had the tying run on second with no one out when Orosco entered— shades of Dale Long and Mickey Mantle in the bottom of the ninth in Pittsburgh. But suddenly the revels ended: the 1986 post-season goblin had played his last trick.

Most baseball games are routine. Most seasons in a team's history are humdrum and indifferent. For a franchise only twenty-five years old, however, the Mets have found themselves in a couple of centuries' worth of bizarre games and unlikely seasons. Before the 1986 playoffs even began, they could supply a resumé of marathons—twenty-five innings against the Cardinals in 1974, twenty-four against the Astros in 1968 (ending 1-0), twenty-three against the Giants in the second game of a doubleheader in 1964—they lost all three quirkily, the Cardinal one on a wild pick-off attempt by Hank Webb. In their nineteen-inning "twilight zone" march in Atlanta in '85 the Mets tied the score against Bruce Sutter in the ninth and took the lead twice in extra innings, only to have the Braves retie it each time on home runs. The second such homer, with two outs in the seventeenth, was swatted by pitcher Rick Camp (because the Braves had run out of pinch hitters). Camp came to the plate with virtually no chance even of getting a hit, let alone hitting a home run;

he had one of the worst batting averages in the history of baseball. (A footnote to the absurdity was that Tom Gorman, the victim of both extra-inning shots, thought he was facing a somewhat less terrible-hitting pitcher, Gene Garber, at the time.) The Mets did finally win, 16-13, but not before Camp came to the plate again as the tying run (against Ron Darling this time) and, after an ominously loud foul, made the final out.

The Mets' 1962 season was a malediction of blown ballgames and unlucky losses defying the law of averages. Then in 1969, against 100-1 odds, they won the first Eastern Division Championship of the National League in a charmed late-season run that included a doubleheader of 1-0 wins over the equally resurgent Pittsburgh Pirates (with the pitcher driving in the only run in both games) and a victory over Steve Carlton in which nineteen Mets struck out but Ron Swoboda hit two two-run homers. Wayne Garrett and Al Weis then rose from obscurity to get unlikely hits off all-star pitchers and lead the team to the Pennant and the World Championship (are we being led on indeed?).

In 1973 behind Tug McGraw, the Mets came from under .500 and just out of last place in September to win the Division. In one improbable game they outlasted the Expos (who twice loaded the bases with less than two outs in extra innings without scoring). The Mets rallied from two runs down in the ninth inning against ace Dave Giusti and the Pirates, winning on a single by Ron Hodges; they beat the Pirates two days later, aided by an extra-inning Pittsburgh "home run" that bounced off the railing into Cleon Jones' glove (the base runner was thrown out at home). They then survived the Big Red Machine in a hectic five-game playoff and, on the heels of a Koosman gem, took a 3-2 lead in the World Series out to Oakland. However, it was not until thirteen years later that the franchise won its next Series game.

Do teams have their own myth cycles? Players vehemently deny any jinx from prior seasons (especially ones played before they were on the team or, for that matter, born). Yet there are curious recurrences:

the Red Sox of the supposed "Harry Frazee" curse are the franchise that sold Babe Ruth and other stars to the Yankees (leading to the American League dynasty of the 1920s and 1930s); they are the team that was paralyzed by Enos Slaughter's inspired dash in the eighth inning of the seventh game in 1946; that lost the seventh game to the Cardinals again, behind Bob Gibson in '67; that blew a one-game lead to the Yankees with two games left in 1949 (giving Casey Stengel his first pennant and initiating a record string of New York World Series appearances over the next sixteen years); that was turned back again in the seventh game of the '75 Series by Tony Perez, Pete Rose, and the Reds after their own miraculous sixth-game win (New England's entry for the greatest game ever played); that were the victims of the Yankees' late-season dash of 1978, culminating in the unlikely Bucky Dent home run in the one-game playoff (New England's singlemost game of infamy until 1986). Many a Boston fan considered their own team legitimately the one with soul in '86, the Mets another New York ogre. A sign at Fenway during the third game of the Series heralded the conceit: Red Sox 2, Mets 0; Yankees: No Game Today.

The Yankees have their own Ugly American/carpetbagger heritage (their very name resounds through Latin America in "Yanquis, Go Home"). George Steinbrenner was able to resurrect this legacy by buying the franchise and then Catfish Hunter and Reggie Jackson (just as Babe Ruth, Lou Gehrig, Joe DiMaggio, Mickey Mantle, and Yogi Berra were purchased before them—I mean these guys weren't exactly draft picks).

The Cubs have a sentimentally downbeat tradition, from ancient World Series folds, to the fade of '69, to Leon Durham's catastrophic error in the '84 playoffs, the latter highlighting the collapse of what seemed an unstoppable pennant surge at Wrigley just days earlier. (How did the invincible Sutcliffe, Dernier, and company all turn into wimps and hand the momentum over to Steve Garvey, Tony Gwynn, and Andy Hawkins at precisely the failsafe point?)

The Cardinals of 1984, with Willie McGee and Vince Coleman, were a true Gashouse Gang throwback, streamlined and funked up for the '80s. The Dodgers of Valenzuela, Hershiser, and Bob Welsh recall the interregnum of Don Drysdale and Sandy Koufax who, in turn, recall the Brooklyn duet of Carl Erskine and Clem Labine. (On the other hand, the Pirates and Phillies of the '70s seem quantum breaks in the myth cycles of their franchises.)

The 1986 post-season played itself out within the established traditions of the teams involved. The Angels blew the big game and then self-destructed. It was the all-time frustrating miss for a franchise whose most heroic identity remains the expansion team of Ken McBride, Leon Wagner, and George and LeRoy Thomas.

The Red Sox saw the ghosts of 1946, 1949, 1967, 1975, and 1978. How often can you miss from that close?*

---

*Both teams were building unawares toward miracle comebacks in the years after this piece was written. In 2002 the Angels overcame a 5-0 San Francisco Giant lead in the seventh inning of the sixth game of the World Series, then went on to take the seventh in a rout. This was not unlike the 1985 Kansas City Royals bludgeoning the Cardinals' '82 Series pitching star, Joaquin Andujar, after "stealing" game six with a ninth-inning comeback after umpire Don Denkinger erroneously ruled that Jack Clark's flip to Todd Worrell covering first was late and awarded Jorge Orta the base. The winning run was driven in subsequently by another Cardinal '82 Series hero, Dane Iorg, now on the other side.

The Red Sox finally captured a Championship in 2004, a sweep over the Cardinals after becoming the first team in Major League history to rally from a 3-0 deficit to take a seven-game series (no team had ever tied such a series at three games apiece, the Mets coming closest at 3-2 led by Melvin Mora against the Braves in '99). Appropriately the Bosox' victim in the American League playoffs that year was their long-time tormentor, the voodoo-wielding Yankees.

Meanwhile the Giants are still working on their own hex, from McCovey's line drive to Bobby Richardson ending the '62 fall classic to Scott Spiezio fouling off pitch after pitch from Felix Rodriguez in '02—even as he would

(footnote continued on next page)

The Astros enacted their own unique tradition with exquisite precision. From the time they were born simultaneously with the New York Mets in 1962 (as the Houston Colt .45s) they have been locked in a transcendental pitching duel with their twin, supplying the likes of Dick Farrell and Mike Cuellar, Don Wilson and Larry Dierker, James Rodney Richard and Bob Knepper. The Mets were at a disadvantage until the era of Seaver, Koosman, and Gentry, reenacted by Gooden, Darling, and Ojeda. (Ironically, the two most dominating pitchers on the '86 Astros were ex-Mets, Mike Scott and Nolan Ryan.)

Insofar as the 1986 National League Championship Series was enacted by two teams locked in a millennial pitching duel, random—almost incidental—plays took on ultra-critical significance. The Met pennant was the result of a conspiracy of dozens of infinitesimal episodes, any *one* of which going the other way could have tilted the series to the Astros. As the winning team, the Mets entered twenty-nine of the sixty-four innings tied, another twenty-nine behind, and only six ahead. All of those six were in the second game of the series! They never began an inning ahead during all three games at their home ballpark, yet won two of them!

How many times do we hear that a team is presently 40-1 or 85-2 when they hold the lead going into the ninth inning? Yet three times in twelve *regular-season* games the Astros were tied by the Mets in the

---

(footnote continued)

four years later against Guillermo Mota—before finally smacking a three-run homer. The Jints still have not won a Series in San Francisco, their last coming in New York in 1954 when Willie Mays set the tone by outrunning Vic Wertz' mammoth opening-game drive.

Spiezio's matching at-bats against the Giants and then the Mets, like Keith Hernandez' come-from-behind hits precisely two decades earlier in seventh games—for the Cardinals against Milwaukee ('82) and for the Mets against Boston ('86)—reveal a lurking archetype; someone in the dugout should have interrupted the '06 playoff game and warned Willie Randolph in time. What a tangled web this is!

ninth or tenth (though they recovered to win the last two of those in Houston). Darryl Strawberry's ninth-inning homer off Dave Smith tying the eleventh game of the regular season between the two teams was prescient of Len Dykstra's walk-off home run off Smith, turning defeat into victory in the third game of the playoffs. Home runs by Strawberry and Knight respectively tied and then won a July game in the tenth inning at Shea—much in the fateful way the Mets came from behind late in the third and sixth games of the playoffs. In the fifth playoff game, only one well-timed swing by Darryl Strawberry prevented Nolan Ryan from shutting the Mets out and sending the series back to Houston with the Astros ahead. That homer kept New York in the game until Gary Carter could punch a tenacious seeing-eye grounder through Charlie Kerfeld's spastic legs in the twelfth. (Meanwhile, detractors of Strawberry's post-season play tend to overlook not only that home run off Ryan but the three-run shot off Knepper that tied the Dykstra game and then the solo homer off Nipper that clinched the seventh game of the World Series. Strawberry could have struck out every single other at-bat—and almost did—and still have had one of the great post-seasons of all time. His first two homers were game-transforming shots off pitchers in outright grooves.)

As unusual as the '86 playoffs were, the Astros must have had the feeling they had been there before. For Mike Schmidt, guest-announcing the post-season on the network, it was *déjà vu* 1980, fourth and fifth games (under the old five-game format). The Phillies won the first game of that series at home and almost took the second too. As Astro pitcher Frank LaCorte trudged dejectedly off the mound, Bake McBride, carrying the winning run, was inexplicably held at third by Coach Lee Elia. Houston scored next, setting the stage for everything that would follow.

The Astros took the third game in eleven innings and, when they carried a lead forged against Steve Carlton into the eighth inning at the Dome, it looked like curtains for the Phillies.

No! The Phils scored three runs to take the lead; then the Astros countered with one in the ninth to send the game into extra innings. In the tenth, pinch-hitter Greg Luzinski doubled to left, and Pete Rose scored all the way from first with a forearm to Bruce Bochy's face.

The next day the Phillies found themselves in an even worse predicament—down 5-2 going into the eighth inning against Nolan Ryan in his prime. Then, keyed by Del Unser's critical hit, they exploded for five runs; the Astros miraculously answered with two in the bottom of the inning—shades of Jim Coates and Hal Smith, Dale Long and Mickey Mantle (diving back into first base in a stroke of spontaneous genius to confound a game-ending double-play). In 1960 Garry Maddox drove in Unser with the pennant-winner.

After watching the Mets and Astros carry their monumental sixth-game battle into extra innings (and the evening) at the Astrodome, Schmidt recalled his personal desperation in 1980: "It was the Astrodome, where they believed they were unbeatable; it was Nolan Ryan; they had us by three runs; we had two shots left; there was no way they could lose. Same thing today; only it was Bob Knepper and he had the Mets beat through eight innings."

Dramatic turnaround at the point of victory (or defeat) was the hallmark of the 1986 post-season. (It perhaps began with the Kansas City Royals' stunning reversals over the Blue Jays and Cardinals in 1985. The sixth game of the '85 World Series was the only time all season that the Cardinals' bullpen blew a lead in the last inning—and even then the umpire had to provide inimitable help.)

How many times does a good team carry a *two*- or *three*-run lead into the last inning and lose? Yet it happened four times in twenty post-season games in 1986, including twice with two out. Perhaps these playoff dramatics reflect a level of intensity missing during the regular season. Players enter an almost psychic state, pushing their telekinetic abilities to the limit as they try individually to wrest the outcome. Some players anyway. . . . Or maybe an undiagnosed archetype prevails.

The way Houston (and Mike Scott) finished the regular season, the Mets were walking open-eyed into a buzz saw. The Astros should have been heavy betting favorites over even the '27 Yankees. Their conjunction with the supersonic '86 Mets in the playoffs could have occurred inside the baseball equivalent of a cyclotron for the way it produced quantum effects and even uncertainty results. By making it through the buzz saw, the Mets defined themselves as a team.

Then a softer version of the same curious puzzle was thrown at them in the Series (with Bruce Hurst replacing Mike Scott) and, in solving that, they completed a mythic season.

Let's review that epic ninth-inning rally in Houston: The Mets had gone down that afternoon without even threatening for eight innings (and essentially the preceding twenty-one in New York). They opened the ninth with Lenny Dykstra, a left-handed pinch hitter (because there were no viable right-handed ones left) against a tough left-handed pitcher. Lenny drove a triple to right center field. Perhaps Billy Hatcher should have caught it, but he certainly wasn't playing Dykstra to pull Knepper. Billy Doran *could* have caught Mookie Wilson's soft liner if he had judged his leap properly. When Hernandez hit a shot to center one out later, the tying run was on second. Dave Smith came in again and somehow walked both Carter and Strawberry; now the flow of energy had turned in the Mets' direction. Ray Knight's ensuing at-bat was the key. First, Knight almost walked and was furious at the umpire's read of the pitch; then he almost struck out. When Astro catcher Alan Ashby challenged this second call, Knight turned and started yelling at *him*. It was no more big salaries, primetime showbiz bullshit now; these guys were playing hardball. Knight muscled a shot deep enough to right to bring in Hernandez for the tie. Danny Heep could have ended it all by taking four balls, but he fidgeted through his customary half-swings and struck out.

Now the game marched off into never-never land, locking baseball fans in a trance for almost the duration of an entire second game under sudden-death conditions. It was the gist of what baseball is. The background intensity—from game to game, season to season—had flooded into a single contest and ruptured from the stadium into the world, paralyzing entire cities.

When Wally Backman singled home a run in the fourteenth inning, a Met pennant could almost be tasted. I hung before the TV, waiting. Orosco struck out Billy Doran to open the bottom of the inning. But suddenly and without warning, Billy Hatcher whacked a tremendous home run just fair down the left-field line.

There was no way out of this game. Exhausted players were on the roller coaster and they had to ride it to the end.

Over the next inning or two Keith Hernandez rhetorically asked a number of Astros on the base paths, "Whatever happens, isn't this a great game?" It was a noble thought, but there was no way for the teams to declare it a tie, shake hands, and walk off the field. The ancient ballcourt had two distinct exits—life and death—and eventually everyone on that field, and every fan following the two teams, would take one or the other. Yet it was also a collaboration, and the teams honored each other merely by being on the field together.

Writer George Leonard compares such a moment to an aikido black-belt exam: "[E]very last spectator realizes at some level that what is happening out on the field is more than a game, but rather something achingly beautiful and inevitable, an enactment in space and time of how the universe works, how things are."

Otherwise, it was just a bunch of men locked in a contest on television.

When the Mets went to the well for the pennant against the Astros in the extra innings of that sixth game, I was transfixed in the tension. As in any ceremony, the significators were hidden, the deeper image concealed in simple fluctuations on the surface. The whole Mets team history passed before me, a hologram reflecting hundreds of other games over twenty-five seasons. The digest of an ordinary baseball match couldn't contain the traces radiating through it. An aura surrounded the field of play and raised it to the level of epic and legend, so it was like looking at a dance of gods and goddesses on Olympus, watching the creation of totems and clans in the crucible of war. Seasons upon nondescript seasons are enacted in order to achieve such an apotheosis.

When you participate in a millennial game, as player or spectator, you are illuminating the legacy of prior campaigns, the subtext of their innings and players. That's what Hernandez didn't want his fellow players to lose in the heat of combat—that, whoever won, this was special, the mere fact of being inside its sine wave was what they would remember for the rest of their lives, and beyond.

The true follower of a team observes unrequited seasons through the imagined crystal of this ultimate moment of truth (whether or not it ever happens), for it is the *potential* of winning the Pennant and Series that gives each season its taut boundaries and keeps the games meaningful. Hundreds of players, thousands of games, and hundreds of thousands of pitches and other nuances, come to their quintessence and resolution there.

Thus, Jesse Orosco pitching for the Mets at the epochal brink was also Jesse Orosco of 1979 and 1982 who failed as a rookie after coming over in a trade for Jerry Koosman, who worked his way back through the minors and then ran off a marvelous skein of saves and wins in 1983. It was the same Jesse Orosco who gave up several game-tying and -winning home runs over the years, but who also regularly got the game-ending strikeout with the tying or winning runs on base. He would never again be as good as he was in '83, but by the time he took the mound in Houston he had a complex history, he had individuated—and, in the end, he was just good enough.

Mike Scott in 1986 may have been better than anyone the Mets had, but the game wasn't in Mike Scott's hands. Jesse Orosco in the Astrodome (and in the ninth inning of the seventh Series game at Shea) was also Jay Hook, Randy Tate, Rick Baldwin, John Pacella, and Scott Holman. All of those pitchers on the mound in Met uniforms flow together in one trope. Likewise, hundreds of shadow Wally Backmans and Mookie Wilsons—Ron Hunts and Benny Ayalas—combine in the puppetry of an afternoon.

The Mets were not born contending in 1984; they do not take their identity from only the triumphant season of 1986. All the players who didn't make it to Houston are still present. Jim Hickman, Steve Henderson, and Hubie Brooks are there; how could Hubie not be a part of it? Though long gone, Henderson struck an ecstatic three-run homer off the Giants' Alan Ripley one June night in New York. Recalled from exile, Lee Mazzilli represents Rod Kanehl, Chico Fernandez, Frank Taveras. But everyone else also participates, from Ed Bouchee to Terry Blocker, from Craig Swan to Leon Brown, from Grover Powell to Bruce Boisclair, from Galen Cisco to Greg Harris, from Charlie Puleo to young erratic Mike Scott and Jeff Reardon. If they weren't there, it wouldn't be the Mets; it would just be some good team winning the pennant, the same thing some good team does every year.

John Stearns is there, kneeling in the dust by home plate, his fist clenched while runs pour across, never losing his fire or dignity. That defeat was waiting five, eight years, to be redeemed in this game.

No matter how physical and concrete the bats and balls and collisions of men are, their real truth lies in the spirits not the bodies of those that play. (Do you doubt that if the New Jersey Nets ever win the NBA Championship, however many decades in the future, Buck Williams will be there rebounding . . . for all his vaults from beyond exhaustion in the fourth quarter, for all the hopeless games and meaningless seasons in which he refused to give up?)

I think you must look inward, because "inside" is where it's coming from; otherwise, what would the game mean but tin soldiers on a toy field, or data pouring through computer terminals? Yes, we are in an era of "acting out" and externalities, from jihads and nuclear bombs to heavy metal, venture capital, and quick sex, but it is the human experience of those things that gives them texture and power over us.

Throughout those extra innings I kept asking myself—Why? Why does this (which means nothing at all) mean so much I can barely breathe?

Inured insights replayed themselves—the joy of collective participation with the many other fans identifying with the Mets . . . projection of my psyche into a certified mythic pageant . . . transference of my anesthetized sympathy for everyone to just these players.

But none of these metaphors or psychodramas does it justice. My participation in the Mets is finally unconscious, or semiconscious at best. At one point during the 1986 playoffs my wife Lindy remarked that the intensity of her husband and son was both troubling and absurd to her. "Who cares?" she demanded. "This matter doesn't affect or interest me, and it's an intrusion on my life." The next evening she added in exasperation: "I don't get it. Are we somehow involved in professional baseball? I didn't get married to have a baseball game imposed on me."

I was mortified; it *did* look ridiculous.

Put under the gun by her as much as myself, I couldn't just watch passively. At least if I was going to be there, I needed to answer some of her questions. Given the world situation, the existential life situation, given the mortality of everyone involved, how important could this game be?

If I wanted to go deeper, I needed to expose not only the myth of baseball but the game in which I was a player:

Watching myself watch the Mets and Astros was a like a zen koan. Although a game isn't real in the way it seems to be at the time, neither is life, which is conducted in atoms made out of subtle vibrations and gaps, creating trances tuned like dreams. Yet you are called upon to participate in this event at the most profound level.

A ballgame shadows life and gives it a sort of counterweight. Baseball generates an intrinsic (if illusory) significance to disguise the fact that the world itself is mysterious and open-ended. Our need for some ultimate confirmation falls on the field of play because it can never fall on us for a resolution.

How strange! Creatures in a dream invent a tournament with a grand prize to relieve themselves of the terror of the dream itself.

In that sense, American baseball (like soccer—called football—in the rest of the world) gives symptomatic relief from the tyranny of time by creating its own cyclical universe. Far more than a rite of spring, it is a complete sacred calendar, a mnemonic device for keeping track of events in secular cultures. (Sometimes, in thinking of death, one of my yardsticks is that the Mets will go on playing games the results of which I will never know, with players I have never heard of.)

But baseball is not only a practice of life; it is a practice of practice. I seek not only for the obvious symbols that baseball philosophers are fond of pointing out in America's frontier psyche but also the very nature of my attachment to those symbols.

Deep in extra innings against Houston I perceive a subtler level: I am fragmented and contracted, not a coherent organism. The part of me that is locked into the game is isolated from real hungers and desires, so it thrives on the exercise of strong emotions bound in this event. Not capable somehow of the full tenderness of life itself, "I" prefer a boost from outside that's at least partially real, not a story or a patent fantasy.

The reason, for instance, my players can't be movie stars or rock singers is that those protagonists "win" every time, whatever they do; their mere persona is a celebration of triumph. A game is different from a play, or a dance, for its outcome is unknown; its moves are not scripted by any playwright or choreographer. It is an unscripted play caught in eternal probability theory, unfolding as the universe of molecules does, giving shape to itself instant by instant according to axioms known as laws. The advantage of a game is that its players become heroes—or in fact anything—only through events that can at most be partly determined by them, events that are also random, entropic, and fortuitous (or not).

A game is an algebraic, disequilibrated network like the one from which simple cells or the universe itself once arose. It must be "played"

for us to get at what's inside it. It is completely adventitious and con-
tingent, so we watch it unfold magnificently, like a butterfly out of a
chrysalis. Meaning is created act by act until its unpredictable shape
is complete—the final box score.

The bogus "high" of a game, and its complementary false "low,"
occur upon soils of geology under skies of meteorology (along with
earthquakes and rainbows), apart from anything we can intervene to
change—which is why rotisserie leagues are sterile to me: who cares
about imposing the aggrandizing, manipulative self (and a mere human
algorithm) on a self-generating phenomenon that has its own ground
integrity. Baseball is interesting solely because it is both tangible and
etiological.

It's not just that baseball involves a fragment of my personality. The
game brings together two fragmented selves that I spend much of my
life trying to meld. There is (one) the positive visionary self, who writes,
who cultivates spiritual and artistic discipline, who communicates
from the heart not the mind, who is capable of love, who feels the
poignancy of the ceremony on the field.

But my more primitive aspects (two)—including the reptilian lobes
of my brain that are still involved in long-ago battles of lizards—have
not evolved to that level. They encompass a fearful, anxious part of
me, a self that is troubled by the danger of the streets at night, the
threat of nuclear war, the ever-nearness of disaster and loss. Those
facets of my inner life stand in dynamic duality with the rhapsodic
parts. Their modus is to move from one dread to another, to be
assuaged only when some imagined catastrophe doesn't occur—a '50s
hysteria of continually postponed air-raid sirens.

The "sudden death" of the Mets-Astros playoff game is an occasion for both selves to practice each other. Every time the Astros come
up I "practice" my anxiety and observe it. Every time the Mets come
up I yearn for my visionary high in the form of the Pennant. I go back
and forth between the two trances and experience their collusion. I

realize that it has always been this way. The opposing intensities mark the emotional boundaries of my life, and the game allows me to project them outward and enjoy their oscillation.

However I get there, this deeply charged state is crucial to me. It is why I get a "rush" out of games: to try to heal myself by proxy. Real transformation doesn't happen, but at that moment it doesn't matter, the semblance of it does.

Just because it's baseball, I might have told Lindy, is no reason to trash it; we little enough understand the sources or accessibility of the tremendous energy we each contain. If I were an Australian Aborigine, the occasion might be an Emu Dance or Kangaroo Ceremony— no more, no less crucial to the mitochondria in my cells. All across the planet (and on other planets) different rituals hold creatures breathless, on the edge of their seats (or rocks), agog to see what will happen next. Today, on Earth, it is a baseball game, the sixth in the ordinal series between the Mets and Astros, the former Metropolitans and Colt .45s. I am here, alive.

For my teenage son it is not quite the same. Like Keith Hernandez, he enjoys the sheer fact that the Mets are in this game and, though he will be depressed and teary if they lose, he is not frantic during it. In fact, I drive him crazy through the eleventh, the twelfth, thirteenth, fourteenth innings, kicking the ground, drumming with my leg, hitting the chair every time a pitch doesn't go right. I am insensible to these gestures, but he tells me, so I leave the garage and go to the TV inside, where my twelve-year-old daughter Miranda is reading a book and cares only insofar that if the Mets win, I have promised a walk to the bakery for a victory cake.

When Knight singles in Strawberry in the top of the sixteenth, I go back outside for the rest of what-turns-into a three-run rally. I flee again when the Astros uncannily come back to life in the bottom half. This game is the epitome of "no control," with the history of the Mets seemingly at stake. The Astros get to within one hit of an all-time miracle comeback recalling Bobby Thomson's 1951 home run, and I can do nothing but pace in stunned silence.

Later we learn that, at that precarious moment, Keith Hernandez came to the mound and jokingly informed Gary Carter, "No more fastballs, or you'll have to fight me right here." (Carter later denied this and attributed it to Hernandez' buoyant post-game mood when he talked fast and loose, as one is inclined to do in the giddiness of such a time. When reality has transcended myth, it has become myth, and one is tempted to create an archetypal version of what happened because it alone seems true.)

But the point is: Hernandez is thinking all the time about the evolving situation. He never brain-locks. There are very few players who are so present in the game that they become the game. Hernandez is the baseball equivalent of an aikido master; his intelligence does not require thought. That's why he went promptly to second to nip Hatcher on Denny Walling's grounder in the hole that final half-inning. If he had taken the easier play at first—which is what most infielders in the history of the game would have done—Glenn Davis' ensuing single would have tied the score (another of those intricate subsets of possibility that propelled the Mets rather than the Astros into the World Series).

In another sense, that "game intelligence" is why Hernandez measured a key ninth-inning double off Knepper after not hitting him all day; it's also why he was the one who broke the ice off Bruce Hurst in the seventh game of the Series with a bases-loaded single, precisely the hit he laced for the Cardinals against the Brewers, seventh game, 1982 (off another difficult lefty, Bob McClure). When whole seasons come down to single quanta, it is these bits of disciplined mentality on which the result turns. Of course, Hernandez would perceive "all curveballs" to Kevin Bass (Bass would finally swing and miss strike three—pandemonium, release at last from this game!).

Afterwards, Mike Schmidt's first observation concerned Bass. "Only by failing in that situation," he said, "do you learn how to succeed the next time. When you succeed, it's not some out-of-the-blue thing. You reach back inside yourself into the previous failure and that's the place you succeed from." He was telling us a secret. When he struck out with the tying run on third in the fifth game of the 1980 playoffs, that was the spot from which hundreds of Mike Schmidt clutch hits would later come.

The Mets started the World Series the same way they started the play-offs, losing 1-0—although in a lower-energy, sloppier game decided not by an early home run but a late ground ball through Tim Teufel's legs. Bruce Hurst's looping curve was just as inscrutable as Mike Scott's split finger, and the Mets had no answers at the plate. They lost the second game too, 5-1, when Dwight Gooden was soundly thumped. Forces at large seemed profoundly opposed to a Met championship; in the fourth inning, tremendous shots to right field by both Strawberry and Howard Johnson died against a cushion of air. It was as though the Sox were swinging against the moon's gravity, the Mets against Neptune's.

To many observers, including ones who had predicted a Met sweep, it was all over. But not to Mike Schmidt, who said that if he were the manager, he would tell the players, "All you have to do is win two in a row. How many times have you done that this year? Forty maybe."

The Mets went up to Boston and did precisely that. They didn't wait for a chance to fall behind again. As the first batter in game three, self-activating Len Dykstra stroked a home run; then the Mets scorched Oil Can Boyd for three more first-inning runs and, though he held them off from there till the seventh, it was enough.

The following day Gary Carter found a left-field screen clearly made for his stroke, twice. The Green Monster, like the wind at Shea, became the ally of the visitors (Mookie Wilson played it like a lifelong New Englander, nailing Rich Gedman trying for second base). Carter, Ojeda, and Darling had come home victoriously (I am counting the Kid's years in Quebec). The Series was tied. But the biggest hurdles for the Mets were ahead.

"Darling on three days' rest doesn't worry me," said Schmidt.

"Gooden on three days' rest does. If I were Dave Johnson, I'd give the ball to Rick Aguilera or Sid Fernandez and say, 'Son, go out there and make a name for yourself.'"

Johnson, though, had lost his patience with gopher balls. Fernandez wasn't as notorious as Aguilera (and Rick still had to pitch to a guy named Henderson in the tenth inning at Shea), but El Sid had thrown an unnecessary one to Alan Ashby in the fourth game against Houston, and he had been no mystery to the Sox in Game Two. So Gooden returned from his shelling on short rest. (Ironically, Fernandez was to appear twice more during the Series—not in a starting role—and the Red Sox were to find him nothing short of the second coming of Sidd Finch.)

Gooden, though, was everything Schmidt feared. Here was someone who, for two whole seasons, controlled the universe of baseball from the mound. He went back and forth between raw heat and Lord Charles, allowing little more than a run per nine innings and striking out a routine ten or so along the way. As games went on, he simply got stronger. If a runner should reach third with no one out, Dwight had the focus to throw nine strikes by the next three hitters (as the Dodgers learned many times). He even taught himself to hit and probably could have gone to the minors and returned in two years as an outfielder with power. He was the prototype of the guy who came down from a higher league. The fact that he didn't get to pitch in the playoffs or World Series was one of the main regrets of 1984 and 1985.

But in 1986 Gooden was not the same pitcher or even the same man. Despite Met denials that anything had changed, he was erratic and, at times, hit extremely hard. He seemed confused on the mound. He tired late in games and, on a number of occasions, yielded ninth-inning tying homers. He became like a raw rookie struggling for even the inklings of mastery more often than at any time previously in his career (except maybe for a few innings at Kingsport and Little Falls in 1982).

During his first two years in the majors, Gooden was like a kung fu master—a frisky child assassin. He emerged from the underbelly of American rap culture, and he transformed its chaos in himself into a functional veneer of calm. As ballplayer he was gallant and spare. He hardly spoke, and what he did say was pragmatic and modest. He had no news to give; he simply fulfilled the requirements of public utterance. For all the effect of his pronouncements, he might as well have taken a vow of silence.

Who needed Bill Lee's yogic relief pitcher making the baseball disappear and reappear? Doc was the eye of the storm.

In 1985 at Candlestick I sat among Gooden's family. His father was as impassive as Doc, but his young cousins or nephews must have thought Dwight was supposed to be Michael Jackson. They wanted a strikeout on every batter, and when anybody put the ball in play, that was an outrage, a "shuck." A hit was a mistake—"You can't do that; no one can hit Doc!" At one point a friend or relative came down with a few baseballs that needed autographing. The family member sitting beside me acted as though he were expected to haul them out to the mound on the spot. "Didn't I tell you never to bother the Doc when he's at work. Can't you see, man. Doc's operatin'. He's conductin' business; he can't sign no baseballs now."

These kinfolk didn't even know that their boy was playing Cooperstown-version baseball; they wanted domination, break-dancing, triumph of the *nouveau riche*. Dwight even did a rap record for them, an embarrassment to all involved.

The explanations for what happened to Gooden in '86 ranged from the banal to the nuts and bolts to the supernatural: the hitters adjusted to him; he didn't have control of the curve anymore; he ruined his motion trying to cut down on his leg kick; drugs and other personal-life distractions drained him; he lost motivation with the Mets not needing him to win every time; he had a physical injury (the mysterious ankle?), an undiagnosed disease; an opponent hired a sorcerer to point the bone at him or stick pins in a Dwight doll; or maybe it was simply (Bob Gibson said) that no one's that good.

Perhaps no single thing caused the change. After all, mastery is not iron domination of strength; it is a subtle combination of speed, rhythm, and control. Other pitchers throw harder; other pitchers have as sharp a curveball. Dwight put it all together in an ensemble.

Even before rumor of cocaine use came out, some people knew. Apparently the kids in the playgrounds of Tampa got the word, but those playgrounds are a long way from corporate headquarters, and there are very few commuters to run messages. A local friend whose job involves working with athletes who have cocaine problems told me he was *certain* that drugs were Gooden's issue after watching the Giants bomb him one afternoon at Candlestick. He saw a slight distraction of timing and pace, a laboring that wasn't there before, a familiar mild bewilderment in Doc's eyes—because he had never fallen so out of sync before.

"What chance did he have, really?" my friend asked me. "He was young, black, wealthy, educated, suddenly famous, and he lived in Tampa." But Dwight protested such accusations all season and even had a drug-testing clause put into his contract.

It makes you wonder if the disease is the drug—or the denial. It also casts a different light on Vida Blue: maybe he never had a chance either. If the great Bob Gibson closed out one era, then Vida unwittingly opened another.

But it will be many a season before we close this one out, for American baseball is a fifteen-minute-old puppet show against the millennial games now being played in Iran, Afghanistan, and Colombia. And most ballplayers are simply grown children, educated by a pop culture for which they are heroes. They are given mentally draining jobs with lots of hollow, meaningless time and plenty of money. Surely they are set up to be the victims of every big-time global and playground scam; after all, how are they going to outwit poor South American and Southeast Asian farmers or urban drug lords in the battle for the planet's resources? They are worried about "Cardinals" and "Cubs" and how to spend the cash fast enough. By the time cocaine reached suburban Tampa, it was already dressed like the next-door neighbor, and it spoke in whatever street lingo it needed to get in. Ballplayers might read the papers but, after their discord with sportswriters, they totally mistrust the information there. They glide right through the warnings.

In any case, drugs are not their own explanation, nor are they a psychological monolith, transcending all the events of personal history and culture. Whatever the proximate cause of Gooden's struggle (cocaine or some other malaise), an aspect of his unresolved past must have engulfed Doc. He couldn't transform chaos and deprivation into mastery indefinitely. Every act casts a shadow, and Dwight's first two campaigns required some compensation, psychological and physical. For two seasons he coasted on raw talent with the blessings of both Athena and Zeus; in 1986 the gods opposed him, and look what he still accomplished! Destiny prescribed that he would lose not only the All-Star Game but two World Series games; sheer guts and ability won seventeen starts during the regular season and dueled both Mike Scott and Nolan Ryan by the breadth of a run in the playoffs. With the Devil himself leaning on him for his due, if Doc hadn't summoned every ounce of remaining energy and skill to force Ryan into extra innings in the fifth game of the playoffs, the Mets never would have made it to the Series.

I don't buy for a moment what the Red Sox said after the fifth game: "No one beats us with two pitches." The Dwight Gooden of 1984 and '85 beats them with *either* the curve or the fastball. The Dwight of 1986 was on a mission to the Underworld; he was thrashing through shadows he magically suppressed for two seasons (the same shadows Oil Can struggles with, less successfully). Dwight was a wounded pitcher in the World Series, although we could not see the wounds or know the degrees to which they were physical, psychological, or spiritual. He was on the most perilous leg of a pilgrimage, far more serious than the game; I mean, two months later he could have been shot dead or had his arm broken on the streets of Tampa.

With Dwight hurling his bolts as the gods set themselves against him, hits rattled all over Fenway. We don't put much stock in celestial interference these days, but archetypally that was the work of Zeus, in partnership with a malefic Saturn. No wonder the man couldn't pitch. That he even lived is a statement of his magic. ("The sudden fame and fortune he achieved is nice," Frank Cashen would say six months later. "But we sort of robbed him of his youth.")

So, the Mets had to overcome not only their exhaustion and lethargy, and the Sox' two-game lead, they had to play through the deflation of Gooden's invulnerability in the fifth game, a myth so central to the 1985 Mets that it had become almost their identity. They had to win the big one without him.

To what degree was the World Series uphill for the Mets? Although they did not trail in runs within individual games quite as often as they did during the playoffs, they were behind the Red Sox in the Series itself entering fifty of the sixty-four innings (all except the first seven innings of the first game, the first two innings of the fifth game, and the first two and last three innings of the seventh game). They actually led in games (plus score) in the whole Series for only its final three innings. Several times in the bottom of the tenth of the sixth game they came within one strike of extinction.

Mike Cieslinski, the inventor of a statistical board game called Pursue the Pennant, tried to recreate the Met comeback in the tenth inning of the sixth game. Using cards representing actual players and dice to randomize outcomes, he sent Carter up to bat against Schiraldi with two outs and no one on. He played all night, but the Red Sox won the Series every time. In his own words, "With two outs—even if you get one or two baserunners—you usually get an out. That's what kept happening: I kept getting an out. Actually I had thoughts of this never happening."

But he went back at it the next morning: he rolled the dice 100 times, 200 times, until finally, on his 279th try, the Mets rallied and won. That puts the odds against a Met comeback informally at 278 to 1. Which means you watch the game from the Carter at-bat 279 times (more than a season and a half) and the Red Sox win 278. Why did we get the 279th game on our only try?

Even the one Met who truly walked on water in '69, Ron Swoboda, was astonished. Asked to compare World Series teams, he did some philosophizing and reminiscing: "The champagne dried a little bit and the years went by, but I really enjoyed watching these guys do it because they put their own signature on this one. I can't believe it. They almost killed me. . . . When it was two outs in the bottom of the tenth, my heart was down there in my shoes. I'm trying to figure out some kind of fallback position. I'm thinking, 'Geez, if they don't win it, well at least we're the only ones who did'—all kinds of rationalizations—and all of a sudden you get three base hits, a wild pitch, an error, and I'm screaming, you know, I'm screaming."

When the Mets had two outs and no one on, I stood up and approached the TV, ready to turn it off because I didn't want to watch the Red Sox celebrating. Apparently Keith Hernandez felt the same way because he went back to the manager's office—where, half appareled in street clothes (in no state to return for the eleventh if Mookie had popped up*), he witnessed the most miraculous World Series comeback of all time. In normal circumstances no one comes back from there; in the sixth game of the World Series, forget it.

All along Robin was telling me no, not to worry, that they couldn't lose. Hit after hit proved his faith. He kept saying, "Rich, sit down. Don't even think of it." So much positive energy, it seemed, in such a hopeless cause. Then, as Kevin Mitchell scored the tying run, I yelled myself hoarse; I had watched baseball all my life trying unsuccessfully to root a wild pitch with the tying run on third. Why now, when it mattered most?

---

*He also wasn't budging. He figured he had found a lucky chair and it still "had more hits in it."

Mookie Wilson was so faint afterwards he could barely talk. This was just baseball, but it seemed more as if a UFO had descended on New York City. The fans stayed and cheered the visitation. On an evening begun by Paul Simon singing the National Anthem and punctuated by a comet-colored second-inning sky-plunger, the inevitable ending had been wrought.

Too often, in the months afterwards, Mookie has been cheated out of the wonder and accomplishment of that at-bat. In a batting slump, with the whole season on the line and no strikes to give, he fouled off two biting Bob Stanley sinkers, dodged the game-tying wild pitch, and made contact with another sinker, sending it toward first. All that work, plus his intimidating speed, led to Buckner's error. "Mookie the whiff," sniffed a Red Sox fan in typical contempt for both the batter and the pitcher, in an attempt to minimize what happened and make it tolerable. But Wilson well described the challenge and intensity inside himself: "When I was up there, I felt like everything was happening in slow motion. I didn't hear the crowd. That was the most I concentrated in one at-bat in my whole career. That at-bat was my career. When it was over, I was drained. That's what I've played all these years for. You dream about that situation, up with the game on the line. Everything went down to one at-bat. It was the difference between winning and losing. It was perfect."

The parallels between seventh games of two Series eleven years apart run so spookily close that they suggest the synchronicities of the Lincoln and Kennedy assassinations. Both games followed historic extra-inning contests of sudden reversals of fortune. In both seventh games the Red Sox had a 3-0 lead entering the sixth inning, with a left-handed pitcher seemingly in command. In '75 Bill Lee threw the Moon Curve to Tony Perez and suddenly it was 3-2. In '75 the losing pitcher was Jim Burton, who finished his career on the Mets' Tidewater farm club. In '86 the losing pitcher was Calvin Schiraldi, who spent much of the previous season on Tidewater. (In fact, it seemed a particularly bad omen for the Sox that in a tight seventh game of a World Series they should twice go to the bullpen in late innings and come up with two of their opponent's least effective hurlers in a 26-7 loss to the Phillies the season before, not only Schiraldi but Joe Sambito.)

I would like to think that, over the history of baseball, the Mets and Red Sox are more allies than adversaries—and that the Series will not leave bad blood. The taunting of Darryl Strawberry by white fans during the fifth game in Boston ("Dar-ryl, Dar-ryl!") and the anti-black rioting that swept rural Massachusetts after the seventh game were ominous signs. Marty Barrett and Mookie Wilson visited college campuses together to try to heal some of those wounds—but Al Nipper, still brooding over the fact that Strawberry took his time rounding the bases on his culminative seventh-game shot, threatened to drill him the next time they met, and then did so with his first spring-training pitch to him. Should Rick Aguilera now go after Dave Henderson for cavorting disrespectfully on his home run?

Raw Feed Transcription

After midnight in the Met locker room, Sal, the weary local announcer, stands in front of the large white World Series 1986 banner, a hand to his earplug, a towel around his neck, mike held limply, still trying to send up newsfeeds. He goes through Carter and Mazzilli, Hernandez and Knight: ("Fuck the highlights!" Keith says, hugging his blood brother. "You've got the star right here!"). Sal frantically waves for another player to join him, but everyone is too far into the partying. Then Tim Teufel comes by, still in uniform, carrying the requisite champagne bottle in his fist.

"How do you feel, Tim?" Sal asks, throwing an awkward arm around him.

Teufel shakes his head, smiling impishly, then crosses in front of the camera and summons another player. It's Kevin Mitchell, the Mets' gravity third baseman; he's wearing a baseball visor, a gold t-shirt cut off at the shoulders, and orange wrist bands. Teufel slides his right arm around Mitchell's neck and, gesturing with his fingers on Mitchell's shoulder, says quietly, "Sal, they wrote us off, and we proved them wrong. That's the bottom line." Silently affirming his own sentiment, he stands there, trying to look diffidently professional, crooking a finger around his bottle, signaling to passing teammates. Something catches his eye: "How about the NBC cap?"

A technician hands it to him and he adjusts its strap for his head size. Meanwhile, Bobby Ojeda, wearing a white Mets cap and a jacket, slips in behind him. Smiling sheepishly, he puts his arm around Teufel and signals Number One with his finger. They all stand there nervously as though posing for the family album.

"Okay, we're in the Weather, and then it comes to us," Sal finally declares, milking communication out of the plug with a finger against it in his ear.

Teufel throws back his head, takes a drink, and stares bemusedly at the bottle. Then he flips it semi-consciously to the side and lets Mitchell imbibe.

Sal becomes aware of Ojeda who has circled in front of them, and he shouts, "Bobby O!"

Teufel adds, "The Eatery!" He pulls the NBC cap down over his eyes and repeats the phrase to himself.

Ojeda is trying to find his way back into the group from behind, but the banner is in the way, and Teufel and Mitchell are searching for him behind it, lifting the material and tossing it around. This state of bedlam worries Sal: "Hey, get out of this! Come over here!"

Ojeda suddenly returns under the banner and asks, "Is this live?"

"Yeah," Sal confirms, "we're coming through this live."

Now Mitchell leans in front of Teufel, lets out a squeal, and squirts beverage right in Ojeda's face. Ojeda stumbles forward and struggles to wipe his eyes.

"Here's a towel," Teufel says to Bobby O. "I hate that shit, man," turning to Mitchell in sham outrage. But Mitchell is spraying again, and this time he soaks both Teufel and Sal with a mouthful.

Teufel wipes his own face on the announcer's towel, yanks the bottle away from Mitchell, and says, "You're damn getting crazy. This stuff gets in his eyes he can't do the interview." Mitchell is unimpressed; he simply wants to reload.

"You guys should sing 'New York, New York,'" says Sal, as though to suggest something also crazy but a little less raucous.

Mitchell now has taken on the persona of a show wrestler; he shoots out a forearm, swatting Ojeda squarely on the top of the head. "Put on his gargles!" he barks. "Let him put on his gargles."

We see that Ojeda is wearing plastic goggles on a band around his neck. Mitchell has gotten a hold of them and is trying to pull them up onto his face. Ojeda is not so much resisting as continuing to press the towel into his eyes, trying to get his eyes opened.

"Let me check 'em out, man," says Mitchell. And then, to counter any objection in advance, he quickly adds the reason he needs goggles: "I'm going swimming."

He pulls the goggles off Ojeda, but Ojeda yanks them back and adjusts them in place over his eyes. At this moment, with players wrestling before the camera and Sal pleading, "Wait, wait!" into the microphone, Danny Heep arrives, puts his hand on the ear plug, and asks deadpan, "You got a problem here?" They all laugh.

Mitchell reaches for Heep's bottle: "Hey man, let me get one sip." Ojeda, goggles on, stares blankly out into space.

Suddenly they are on the air.

"We're back in the Mets' clubhouse: Danny Heep, Bobby Ojeda. Kevin Mitchell—" Sal gesturing to each one as he pronounces his name. But the players have not yet noticed this change of focus and are continuing to wrestle with the bottle.

". . . and Tim Teufel, who was classy enough to come on after his big goof in the first game. . . ."

Mitchell grabs a can of beer from Ojeda's hand, fills his mouth with suds, and then explodes them in Heep's face.

"...but now he's a world champion."

Teufel realizes all at once he's been addressed: "That's right. I'm a world champion; the whole team is, and we're all very excited. Whatever happened in the first game" [petulantly] "is all behind us." While he is speaking, Heep has recovered, ducked, and deftly shoved Mitchell away. So Mitchell sprays Teufel and Sal.

"O-kay!" says Sal with tired jubilation. He looks around nervously for who's next. "Bobby Ojeda! Here's Bobby Ojeda," he almost shrieks.

Ojeda steps forward, so close to the camera that he is out of scale, goggles on, eyes staring flat out, his right hand raised Hi! as if an outerspaceman saying hello to Earth. Beer cans and bottles are passing back and forth in front of him, and Mitchell squirts him squarely in the eyes as he waves to New York. The goggles are protecting him. "Hi folks," he says, walking forward into the camera, hair soaked, foam dripping down his face. Then Danny Heep pulls down the white banner and tosses it on his head.

"I have ... I have ...," says Ojeda, pointing to his goggles. Then he presses his face up against the camera, totally out of focus, grimacing.

When he pulls his mug off, Sal is gone, the banner is gone, and a professional-acting Teufel has the microphone and is approaching him anew, as though for the real interview: "Bobby, Bobby, how does it feel?"

Ojeda is staggering backward holding up the beer. Then he hears the question: "It feels incredible, Mr. Teufel...."

Mitchell steps up, face to face with Ojeda, and spits beer all over him. "It's because he's swimming," the huge third baseman snarls.

"Yes, I *am* swimming," acknowledges Ojeda. "But I don't feel it. I don't feel a thing."

Heep is pouring beer on his head from behind, but Ojeda is grooving now; he points to his goggles and says, "These are shatterproof, they're ..."

Mitchell spits in his face again.

"Will you quit drinking my beer, Mr. Mitchell."

Undaunted, Mitchell fills up and squirts him yet again. "Do you always act like this, Kevin Mitchell?" asks announcer Teufel.

Protected in goggles, Ojeda points to his own face: "I don't feel a thing. You can buy this at your local supermarket. These are breakproof ... shatterproof..."

A new barrage of beer.

"... spitproof... "

"This interview is now over," declares Teufel.

"Poof ... poof ... poof...," continues Ojeda; then: "You better cut this."

He staggers away and Mitchell steps forward, turning to reveal the back of his t-shirt on which is sewn in script: "I ONLY HIT ROPES." He shakes the can of beer empty, then points to it and growls, "I'm through with you. You're fired!"

So, the 1986 season rushes out through its last ragged end.

With acknowledgment and thanks to the following sources for quoted material: *Mets Inside Pitch* (Mookie Wilson), *Baseball America* (Mike Cieslinski), *The Silent Pulse* (George Leonard), and Sportschannel/New York (Mike Schmidt and Ron Swoboda). The locker-room dialogue was transcribed from Satcom 1.

Public and Private Baseball: Ethnography of the 1984 Season

Year Written: 1984
Mets Seasons Referenced: 1962–1984

1.

My baseball interest began in 1952, so while I have no memory at all of Joe DiMaggio as a real player (he had only *just* retired), his hits were still echoing. During the seventh game of the World Series at the end of my first season as a Yankee fan, I somehow got so sick at school that I was sent home; I was lying in bed listening to the radio as Bob Kuzava pitched out of a bases-loaded seventh-inning jam against Brooklyn. While everyone else suddenly froze, Billy Martin raced across the infield at the last possible moment to make a shoestring catch of Jackie Robinson's towering two-out pop-up, two Dodgers in motion on the 3-2 pitch having already crossed home, a third right behind. By then it seemed as though I had been following the Yankees forever, so steeped in pinstripe history and lore had I become: from Joe Dugan and Waite Hoyt to Charlie Keller and Joe Page. When the Indians beat the Yanks in a battle of behemoths for the 1954 Pennant, I experienced it as a Götterdämmerung equivalent to the fall of Rome—the end of an era, even though I personally witnessed only its last two years.

My stepfather got tickets to the opening World Series game at the Polo Grounds that year—my first in person. As an American League loyalist, I rooted for the Indians. When Cleveland rallied late only to have Willie Mays run down Vic Wertz' colossal shot while racing back to home plate, I remember the pandemonium of the rising crowd and my disbelief and disappointment afterwards that the ball hadn't fallen in. I didn't see the catch itself.

I was at Yankee Stadium seven years later when Roger Maris cued his sixty-first homer off Tracy Stallard. Hard to believe that in that short time I had metamorphosed from a third-grader unable to see over the adults to a teenager on his first date, having found a girl at summer camp who followed baseball. I was now the adult who stood instinctively as the parabola descended against the right-field stands.

For years growing up in New York I lived at the heart of the American League, the crucial showdowns between Yankees and Indians—Allie Reynolds, Vic Raschi, Eddie Lopat, and Whitey Ford (the kid) against Early Wynn, Bob Lemon, Mike Garcia, and the ghost of Bob Feller. I saw Bob Grim win his first game at Yankee Stadium in 1954, and I made him my second-favorite player after Gil McDougald (Grim was to notch twenty his rookie season but do little thereafter). I saw fireballer Jim Bouton, throwing so hard that his cap fell off, make his first Major League start in 1962. Between the debuts of Grim and Bouton my Yankee staff included Bob Turley, Don Larsen, Johnny Kucks, Tom Sturdivant, Marshall Bridges, Luis Arroyo, Art Ditmar, Bud Daley. The sounds of those names loose a mêlée of memories and landscapes. I see lakes and lawns, flowering bushes and tomato plants, but not baseball games. Likewise, Ray Scarborough, Tom Morgan, Danny McDevitt, Rhyne Duren are charms striking distinct chords of my emerging consciousness.

My brother Jon and I sit forever in Central Park with our boxy brown radio, listening to changes in fortune, the progress of games into late innings—Phil Rizzuto working out a walk, Gus Triandos dropping a gem of a hit, Willie Miranda going in to run for him, then Irv Noren delivering a clutch pinch double into the left-field corner, as the roar of the crowd drowns the announcer's voice and we dance a jig and yell together.

Through lonely years of summer camp my radio was a touchstone to the center of a more luminous and composed universe—dart-throwing Bob Wiesler trying once again to gain his control, slugging pitcher Larsen batting eighth ahead of Willie Miranda, Tommy Byrne lining successive singles in a start, Mickey's godlike homers, Eli Grba capturing that crucial fourth game of a series against the White Sox, Joe DeMaestri's soft pinch single turning a comeback against the Tigers into a win, Gil McDougald's two-home-run game late in his career, and third-string catcher Johnny Blanchard electrifying pinch homers that rescued the 1961 season.

In an average year between 1952 and 1962 (when I finished high school) I attended about thirty games at Yankee Stadium. My father's company shared a box behind the visitor's dugout with singer Eddie Fisher's Ramrod Productions and, although I didn't spend much time with my father himself during childhood, I was able to claim the unused tickets at his New York office. As I got older and mastered the subway, I enacted this routine more often, inviting a variety of friends. That is how Jill Lewin and I happened to see Maris connect for his sixty-first.

In earlier seasons, before I was old enough to get around, on a few magical nights my father showed up unexpectedly at our front door to take me to a game. I remember two contests with him that went into extra innings. In the first, Gene Woodling homered in the eleventh to win one for the Yankees (and my father's crony handed him a twenty to settle a bet even before the risen crowd sat down). Years later, Al Smith capped an Indians comeback from an eight-run deficit with a home run in the tenth (though we were in the parking lot when he cracked it because my father declared, "Nine innings only when there's school tomorrow").

In fact, on November 3, 1952, my eighth birthday, I went to dinner with my father for the first time after learning his identity, and he took me to Al Schacht's baseball restaurant where the menu was all in puns (like Yogi Berries and Ty Corn on the Cob). The banister was made of bats and balls, and two Yankee players, Joe Collins and Charlie Silvera, met us at our table for the meal.

In 1962, a lifetime later, I took a Trailways bus down from Amherst College to watch Bill Stafford outduel Billy Pierce in the third game of the World Series. Stafford almost tossed a shutout that afternoon, Ed Bailey's shot in the ninth ruining it. After the game, my father, stepmother, and I joined the winning pitcher and his wife for a barbecue at his house with Eli Grba and, now that they had a 2-1 lead in games, the two pitchers talked of finishing the Giants off quickly.

The next day my family returned to the mountains, and I went to the Stadium alone to see Chuck Hiller ruin that plan by smacking a grand slam into the right-field stands off Marshall Bridges; then I took the late bus back to college. It was the height of my Yankee commitment, so I could hardly have suspected at the time that it would be my last visit to a ballpark for eleven years, longer than the time I had been going.

A week later, after multiple San Francisco rainouts, I stood in a basement television repair shop in Amherst by invitation of its owner, Mr. Mientka, viewing the seventh game on the store set. I paced in anxious anticipation as Ralph Terry worked to Willie McCovey, two men on and the Yankees leading 1-0 in the bottom of the ninth.

"If you care that much about this game," offered an unsolicited repairman, "I feel sorry for you."

Caring is not always what you think it is. At that moment a Yankee win was the breath of life, the key to unadulterated happiness instead of utter misery. I imagined myself a fan forever because I assumed unconsciously that things would be always the same. Yet 1964 was my last season rooting for the Yankees. Life changed, and I became a different person to myself. Soon I was thinking more about the Cuban Missile Crisis, summer jobs, writing, and girls, while scripting an escape from the dysfunctional family in which I had grown up. With survival itself at stake, baseball became unimportant.

I had rooted for the Mets too, from their creation in 1961, but with a different piece of myself. As they competed for nothing, I could follow them with a purity of intent, a probity that encompassed my readings of Carl Jung and William Butler Yeats, my initiations into tarot cards and alchemy. The Mets were, if not explicitly, then at least intuitively related to the Queen of Pentacles and the collective unconscious; they shared territory (figuratively) with the mandala bitten by the ouroboros, the transformation of mercury into gold.

During the winter before their first spring training, I played an imaginary season with a spinner game, using the roster of the team drawn from the draft (plus free agents) along with their equivalents from the Houston Colt .45s. Baseball personae for Bobby Gene Smith, Ray Daviault, Chris Cannizzaro, and Craig Anderson were already familiar to me by the time the season started, though I had to reconcile them with reality. For instance, Cannizzaro won the home-run championship in my league, but during the regular season a young Howard Cosell (who hosted the original Mets post-game show with his sidekick Ralph Branca) sat pleading with the real Cannizzaro, almost in tears—Howard consoling the tragic youth after yet another disappointing day, telling him that he could still learn to hit.

"I know I can, Mr. Cosell," replied Cannizzaro, "I just know I can." I believed it with all my heart too, for I had seen it all winter.*

Rod Kanehl became my first favorite Met when he hit a single in the team's second exhibition game. He was the first player to appear on the team who hadn't been in my own "season." In fact, I had never heard of him. No one ever made the Yankees without me at least knowing who they were and where they came from.

I was charmed by the notion of strange players entering a league I had never followed. The Mets were like unknown orders of worms and snails from forest ponds suddenly set into the immediate sunlight of American life. I had witnessed rotifers swimming like dot-sized

---

*Canizzaro never hit a homer in 581 Met at-bats over four seasons.

lobster-cats in water I collected in an old honey jar and placed on a slide under my toy microscope—identical to the line drawings of them in my textbook. I wrote my biology term paper on their ancillary phylum. Asked to select a play of Shakespeare's for an English term paper a year later, I alone discounted *Hamlet, Macbeth,* and *The Tempest* and chose *Troilus and Cressida*. I was a natural Met fan.

The Yankees had been an intimate family affair, first with my stepfather and brother, later with my father. From going down to the field as Paul Grossinger's son to shake hands with Andy Carey and Gil McDougald, to ice-skating at his hotel beside Whitey Ford (and having Whitey help me up when I stumbled), to watching the Yankee-Dodger World Series in the TV room with Al Rosen and Jim Hegan, to joining Stafford's barbecue, the Yankees were a map of my body and psyche from ages seven through eighteen. They carried the weight and expectations of my whole insane childhood; they represented the elders and their giant, powerful city.

The Mets, on the other hand, stretched into my unknown future; they were my own—the seeds of my own emerging nature, the possibility that I was someone different from the person my family had tried to raise. When I took the subway to the Polo Grounds by myself and cheered as daffy Elio Chacon never stopped running, stretching a single into an "inside the park homer" on errors, I was already breaking with authority. I bought my own tickets and sat in the grandstand—eight times in '62—and watched the calamity Mets go seven and three (two were doubleheaders). I can still visualize ex-Pirate farmhand Al Jackson, a compellingly compact little lefty, snapping off fastballs and curves unlike any player the Yankees ever had—wiry and indefatigable, bearing down with the lead in the late innings of tight games against formidable rivals despite the fact that he was a mere expansion-draft refugee. I can call up the image of Hobie Landrith beating a startled Warren Spahn 3-2 with a two-out ninth-inning homer that nicked the short ledge in right as it descended.

During the Mets' early years I had high hopes for Jesse Gonder, Jim

Piersall, Carlton Willey, Don Rowe, Ed Bauta, Ted Schrieber, and Jim Hickman, and each of them had his moments. (When Piersall ran the bases backward after hitting his only Met home run, he was also signing his ticket out of town, for as Casey Stengel noted at the time, "There's room for only one clown on this team." Conversely, there were some days on which Hickman was the Mets' reincarnation of the Mickey Mantle of my childhood.)

The team might not have been a contender, but it provided something more profound than victory—identity and hope. I found myself relishing more and more Met games and ignoring the Yankees' essential contests. I may have staked my happiness on the Yankees of 1962, but I hardly cared by the time the Dodgers steamrolled them in '63. They had become mysteriously irrelevant. Deep at the heart of myself, a primordial link had been snapped. I had erased a signature that for some is as deep as DNA.

After the crucible of Mientka's TV I no doubt would have startled the repairman by the swiftness of my apostasy. In his presence I was a terminally obsessed Yankee fan but—unknown to either of us—I was also a changeling, a child of Scorpio: death and resurrection. The '63 Yankee season (during my sophomore year in college) was my least attentive since I started following the team in first grade. The only thing that kept me going through 1964 was loyalty to Mel Stottlemyre, the last rookie I tracked up through the Yankee chain. When the Cardinals knocked him out of the seventh game of the World Series, it was over for me, though I became aware of it only gradually. I entered a dark period that winter and struggled with sanity itself for the next eighteen months. When I awoke from the nightmare, the Yankees were gone.

In less than two years, I was an adult, married and headed for graduate school in Michigan. As I recovered an interest in baseball in 1966, the Mets alone held my attention and loyalty. They were an antidote to existential despair, a reawakening to ordinary life. Unlike the Yankees who held a time capsule of habitudes and nervous tensions from the '50s and early '60s, the Mets were "young love," unlived life, a natural complement to Lindy's and my honeymoon in Shiprock, Arizona (during which we heard a ballgame in Navajo on the car radio, suggesting the esoteric New World origin and White Thunder Boy/Cornbeetle Girl prayerstick magic inside the game).

I was living through a change of identity so profound that I felt like someone who had traveled to another planet. The ballgames were at least stable; they provided an anchor to the remote past and an old familiar self. While I avoided any Yankee baggage, during the fall of '66 I enjoyed listening to the Mets at night from our attic in Ann Arbor, as I worked on tiny kodachrome strips of my 8-mm films; their players included Ken Boyer, Hawk Taylor, John Stephenson, Jack Hamilton, Bob Friend, Bill Hepler, Bob Shaw, Gerry Arrigo. They were going nowhere, and I didn't care. I appreciated their music and masque.

The 1967 and '68 Mets provided a copacetic scrim to my life, to our stray cats and used bookstores and walks along the Huron River as well as the sand-painting ceremonies and Dreamtime myths of my graduate seminars. For an anthropology student and an apprentice in the traditional occult, the games were a secular counterpart to arcane hierarchies of symbols—a balm and magic like the marigolds and horsetails of my ethnobotany workshop. The Mets were not a lost alchemical text or a Hopi kachina ceremony, but they *were* a taxonomy, constructed in layers of names and sacred numbers in the same way, and (I suspected) they were gathering toward an astrological transit, a moment in which their own history would synchronize with a cosmic cycle, and their secret identity would be revealed.

Of course there were new Yankee teams, but they didn't have to do with me. The Highlanders and Bronx Bombers had already happened; their history of my childhood was complete, archived back in New York with subway odysseys, Hare and Hounds, and Sundays in Central Park. Their cycle of games had passed into legend and myth. I never lived in the City again, but its landscape was mutated and reborn in a mural of Met games. The old Yankees flowed into and became the current Mets, ending the Mantle-Maris legacy for me at 1964.

I rooted intensely for each Mets' win during those formative years, but it was the gradual accumulation of lore that fed my imagination. The team was mercurial and novel, its rosters constantly changing. The movements of players and their unfulfilled partial careers tenanted a bittersweet cosmos—season by season, player by player—Larry Stahl, Amos Otis, Ron Taylor, Greg Goosen; box score after box score: Kevin Collins, Duffy Dyer, Bill Short. Soon it was Rob Gardner and Dennis Ribant, the foundations of a new pitching staff, outfielders Johnny Lewis, Joe Christopher, and Cleon Jones.

My wife Lindy was not a fan, so I kept the Mets a quiet and private practice. I read box scores and tracked their games, mainly at night, in Michigan and then Maine and Vermont—even those often took juggling with a radio, searching for power spots and tilting the solid object between invisible airwaves and competing stations. In Ann Arbor I had to stand in the shower holding the radio to the ceiling for Pittsburgh, but I could get Chicago in the daytime on the car radio if I parked at a particular spot at the end of the driveway.

On the field the Mets were becoming a better team, almost imperceptibly: Tug McGraw, Dick Selma, Bud Harrelson, Ron Swoboda. Add Koosman, Seaver, Ryan, Boswell; Cardwell, Taylor, Agee in trades, and we arrived at 1969 and a ceremony no one had seen coming: Moon landing, Woodstock, the birth of our first child, our migration back East to an island off the coast of Maine, the Pennant, the World Series—the first harmonic convergence of the Age of Aquarius.

The year before, 1968, our Michigan neighbors cheered for Denny McClain and Willie Horton and a World Series in Motown. "Tom Seaver will be a better pitcher than Denny McClain by next year," I declared, and they guffawed—but my "last laugh" was only in the imagination, as we were long gone by the time it happened.

Robin was born on June 19, and in August we drove to Maine. On the way we stopped at my father's hotel in upstate New York with a U-Haul full of cats, books, a few pieces of furniture. It was there that I watched the Mets catch and pass the Cubs, Tommy Agee barreling through Randy Hundley with the first big run in the climactic head-to-head series.

From then on it was the Maine coast, starry nights, a tiny baby crawling on the living room floor, and those final games of the '69 rush from anonymity to the first championship—not at all like the Yankees whose succession of dynasties I was born into. The Mets I had woven out of my own transition from child to father. Their transformation and joy were all my own.

We moved south to Cape Elizabeth, and I taught at the University of Maine in Portland. I followed the '70 and '71 Mets on an FM station, available even in the daytime. I would go to Crescent Beach with Lindy and Robin, in between innings running into the waves and back, holding his hand. Or I'd lie in the high grass outside the barn with a book while he threw plastic toys into the wading pool—trying to overcome the Pirates in the late innings with Jim McAndrew hurling, and never quite making it. My memories of my early adult life and then the childhoods of my children are submerged unfathomably within the seasons of the team.

Those were dreamlike idyllic years of a young family, before we moved to the mountains of northern Vermont in 1972. The Mets gradually molted too. Nolan Ryan, Gary Gentry, Ed Charles, Amos Otis, and Ken Boswell departed. Jon Matlack, John Milner, Ray Sadecki, Ken Singleton, Dave Schneck, Teddy Martinez, Rusty Staub, and Don Hahn arrived. Though the lingering promise of '69 was unfulfilled, we were building toward the Indian summer of '73.

The Miracle Mets of 1969 were a harbinger of the brief American Aquarian Age; the Miracle Mets of 1973 provided a single Earth Day before America dove into home computers, punk rock, designer jeans, and yuppie supply-side culture.

2.

As years and then decades separated me from my childhood in New York, the Mets came to stand for the mythic land of my origin, a native country that was otherwise obliterated by the impersonality of concrete and the changing occupants of apartment buildings. The Mets represented the indigenous spirit of the ancient boroughs, the layers of New York that were idiosyncratic, small-town, and tribal—as much African and European as New World. The brief glimpse of Shea Stadium in Wim Wenders' film *Alice in the Cities* reminds me that New York is as hieroglyphic as a Peruvian village if viewed totally from the outside.

The Mets also represented the vitality of the streets and my generation's belief in itself. When they were terrible, we accepted their losses with compassion and understood them as a process deeper than baseball. When they turned their destiny around, they did it swiftly and gracefully in one season—as abrupt as the landing of a UFO in Times Square. They met the crucible of Woodstock and Vietnam resplendently.

The Yankees, on the other hand, came to stand for the New York I had fled and now denied in myself—the arrogant, provincial capital of corporate hegemony. They personified the obsessions and cruelties of my elders, both in my family and at school and summer camp—fascist bullies all. Yet I missed the old loyalties too. A journal note from the early '70s captures the nostalgia of my transit:

> In a certain distance the Yankees play for another pennant, too late. I can loosely want it, the Yankee Stadium of October time, and my childhood, my brother and me there (now merely old photographs), and everything on the line in the excitement of cosmic Yankee things. As the crowds move through the cigarette smoke, past the scalpers, into their seats to watch history.

My old team gradually came to represent high-rise Manhattan, Madison Avenue—*"king of the hill,/top of the heap"*: the New York of the crass self-promoter, the public-relations showboat, the carpetbagger who rebuilt his dynasty by stealing the players and the souls of other teams—first Catfish, then Reggie and Goose. They were owned by win-at-all-cost imperial America; thus their victories were neither sympathetic nor honorable. They could play Sinatra at Shea, and I heard: *"These vagabond shoes/are longing to stay."* They could unleash that same recording at Yankee Stadium and I pictured *The Godfather* and a bar full of off-duty cops making racist jokes while rooting for Chris Chambliss and Oscar Gamble.

Living away from the City, I sometimes wondered what happened to my fellow original Met fans in the years after '73. I could not believe that so many of them had turned into Yanquis; yet even people who once only idly followed the pennant races except to hate the Yanks had turned into closet (and "outed") Yankee-rooters, accepting Steinbrenner as some inevitable conquering savior—a marquee that read: *The Return of the Jedi.* Socially conscious Yankee fans argued their case eloquently: it was the Yankees who went out and aggressively acquired important African-American and Latino players—Willie Randolph, Ed Figueroa, Roy White, Reggie Jackson, Mickey Rivers; the Mets meanwhile were publicly embarrassing Cleon Jones and dumping Ken Singleton and Tommy Agee. You could hardly argue with Spike Lee or Rudy Giuliani on that one.

The Yankees were also rich in folklore, bringing together good old boys like Catfish Hunter and Ron Guidry, and offering a forum for the expression of such diverse talents as Thurman Munson, Reggie Jackson, and Graig Nettles. The crosstown Mets sent off Tom Seaver in the night and dealt Tug McGraw (for Del Unser, Mac Scarce,* John Stearns) quickly before anyone learned of the tumor on his arm. They were in

---

*The scarcest of all Mets, he faced one batter in early 1975, Richie Hebner, and gave up the game-winning single—his entire New York career.

the process of trying to ditch Stearns and Craig Swan at the moment ownership was changing. (Oddly all four principals in that hexed and uncompleted trade, Willie Aikens and Dickie Thon for the Angels, were to have their careers prematurely curtailed.)

Anti-Met new-breed Yankee fans argued that Steinbrenner at least was creating a real team, expressing a gratuitous intention toward ethics. The Mets didn't even offer gratuitous lip service; they were feuding with their players and still in baseball's Stone Ages on labor practices and overall ethics. How could anyone under the reign of M. Donald Grant complain about Steinbrenner's vulgarity, bullying, and greed? Yet that's the story of the Mets until 1980.

During the ten years that followed the Mets' last pennant they got less and less coverage in New York papers. Even the *Village Voice* considered the Yankees the only team worth deconstructing. To me, the Mets may have been in exile, but the soul of New York was still with them. The Yankees were simply a well-orchestrated advertising campaign, glitter around a spiritually hollow snow job.

What now, Mr. Mientka Repair Guy, of a college kid who stood in your shop in Amherst and let out a whoop of relief as McCovey's shot was corralled by Bobby Richardson? No doubt I had been transformed at core, but the whole American landscape had changed too. In twenty years hard drugs, free agency, and tribal war had corroded the possibility of a baseball moment so pure.

I had stopped going to the ballpark, too. After the 1962 World Series it never occurred to me to follow the Mets in any way other than on the radio and TV. Perhaps, with my beard and long hair, I had absorbed too much counterculture; I lost a tolerance and appreciation for the commonality of spectators in their hippodrome. The ballpark had a tinge of the right-wing enlistment of my peers, the pro-Viet-War mainstream, the Selective Service of Kafka's Amerika, as well as the desolate confinement of the required academic classroom. It was a scene as much to be avoided as a George Wallace rally. Shea Stadium had become, in the words of poet Robert Kelly, "a more disreputable place than a whorehouse."* A visit to the actual diamond had come to feel like conscription rather than pleasure, and I dreaded the *hoi polloi* of fans and their mindless pogrom. They would probably stare and turn on me.

Gone was the child who once enthusiastically attended games and cheered for my New York teams. Baseball was now my private ceremony, and the Mets were more like a tarot deck than an enterprise related to *"Take Me Out to the Crowd."*

Finally, in June of '73 Lindy and I left Robin with a schoolmate's family and drove two hours to Montreal, where we met a friend and went to Parc Jarry to observe the visiting last-place Mets against the Expos. For me it was a return from exile, and for Lindy (without an affinity for baseball) an adventure to Quebec capped by evening of street theater.

I may have gotten phobic about going to the ballpark, but in 1973 Montreal, a small neighborhood stadium with French overlay, it seemed possible to go to a game without melancholy for the past or fear of the police state. I saw the clarity of actual players in three dimensions and was captivated by it once again.

Two years later I drove back to Montreal with a student friend to watch Randy Tate, a lanky, bullet-throwing Met "phenom" who didn't pan out, blow a start.

In California I regained my old fervor for the field of play, and I began attending every Met game at Candlestick Park. I occasionally went to other games too—one afternoon in 1978 to see Jim Bouton win his last game with a knuckleball (almost two decades after I had attended his first victory).

---

*A Letter in *Io/10, Baseball Issue,* Cape Elizabeth, Maine, 1971.

3.

From our first visits to the Bay Area in 1975 I tried interesting Robin in baseball, but when I took him to games he was totally bored, mainly looking around for the ice-cream man and mascot clowns. On August 24, 1975, just before driving back to Vermont, we saw Ed Halicki no-hit the Mets in the second game of a doubleheader, but my son was involved only with punching me in the arm repeatedly because I wouldn't leave, as I had promised, when the upper and lower scoreboard numbers filled in to 5 (his sole focus for the previous hour and a half).

After a couple more tries at baseball initiation I gave up, so I was surprised when I found him watching the Yankee-Dodger World Series on TV—twenty-six years after I came home from P.S. 6 to listen to a different Yankees and Dodgers. While I was a city boy who grew up in a neighborhood, he was a rural kid from Vermont, a culture favoring bikes and sleds, and he was also someone carted back and forth between Vermont and California (twice before we finally moved West). When we settled in North Oakland, he was seven, our daughter Miranda was three, and she kept pointing to streets in Berkeley and asking, "Is that Vermont?"

My grade-school friends and I began our baseball careers by collecting Flash Gordon cards—vistas of the Moon, Mars, and beyond. With the change in season, the candy store we called Jessie's Jip Joint offered baseball portraits with gum. I followed the P.S. 6 crew into the new hobby.

For Robin night-sky gods preceded sports figures too, as his peers collected Star Trek cards before baseball ones. His interest initially had little if anything to do with my rooting. In fact, I had stopped following the 1978 season after the Mets were eliminated, and I was somewhat inimical to the Series being on in our living room. Triumphant in his new understanding of the game, Robin was puzzled by my attitude, which translated roughly as: "When the Mets are not playing, there's no game." Yet I was pleasantly surprised that he suddenly knew all the rules, who Reggie Jackson was, and other things like that.

When he began following baseball from the beginning of a full season, 1979, he briefly considered rooting for the A's, but then chose the Mets because of the colors of their uniforms. I told him life would be easier if he rooted for a local team, but he was firm about his decision. Back in our old farmhouse in Vermont we had painted his room childlike blue and orange for reasons having nothing to do with baseball, and during his early years in the Bay Area he longed to return to the lost village. The Mets bespoke his nostalgia for his old room and also his alienation from California. Unlike eccentric Vermont kids, his Berkeley buddies were always chasing the latest fad and "being cool." If they liked the A's, they made them into disco idols indistinguishable from comic-book heroes and rock stars. Robin thought that was stupid.

By contrast to the A's or Giants, the Mets were weird and foreign, and no one in his school knew anything about them. In the world of baseball cards, though, they were as precise and monogrammatic as any team, and Robin naïvely imagined they weren't jive or show-offy. From the moment he adopted them he acted as though the Mets were something he invented quite apart from me *or* his peers: he was rooting for his own blue-and-orange baseball-card team, a team that began at the moment he noticed them. In fact, initially he discarded cards of players no longer on the team.

As the 1979 season began, he counted the days till the first visit of the Mets to Candlestick. We got our prize seats among the Mets' families and friends from Arthur Richman, a club official who traveled with the team, a longtime friend of both my father and stepfather. Once a sportswriter for the now-defunct *Daily Mirror,* Art was burned out from too many years chaperoning a child's game, especially jaded by the antics of the new generation of me-first players. "I've got to be babysitter now for a bunch of spoiled kids," he complained to us that spring.

He was real New York downbeat cynical, seen-everything, just-getting-by—not the jolly fan I remembered as a child. But he graciously provided us with comps at the Will Call window, and sometimes, visiting us in the stands, he let it slip that he liked these guys and was rooting for them to win. More often, though, he felt obliged to apologize for their rude habits and miserable play.

We came to the ballpark the first time a couple of hours early and stood behind the Mets' dugout, watching the warm-ups. From a specific incident, Robin picked out John Stearns as his favorite player: The Mets then had a German calisthenics coach who led the team in exercises and stretches. Before their baseball warm-ups the whole squad had to lie out on the grass and follow his drill. Many of the players seemed either irritated or embarrassed by this public activity, but the one-time Colorado footballer John gave voice to a general dissatisfaction. At the appropriate point in each cycle Stearns moaned: "And oun streeeeetch," mocking the accent and then laughing.

Later that series we ended up chatting with Stearns' college friends from Colorado, gentleman jocks who now farmed in Wyoming. I had previously imagined him a typical jock too, but through their eyes I saw a cowboy hippie, a rebel they called Dude. In the fierceness of his play Stearns had always seemed the heart of the post-'73 Mets; even with all the losses he sustained the desire to win and a fury at being beaten. The image stays in my mind of him kneeling by home plate that week while the tying and winning runs crossed behind him, looking forlornly up at his friends as he grasped at dirt with his fist. They gave him a V sign, and he nodded slowly and then bounced back to his feet and ran to the dugout. I wanted the Mets to revive in time to let this warrior play for a pennant in their uniform.

It is hard to pinpoint Robin's maturation as a fan because it came so fast—from a few cards to a room filled with banners, yearbooks, and signed baseballs. After one year he was trying to collect every player who ever played for the Mets. He kept a checklist of their all-time roster and took it to old card stores, though he realized that some would always be missing (Don Rose, Lute Barnes, Greg Harts, etc.).

When I discovered a source of minor-league cards, he began collecting the Mets' farm system insofar as it was available: Tidewater, Jackson, Lynchburg. (His caboodle had only one non-Met souvenir that he valued, and it was a primo specimen. While he was in school on a weekday afternoon, I traveled to Candlestick in the company of a friend, *Oakland Tribune* beat-writer Nick Peters, to watch the Expos play the Giants but mainly to meet The Spaceman. My mission was successful. I came home with a prankishly huge smile and a signed baseball, "To Robin, Best wishes, Bill Lee, Earth, '79." My son took it from my hand and, issuing an awestruck "wow," held it as I had been to the Moon that day and brought back a meteorite.)

Robin was likewise excited to realize that he had been born in '69, the year of the Mets' Championship, though he was frustrated that he had missed it, and he milked me for details of what it was like. When I thought back to those evenings by the ocean in Maine, I remembered not only the radio, Don Cardwell pitching and Ron Swoboda hitting those home runs off Steve Carlton, but him innocent in his diaper, moving across the universe that precedes this one.

The Mets were at Candlestick on June 19th, Robin's birthday, and Lindy, Miranda, he, and I went to the park together. Before the game Art Richman brought over individual players as well as the manager to congratulate him. Joe Torre immediately asked our son why he wasn't married yet; Bruce Boisclair, when he heard he was one of our favorite players, said uneasily that he would try to get a hit for us. Then at our suggestion Art found John Stearns. Lindy knew already that the catcher was from her hometown of Denver, so after his few moments of ballplayer-to-young-fan talking, she asked, "What high school did you go to?"

They then began throwing back and forth quippy comments about Denver and what she called "Denver dirty boys."

"I know about girls from Kent," Stearns rejoined when he heard which school she attended.

Afterwards Lindy teased Robin: "How do you like that? Your mother not only talking to your favorite player but doing it with some aplomb, I might add."

"That's fine, Mom, but let's not talk about it any more, okay?"

Over the course of the season Robin and I developed an unlikely relationship with Keith Hernandez' father John. Rumored to be both a baseball genius and relentless taskmaster vis-à-vis his son, he was a charming misanthrope and good company for us. We served as an eager audience for his streams of insights and invectives. In fact, we had plenty of challenges for him—by then we subscribed to our baseball newspapers and minor-league reports and knew the Mets' farm system inside out. Juan (as he was addressed from the adjacent seat by his other son Gary) was entertained by our amateur scouting opinions and would set us straight with bemused adages and wry asides, making us fall guys for his critiques of Met coaches and management and "bad" pitchers like Wayne Twitchell and Dock Ellis.

Robin even made it to Shea that season. We flew east as a family for a few weeks in August, and on a rainy night I took him and my brother Jon on the rickety el to the ballpark. It was a dismal game—hardly any fans, continuous rain, and a substantial Met loss to the Phillies. We didn't even stay for the scheduled second game, which was played many hours later that night.

On the way home Robin expressed surprise that the obnoxious people cursing and yelling dumb insults were Met fans; he had gotten used to being in a small island of "nice guys," surrounded by an uncouth mob.

It took him a number of trips in different seasons to see that Shea was still relatively good-humored compared to Candlestick. The Giants of that era evoked racist anger and redneck fervor from an urban area generally thought of as hip and liberal. It wasn't. The South San Francisco gay-bashing crowd were as ornery and mean a group of Americans as there are. Add in the Daly City/Brisbane low-rider tailgate partiers and you have a zoo. I don't think at Shea you'd find the fat woman who sat behind me one day, drinking beer and kicking my seat with some force because I was rooting for the Mets. "You're in public now, you prick," she said, in answer to my objections. "You can't tell me what to do."

Of course, at Yankee Stadium the punks are big-time and come armed to take back Cuba, but that is a different kettle of fish, with Admiral George setting the patriotic mood. Those guys think that the National Anthem is for the home team, so they stand and salute. The visiting teams are all commies and degenerates.

Later that season the Mets came back to San Francisco; they lost the last three games of a four-game series at the end of August, and when they left town for Los Angeles our family followed them down the coast en route to a regional booksellers' fair in San Diego.

We stopped at a motel in Anaheim the first night and took the kids to Disneyland the next day. In the evening Robin and I drove up to Dodger Stadium to watch John Pacella pitch against Dave Goltz, tickets compliments of Art. Two of the three minor leaguers the Mets had just brought up from Tidewater played in their first official game. Wally Backman started at second and hit a couple of shots up the alley; Mookie Wilson played center, got his first hit as well, and ran down some balls to deep center, though he turned the wrong way on one. The Mets lost 6-5, and were swept the next night as we drove south.

The following afternoon in San Diego we stood in the noon sun behind the visitor's dugout as the players warmed up. When Mookie Wilson wandered close enough, Robin called out to him, showed him his Tidewater card, and then congratulated him on his first hit. Mookie was astonished that anyone even knew who he was. When Wally walked by, Robin shouted, "Nice hitting the other night." Backman smiled and came over and jibed with him. A few rows back I was laughing quietly: with these rookies Robin had found his own first Mets.

The Padres came back and beat Neil Allen that day and knocked out Mark Bomback the next game. The following night, thanks again to Art, we sat in a small Mets cheering section behind third base; it included us (with Lindy and Miranda this time); Wally Backman's wife and parents; Alex Trevino's friends and kin from Mexico; the mother and sisters of another rookie, Hubie Brooks, and the father and sister of a Mets Double-A second baseman named Brian Giles who (we knew) had a good year at Jackson—Giles himself sat a few rows down below.

It was an evening of unreserved buoyancy and joviality that could never really be repeated—not as these players got older and their families hardened to the modern game. That night the new Mets played openly to our small cheering section, looking back and smiling. It was the first game for Hubie Brooks, the second for Mookie and Wally. Ray Burris, the Mets' starter, got knocked out early, but all three players got hits. We were an island of pandemonium as the Mets closed to 8-7 before a fine backhanded stop by Ozzie Smith ended the rally.

Far from New York City we were seeing the initiation of a new team; in the midst of a catastrophic losing streak the Mets were suddenly shedding their old skin and crawling away.

All winter Robin and I talked about going to opening day at Shea and, when bargain fares were announced in March, we bought two plane tickets. We would go to watch our rookies open on the home team.

The last weeks before the new season were filled with strange dreams in which my manifold ambiguities and symbols of baseball invaded one another. I was taking Robin the child to a game but, as we sat in our row, he turned into an old man with a beard, and the guards ordered us to leave. Another night we found ourselves in the old underground of Yankee Stadium; there were no Mets anywhere, but Bill Skowron and Mickey Mantle were dressing for the game in a shabby room behind a hot-dog/orange-soda stand.

As it got closer to April I dreamed that we were trying to get from the el to the ballpark, but the exit ramp became a bridge over a vast stretch of ocean; we could see the ballpark far beneath us in an archipelago, minute figures enacting not only the game but a whole season displaced in another space-time.

Then I dreamed the Mets were opening the season against the Red Sox in a city park in New York, a sandlot field without stands and fences. The usher seated us on the grass just outside the foul lines; I was afraid we were in the way. The first batter lined a ground ball foul on the other side of us, and we had to leave. Now Tim Leary, dressed in street clothes, was delivering a lecture.

Closer still to opening day I dreamed that we arrived late at the ballpark to find the Mets playing the old St. Louis Browns in the first game of a World Series. The Browns had jumped to a 3-0 lead: we saw the last run score on a grounder down the third-base line that a fat Met left-fielder (whom I didn't recognize) bobbled.

Two days before we left on the plane, and in the middle of a dream about something else, a line drive was hit right at me; I dove to make a backhanded catch and then looked up to find myself on the field on opening day, the right-fielder. How did I get there? How could I slink away before being exposed as a fraud?

Baseball, like a medicine, was working through my bloodstream to every level of consciousness and unconsciousness.

Actual opening day was rained out, but the next afternoon we took the subway out to the ballpark with a writer friend, Paul Auster, and stood in the pale East Coast spring sun, the chill of winter still in the shadows, the Stadium unopened. Times long ago and time present seemed merged in the clear prism of memory and New York light. I could still access in myself the subway journey with my stepfather to Ebbets Field for a 1956 World Series game—the same chill in the air, the same vendors selling programs, the smell of cigars and old overcoats summoning the peculiar incense of baseball tension, baseball promise.

The Mets had an early season sparkle with Mookie Wilson lining the ball up the alley and running around to third on a bobble, Doug

Flynn then driving in a couple of runs. They beat the Cardinals and the Expos after a loss. Craig Swan threw a strong game, and then Pat Zachry won as the fans stood and cheered the first big moment of the season—Dave Kingman launching it high into the left-field stands to settle the issue. We were sure we wouldn't be embarrassed at Candlestick again with this new young team, but it was always the same story—another disappointing year.

It didn't seem to matter if the Mets were playing well or poorly at the time, they let most games at Candlestick in which they weren't outright demolished somehow slip away, as though there were something about the very shape of the ballpark and Mediterranean climate that made the Giants invincible against the team that had taken their place in the old city. Let the Giants play the Phillies or Expos or Cubs and fall behind by a few runs early, and the game was all but over. For the Mets no lead was safe. The disasters of the late '70s and early '80s all blur together: Jack Clark is homering off a too-young Jesse Orosco in the eighth inning to give him his first major-league loss; Johnnie Lemaster triples in the eighth off Pat Zachry and scores the only run of the game; Neil Allen throws a pinch homer to Hector Cruz in his first at-bat as a Giant to tie a game with two outs in the ninth—Giants win in the tenth; Neil Allen serves a three-run pinch homer to Reggie Smith, turning victory into defeat in the ninth.

I can still see the balls falling against the backdrop of cheering fans in the arc lights, and I remember the frustration and wounded hopes we carried to the parking lot as if it were all one relentless event, like a voodoo cycle, a curse that could not be lifted. Later in 1984 there would be the light-hitting Brad Wellman lofting a two-run homer just inside the left-field foul pole off Jesse Orosco to turn a hard-fought one-run win into a one-run loss and costing the Mets a game in the standings they could ill afford. Robin and I sat there flushed and numbed, shocked not that it happened but that it continued to happen despite the fact that the Mets were finally a contender and the Giants now the worst team in the league. We were trapped on a concourse with No Turns: falling one run short against Vida Blue, one run short against Ed Halicki, one run short against Allen Ripley, one run short against Al Holland.

From the East Coast, Candlestick might seem exotic, the site of late-afternoon and late-night games shrouded in mystery and fog that spill over into the morning of the next day. But in San Francisco itself, in our own time zone, the games were lucid and factual. The Giants were a sleeping dragon aroused by the appearance of the Mets.

Happily, though, the experience of the ballpark went beyond winning and losing. We would drive across the Bay Bridge two hours before game time, collect Art's tickets upon the clattery opening of the Will Call slot, and recline in either the late-afternoon shadows or the late-morning luminosity and watch the players come down from the clubhouse onto the field and warm up.

1982 stands out. We burst out of the stone tunnel into the visibility of ballfield there below like the Earth from the Moon, the late-afternoon sun tinting the grass and the music playing Johnny Burnette: *"She's Sixteen, She's Beautiful, and She's Mine."* Baseball herself.

We walked down the right-field line and reached the bullpen just at the moment the Mets were coming out of the tunnel to their clubhouse. Tom Veryzer walked onto the field with a few teammates, and another expatriate American Leaguer yelled out to him: "Welcome to the big leagues, boys."

When he was younger Robin would go down to the edge of the field and get his yearbook and cards autographed, but gradually the behavior of the other fans discouraged him, spoiled kids and adults pushing people out of the way and cursing at players who ignored their screams for attention. After a while he realized that many of his colleagues currying autographs simply to sell them. He went through a transitional phase of getting them despite his better judgment because he could think of no alternative record of the experience until finally he was satisfied just to stand up close and watch for the memories. It was always a wonder to him to see the cards come to life in full uniform, the names and numbers from the box scores running wind sprints, the new players capturing our first attention—what they really looked like as people.

The Met identities were indelible and eternal; warming up, the guys didn't have to be making stats in a game; they just had to throw a ball back and forth, take their swings in the cage, and walk across the field. That was the game of baseball that never appeared in the newspaper or on the radio. The serene, necessary preparation for the ceremony that followed, it was as much what we went for as the scheduled tilt.

At Candlestick where Art's tickets always landed us in the family section behind the dugout, we enjoyed in-crowd camaraderie. In different seasons we saw (or heard): rookie Mike Vail's parents shooting movies of him every time he came back to the dugout and his mother yelling, "Mikey, smile," as he kept his eyes sullenly downcast after successive strikeouts; Gary Rasjich's brother trying to figure out how Gary could get into the game and telling us about their baseball-fan mother; Wally Backman's wife recalling Tidewater; Ronn Reynolds' wife talking about the interminable season at Jackson; Mike Scott's parents worrying about his future; George Foster's wife and sister in furs (his sister had the same face as George, and his wife kept promising us George would win the game); Leon Brown's father expressing sorrow that his son wasn't as good as Gary Matthews on the Giants: "Now there's a player. If only he could have been like that."

In 1982 during a day game we suddenly realized that we were sitting next to Lou Gorman, the vice president of the team, and over the course of the afternoon, with polite urging, he was willing to run down the individual prospects of the best players in the system: Ron Darling, Doug Sisk, Herm Winningham, Terry Blocker, Jeff Bittiger, Jay Tibbs, and their one great power hitter, John Christensen, "the boy we signed out of Cal State Fullerton." We asked when Tim Leary might come back, and Gorman said he was throwing pain-free but needed a year of rehabilitation.

I couldn't tell if he was pleased that we knew so much about the Mets and the names of so many players in the chain or whether we were just another kind of pesky, over-informed fan to deal with. Our information, impressive though it was, was solely from minor-league newspapers, whereas to him these were real athletes, players with qualifiable talents and histories: we were talking about two different things.

Gorman said that the reliever with the fine record at Jackson, John Semprini, had a trick delivery, a kind of drop, and that when he got it over he was unbeatable at that level, but he needed more pitches to rise to the majors (a couple of years later he went to Seattle in a trade). He said that Greg Biercevicz, a pitcher leading the International League in earned run average, was a prospect he had at Seattle who hurt his arm and now he had re-signed him for the Mets (later, he played out his minor-league option and became a White Sox farmhand). He said that Mike Scott had as good stuff as anyone on the staff, but he wondered if he was teachable and thought they would have to give up on him (he was traded to Houston for Danny Heep after the season). He liked Ed Lynch okay: "Ed's a good pitcher and a fine person. I wish he were a better pitcher because he's a credit to our organization, but we've got some boys coming along that are really special, and they may push him out."

When he mentioned Biercevicz, I suggested that maybe it was like when Whitey Herzog went after Amos Otis after leaving the Mets. I added that it was a pretty smart trade because getting Bob Johnson and Amos Otis (especially with the players who came from trading Bob Johnson later to the Pirates) established a Royals dynasty. For the first time Gorman looked intrigued and, chuckling, said: "That was *me* that made those trades. *I* built the Royals." Then he added: "And how about Craig Reynolds for Floyd Bannister? That's a deal I pulled off at Seattle. Wasn't that a good one?"

He was like an artist discussing the high points of certain periods of his work. He told us that the Mets were one of the best teams he was ever involved in putting together and that it would become apparent when they jelled in a year or two. He paid only on-and-off attention to the game until Jesse Orosco came on in relief with a small lead. Then he leaned forward and zoned in on every pitch. "This is one of the most promising players we've got," he confided, "and everyone wants him. All he lacks is confidence. If he gets that he'll be the best left-handed retriever in the game."

In retrospect, that seems to have been the day that Jesse turned it around. The Giants were helpless against his assortment of fastballs and curves and, when Dave Kingman put one out with men on base to clinch the game, Lou Gorman stood and applauded with the rest of us.

In 1983 the Mets' whole farm system came to life. At their highest-level Class A, Lynchburg fielded one of the best minor-league teams to be seen in many years; its pitchers included Dwight Gooden, Jay Tibbs, Jeff Bettendorf, Bill Latham, Wes Gardner, and, after the draft, Calvin Schiraldi, who had helped Texas to the College Baseball Championship. Dave Cochrane socked 25 homers; Len Dykstra, a swift center-fielder, hit .358. A notch higher at Jackson, John Christensen batted .333, and the third baseman Kevin Mitchell and catcher John Gibbons both had fine years with power. Herm Winningham led the league at .354 before he was moved up to Tidewater. Columbia, a lower Class-A team, had three of the most promising starters in the South Atlantic League— Randy Myers, Floyd Youmans, and Kevin Brown,* and a good young catcher in Barry Lyons. Another draft choice, Dave Magadan, *Baseball America's* college player of the year, broke in at .336.

The Mets got both Schiraldi and Magadan because the Braves signed Pete Falcone as a Type B free agent; it was like trading Falcone not only for Bob Horner and Steve Bedrosian, but to be delivered down the road when needed. Their own first-round choice got them Stanley Jefferson, another fleet center-fielder who went on to be voted the best major-league prospect in the New York-Pennsylvania League.

---

*Not the later, famous one.

Meanwhile, the big-league Mets, struggling through another last-place season, took a gamble on making the future come sooner by dealing Neil Allen and Rick Ownbey, young pitchers with above-average stuff, for Keith Hernandez in the midst of playing out his option. They had made a similar move a few seasons earlier, trading Jeff Reardon for Ellis Valentine, and Valentine neither lived up to his potential nor re-signed with the Mets—so doing it again took gumption.

That summer, our whole family went to a three-game series at Shea, and during the third game Robin and I sat with Fred Wilpon for an inning and discussed the team. No small part of the future would be signing Hernandez, and I asked Fred the obvious: could they convince him the Mets would be a contender on the basis of the farm system? The owner said that that would certainly be part of the pitch they would make: that Hernandez needn't go elsewhere to look for the team of the '80s.

The Mets were already improving in the latter part of 1983, as they swept the Cubs that weekend, Walt Terrell pitching his first shutout.

On the same trip East we got to see another level of the Mets' system for the first time. One evening Robin and I drove from Falmouth, Massachusetts, where we were staying with friends, to Pawtucket, an old Rhode Island industrial town, to watch the Tidewater Tides managed by Davey Johnson play the Pawtucket Red Sox. The ballpark was in a residential neighborhood, and the crowd seemed to walk straight from the houses at game time. A small field with painted signs in the outfield, McCoy Stadium was a throwback to a "Field of Dreams" era.

The game provided a glimpse of the Mets yet unformed. Unfortunately, Tim Leary was very wild and Gary Rasjich dropped a fly ball in right field with the bases loaded, so the Tides got beaten badly. Still, Terry Blocker hit the ball hard every time up, and Mike Fitzgerald homered over the wall in left. Gardenhire and Backman looked lively at short and second in their Tide grays with Pirate-like caps, a conflation of Met past and future. (Backman seemed chronically unable to stick at the major-league level.)

Our real high of the 1983 baseball season was the Triple-A World Series on ESPN. Although finishing in fourth place, the Tides got to represent the International League by knocking off both Yankee and Brave farm clubs. After splitting a doubleheader with the other two teams in the tournament (beating Denver, losing to Portland) in the untelevised portion, they played a Sunday doubleheader against the same two teams, starting Dwight Gooden just up from Class A where he was 19-4 with 300 strikeouts in 191 innings. It was our first look at him—a raw minor-league fireballer in an historic Triple-A setting. He started out shakily, spotting Denver two early runs, but then he built up a head of steam and was overmatching hitters in the late innings. We were ecstatic: the Met future was more than just numbers and names; it was palpable in a teenage pitcher rising to the occasion two whole notches above the level at which he had competed all season. In the second game of the doubleheader, one-time prospect Jeff Bittiger mastered his control and fine curveball and beat a very good Portland team of mostly ex-major-leaguers, Terry Leach following and Brent Gaff getting the final outs.

The next day this team of Davey Johnson's won the championship without playing as Denver beat Portland. It wasn't the World Series, but it was the furthest the Mets had come since we had been following them. We wanted to see Johnson himself as Met manager—no more summoning George Bamberger and Earl Weaver out of retirement. The old '70s skin was almost completely shed.

In 1969 the Miracle Mets had beaten the Dodgers and the Orioles; the 1983 Mets were in the process of becoming them.

4.

Although we now looked forward to 1984 with heightened interest, we were frustrated by the fact that we had no way to get the Mets on radio. But we misread the era: radio was no longer the common person's medium. There was a far simpler and cheaper technology for following the team: WOR, Channel 9 in New York, was on one of the commercial Galaxy satellites, and it carried two-thirds of the Mets' games. Some Bay Area cable systems already included it in their package. For two years I tried to convince our local system to pick it up; when I finally got the appropriate salesman in the home office in Denver, he posed an effectively rhetorical question: "Why pay out more money in royalties when we're not going to add very many new subscribers?"

When we moved from suburban Richmond to Blake Street in Berkeley in 1983, we got a new cable system but the same outcome.

So our direct Mets experience was limited to the twelve games against the Giants (either at Candlestick or on the radio) and most of the twelve games against Atlanta (on cable television) plus an occasional other game on network. As we had no plans to go East, it looked like a down season for following the Mets just as they were getting good. Donald Sutherland might dial in the games of his beloved Expos from a phone booth on location in Italy but, short of Hollywood salaries, there seemed no way to replicate that act.

There was a satellite dish atop a video store on Highway 101 north of San Francisco, and throughout the winter I stared longingly at it. In late March I stopped in and asked the salesman if I could come by and view a bit of opening day. He told me to call the home office of their company, Cygnus Satellite, in Sausalito. To my surprise I got a Met fan, George Grapman, on the phone, and he immediately invited me to watch the game with him in person. So on an April morning I drove across the Richmond Bridge and down 101, then sat enthralled as George punched the correct satellite into the computer. As the dish rumbled across its zodiac on the roof, static cleared into a picture and there were Tim McCarver and Ralph Kiner—as palpable as if I were in New York. This was the genie's lantern.

The Reds jumped on Mike Torrez early and won easily behind Mario Soto; Darryl Strawberry's long home run on his first at-bat was the single high point. But all through the game, as George and I brainstormed strategies, it became clear that, with a group of fans, a dish was afford-able. On the way home I kept dividing $3,000 by numbers of possible members: 10, 20, even maybe 30. George may have been an authentic Mets native of Queens, but he was also a resourceful salesman.

That night Cody's Bookstore, just up from our house on Telegraph Avenue in Berkeley, held their annual bash for the start of the base-ball season, and it was there that I announced the novel concept of a baseball satellite club and put down a sign-up sheet. I explained that the dish was a long shot. If we failed on a quorum, everyone would get their money back.

I hadn't taken into account the emerging fad of rotisserie baseball (people drafting their own imaginary teams and holding fantasy tour-naments all season based on their players' stats). A startlingly large number of fans pledged $100 each. In one night we had half the money needed.

George's boss then offered to install a dish in exchange for that down-payment plus our monthly dues. Now all we needed was a site.

Visits to bars, apartment complexes, and empty storefronts scared up no landlords or property managers willing to mount a free satel-lite dish in exchange for viewing privileges, and there was no rentable space cheap enough, let alone located with a view of the right portion of the sky and outside of microwave interference.

In soliciting bar owners and prospective members I found that I had a basic problem in getting the concept across. In fact, I had just learned myself that it was like the wild West up there in the sky, with technology shooting way ahead of commercial applications. A wealth of baseball was available for free on anyone's private dish, but few people grasped the opportunity.

There were regular channels carrying the Mets, Cubs, Yankees, Braves, and Red Sox, and regional sports networks showing alternately the Rangers and Astros or the Cardinals, Reds, or Royals. Then almost all other teams and many minor-league games were irregularly on one satellite or another.

Most notable of all, raw feeds of *all* games were routinely being sent
back to their home city any distance away—in other words, the uncen-
sored uplinks from stadiums to satellites, with announcers chatting
with each other in between innings, no ads, full field coverage of rain
delays, and often pre-game batting practice from a fixed camera.* A
game didn't have to be on cable to be on satellite, available to the
snooping public. It just had to be transmitted by satellite to a television station too far away for land-lines. One could hijack private signals legally and at will.

During those frustrating weeks when we couldn't find a site, while
April slipped away, I had my eye on an unlikely candidate: a collapsing garage in our backyard. The former owner had offered to raze it
(since it was more termites than wood), but we elected instead to waive
the structure from the termite report. A carpenter friend from Wisconsin, in exchange for a place to stay that summer, put a foil roof on the
building. Since then it had been Robin's woodworking studio.

---

*Back then, before hi-tech scrambling shut down the free fare and DirecTV
and Dish took up the packaging and selling, the satellite nation of baseball
was a flourishing polity. People who used dishes could enhance Game-of-the-
Week selections and national media coverage and avoid blackouts. Baseball
became regional once again, but in a whole new way. Remote areas of the
Northern Hemisphere that once had no television and barely any radio suddenly were able to follow the day-to-day fortunes of most major-league
teams. Cubs fans in Costa Rica watched Chicago television and listened to
Harry Caray. Mets fans followed their team from Guam, Eastern Oregon,
Alaska, and rural Alabama—live. Ballplayers bought dishes for their wives
and fathers. The town of Ukiah, California, erected a dish so that the friends
and relatives of Kelvin Chapman could hang out and watch him.

On raw feeds the announcers were more candid, as they imagined themselves off the record. When Tim McCarver complained between innings
about Brent Gaff's unproductive pitching, someone in the booth told him
that they should send him to Triple A. "I'm not even sure he's a Triple-A
pitcher," McCarver scoffed.

One afternoon George crossed the San Rafael Bridge and worked his way through Berkeley to Blake Street. As we sat in the backyard with tea and cookies, trying to think up new sites, he suddenly jumped to his feet and pointed at our collapsing garage. He was ebullient. Why hadn't I mentioned it? He enumerated the structure's advantages: it was close to everyone (especially us), free, blocked from microwave interference by the student high-rises, and—most fortuitously of all—had a clear look at the satellite-rich sector of sky. To confirm that, he stood beside me on the roof with surveyor's equipment and, position by position, called out the teams we were sure to get. It was—finally—all of them.

Two carpenters showed up Monday morning and hammered plywood to keep the building standing under the weight of a dish. We cleaned and wired the inside and bought an assembled second-hand Heathkit TV from the classified. The next evening a crew from Cygnus Satellite built a ten-foot-diameter mesh pie on the roof, mounted it on a pole, drilled a hole, and dropped wires through it. A hopeful crowd broke into a spontaneous cheer as the video screen became Merlin's crystal and materialized a raw feed of the Cleveland Indians out of static. The engineer pressed a button, activating the dish, and suddenly in a backyard in Berkeley, California, there was WOR, its magical 9 turning into the Met insignia, and the voices of Tim McCarver and Steve Zabriskie were heard within a few blocks of Cody's, Telegraph Avenue, and People's Park. Our wish to see the Mets had finally surmounted three thousand miles of separation and red tape—the East Bay Baseball Satellite TV Club was born.

Setting up a baseball club of this sort with a stable membership remained dicey. Notices in the paper brought inquiries mostly from people who wanted to join without dues or who thought that we could somehow beam the games to their houses. When it came time to buy the dish, only eight of the people on the original list confirmed as full members, and two of those dropped out within the first month and were replaced. Throughout most of the first season we had eight full and eleven partial (half-price) members.

One fan brought stat books, baseball abstracts, and scouting reports, picked the best game (or the only game, even if it was Cleveland-Milwaukee), and sat in one of the old chairs analyzing each at-bat with charts on both the pitcher and batter. After the games he began painting the inside of the garage (bright green) and hanging baseball photographs in frames. Other members brought in balls, bats, helmets, and paintings, and soon the inside of the clubhouse became a little Cooperstown. It was as mysterious as a planetarium, as ceremonial and community-oriented as a Grange Hall.

Groups of adults (plus one child) sat in the dark on a fissured stone floor watching the lit screen, guys chugging beers, occasionally stepping outside to pee in the yard, lots of loud cheering. Lindy wondered how she ever approved such a lodge. For Robin it was the dream baseball clubhouse, a musty old shed with branches growing through planks, a single bare bulb, everyone's donated rotting chairs, Babe Ruth and Jackie Robinson on the walls, adults tossing wisecracks and wry jokes.

Using the dish to search for unexpected games, Robin and I came across Tidewater on a few occasions—once, to see Rafael Santana single in the winning run in extra innings; another time, to watch Wes Gardner pitch several innings of effective relief. We also found Sid Fernandez pitching for Tidewater a transponder away from Dwight Gooden pitching for the Mets on the same satellite one night, so we flipped back and forth. We also found a Tide raw feed of a game with the Maine Guides that included a beanball battle in which both benches emptied and Guides' manager Doc Edwards was ejected, at which point he went across the field and picked up third base and threw it away, then second, then first, and finally he took home plate into the clubhouse with him. After that we watched Jeff Bettendorf finish up and get the win when the Tides came from behind. He was the pitcher stolen from the Mets by the A's in the winter draft, mishandled by them, and then returned to the Met system; his reclamation had been a high point of our season.

Several weeks after the dish was up, a new Met fan joined the club, giving us a majority for choosing the daily game: "I heard there was this garage in Berkeley where you could watch the Mets," Stu acclaimed, as a friend from work brought him by, "but I didn't believe it till now. All I can say is: Wow! The Mets are a big part of my life, and this is heaven."

A conventionally handsome, tanned guy, albeit with a bit of a snarl, Stu seemingly liked baseball more than partying, dating, or general human life—the kind of guy who would go to Spring Training rather than a friend's wedding. A stockbroker on the Pacific Exchange, he told us he decided to move to California while visiting San Francisco after hearing a kid at Candlestick ask his father how it could be raining (as the scoreboard said) in Cleveland if it was summer.

An utterly uncompromising Met fan, he provided an education to Robin in New York sports insanity. For instance, on his first night watching a game with us Stu said that he considered Tom Seaver a traitor for leaving the Mets. I reminded him that he had been traded. "If I were traded to another team," he snapped, "especially a Chicago team, I wouldn't go; I'd just quit."

"Is that what you expect of him?" I asked.

"Absolutely. The only two things that should never happen again is the rearming of Germany and a pennant in Chicago."

"Don't you feel we owe them something for '69?" I teased.

"Owe Chicago anything? A city where everyone looks like Harry Caray?"

The Mets were Stu's intellectual, emotional, and spiritual universe, the persona he presented to the world, and (unlike me) he was unashamed of his obsession. "I am so happy this season," he remarked. "I thought I would be dead before they were good again."

I remember Stu during that maiden season of '84 for a couple of ad libs in particular. First, there was his classic: "Out! What do mean, out? Who do you think you are? You're an umpire, not God."

Then there was the vintage crack from the peanut gallery. On an evening when I was the parent cooking dinner (before the game), Robin came back to the garage from a trip to the house for seconds with a question from Miranda: "She wants to know if she has to eat her spinach."

"Yes," inserted Stu before I could answer. "And give her seconds."

Although he had lived in California for nearly ten years, Stu had never in his life seen tomatoes on a vine until our backyard garden. ("Is that how they grow?") Owning a condo in Walnut Creek and commuting to the Exchange, he had never even been into Berkeley until the club, and he virtually crossed himself every time upon arriving: "What a town! I just drove down Telegraph. They don't call it Bezerkeley for nothing."

Disgusted and affronted by the appearance of any bug, Stu believed that you stepped on all insects and spiders, and he had to be restrained at times, for Robin and I (and in fact most of the members) observed a different ethic.

After Glenn Hubbard put a hard tag on a Met runner, Stu stood and screamed: "The next guy who goes down there on a double play, put him out for the season!" Then he looked at me and said: "The guy's not even gonna be able to walk."

After hearing of Dick Ruthven's arm injury he said, "Six months at least I hope." Same line later for John Denny. No good sportsmanship for Stu. When the Mets were on their surge he delighted in switching to the Cubs' station to hear Harry Caray get the score. "Take that, you bum," he hooted.

He shouted for Mike Torrez (who had already put Dickie Thon out for the season) to drill Gary Carter on his sore elbow; the Expos were coming hard at a Met lead and Torrez hadn't won all year. Then our embarrassing compatriot jumped up with a loud clap and "yeah!" when Torrez did just what he requested. After the game I told Robin he didn't necessarily have to agree with Stu, even though he was rooting for the same team. Robin thought about it and then said: "But he's such a good Met fan."

The chemistry between the two of them was edifying for me to watch. During a year of hard work in ninth grade, Robin tended to retreat to his two favorite things, both in the garage: the Mets and his woodworking projects. He never called a single friend all that summer. Although Stu's personality was the opposite of his, Robin preferred him to anyone else available. "You know why it works," he told Lindy. "It's because there's a part of me that's exactly like him. He's a big child."

Robin was also fed up with the reactions of his yuppie friends, as they loved to taunt him about the Mets. Many of them rooted for whatever team was winning, changing from season to season: the Braves, then the Phillies, then the Orioles. This year they began wearing Tiger caps. Or if they were loyal Giant fans they insisted the Giants were "awesome." When the Giants did badly, they reminded Robin that the Forty-Niners had won more Super Bowls than the Mets. When the Mets were doing well for the first time in his life in '84, they teased, "Hey, Rob, how about those Cubs!"

Stu understood that only if you root for a team when it's down does it mean anything to be on the bandwagon when they're winning—not an easy line to sell in the upwardly mobile Bay Area. But Stu, Robin, and I shared it, and it was the basis of our solidarity.

During the hot streak of June and July when the Mets put together several long winning streaks and soared into first, Stu transported us from Berkeley to a hot bar in Queens. As tense game after game ended in victory the three of us would rise with a collective roar, and Lindy and Miranda inside the house knew the Mets had won. Leaving the mound with a save, Jesse Orosco would be pounding his glove, or Keith Hernandez would be rounding first as Mookie Wilson raced home to vanquish Neil Allen and the Cardinals. It was probably too much too soon, and by the end of July we were confronted by an intimidating rush of the Cubs.

"My whole world's falling apart," Stu confessed at one point in late August as the Mets continued to be pounded by the Cubs while the arch-enemy Yankees put on a fierce belated rally.

He had been denying all year that the Cubs were any good even as it became obvious they were the resurgent Mets' sole formidable foe: "Bob Dernier's a bum; Ryne Sandburg's a bum. They've got one guy who can play the outfield, no left side of the infield. The only thing that's going to fall faster than the Cubs is Bob Brenly's batting average." Wrong on both counts, he remained undaunted: "Next year Sandburg's hitting .220. What's he done the second half anyway."

When we held our final meeting of the club for 1984 after the season, I assessed dues and then asked people their predictions for 1985. There was a brief silence, and suddenly Stu said: "All I can say is you better collect the money from those Cub fans up front because they're gonna be losing interest before we get to All-Star break."

5.

Candlestick Park, May 15

Having a press pass for the first time in my life, I still find it hard just to stride onto the field. I stand in the front row behind the Mets' dugout, invulnerable in the role of Robin's father. As a stream of Met blue pours from the clubhouse, I do it; I open the gate behind home and walk onto the grass. I take a few steps and then look back at the stands, lightheaded: I have passed through the looking glass; I have violated a taboo almost as old as myself. I grip my press pass in my hand like a child with his first movie ticket. I feel as though I am breaking out of jail before 15,000 spectators.

I stand at the batting cage beside Darryl Strawberry, Hubie Brooks, and the rest, eavesdropping on their banter as if it were my own pickup game. The ball is hard, the shots are high and deep, but these are kids, mocking each other's swings, spoofing with exaggerated dances and exclamations, faking "hot foots," and shoving each other out of the box. The crack of the bat and arc of the ball's flight are metronomes.

Seeing the players not only up close but in a situation where I am free to move among them immediately elicits this dilemma: they look totally familiar but don't know me from Adam. I am an intruder in their house. Although it feels impolite to be turning away with guarded glances, that is exactly the etiquette required in this situation. Where the physical barrier between player and fan has been removed, another must replace it.

I recall with some apprehension an incident that happened to my brother many years ago when he was in college in Wisconsin. Physically he had turned into a full adult hippie, with shaggy clothes and much longer hair than I ever dared; yet in a part of his mind he still imagined himself the child-prodigy shortstop of Camp Chipinaw. He had taken a pilgrimage to see the Yankees play in Minneapolis, and before the game he strode into the Yankees' hotel, hoping for a glimpse of Mickey Mantle, his alter ego all through childhood. Boyishly trooping across the lobby, he was frozen by a voice behind him. "Hey, someone is looking for you." He turned around eagerly, expecting somehow to see Mickey. It was Elston Howard and he said: "The barber."

I mingle safely in the coterie of sportswriters behind the batting cage. Familiar Mets are all around: Ron Hodges, Keith Hernandez, George Foster. I had plans to do sprightly interviews for the *Village Voice;* now I find I have nothing to say to any of them.

Jesse Orosco and Chili Davis are off to the side parleying with one another—seems a strange pairing since Chili hits him ultra-well and boasts about it to the press; one imagines them as simply names and opponents to each other. Then Chili finds Darryl Strawberry, and the two of them huddle along the Giants' dugout, hanging out intently until Mets batting practice. They don't seem so much to share words in the sense of "gabbing"; they stand silently together, as though in a show of solidarity against the tyranny of false promise. Joel Youngblood has been hanging around the outskirts of the batting cage, greeting his old Mets friends with exuberance as they arrive. As Wally Backman approaches, he breaks into a big smile; they clasp hands, almost hugging. "Hiya Blood," says Wally.

Kelvin Chapman arrives in a group of players right behind Backman, and Youngblood shouts, "I never thought I'd see you up here again! Ever!" Meanwhile it seems as though half the town of Ukiah is shouting at Chapman from the stands. After visiting with Youngblood, he patrols the edge of the dugout shaking hands, inquiring about weddings, babies, little-league games—this report Robin gives me.

Being on the field reminds me of my first days on the wharf as an anthropologist with lobstermen in Maine: You know that you don't belong, and in matters of their own calling they're sharper than you; one way or another they're going to prove it, prove that you don't belong and shouldn't be there. Even if you prepare yourself for their sword and parry, you are going to get pricked.

The one person standing around unoccupied is Mets batting coach Bill Robinson. He looks friendly and safe, so I ask if we can talk.

"Why not," he says. "I'm not doing anything."

Not sure if he's being ironical, I ask him how the Mets are different from what he imagined coming over here. "Different? It's a whole new organization, new players, new attitude. It's not different. It's just not the same people."

"What changes have you brought about since the start of the season?"

"Well, Mike Fitzgerald's hitting better. José Oquendo's a better hitter than he was. Hey, you're not writing any of this down. If I'm going to talk, you've got to write it down. That's *your* job."

Pen poised, I ask if there are any good hitters in the Mets' minor-league system. "The best are here," he says, looking strained. "But there are some decent hitters down there: Kevin Mitchell, John Gibbons."

I thank him for the interview and retreat to behind the cage. At the plate Junior Ortiz and Oquendo are involved in a batting-practice contest, arguing about what's a hit and what's not. Keith Hernandez is answering questions for a group of sportswriters, so I listen. He says he was very unhappy with the trade at first—he had been a Cardinal fan his whole life. He didn't at all expect to re-sign with the Mets because he intended to be on a contender team. "Just playing out the string is drudgery. You want a chance to win. But they told me they had some pretty good players in the system, and I found out in spring training they weren't kidding. It's a far better team than I realized. I just rolled the dice and came out lucky."

A writer asks him what it's like winning in New York.

"I don't know. I never won anything there. I haven't found out yet."

Up close Hernandez is different from my image of him. There's truculence, almost intimidation issuing from his presence—the drive that gets expressed in every game. Yet, as he jokes with his brother Gary on the field and takes practice swings, he reveals a sunny side, almost like jolliness—he was once this guy's kid brother, a clown. Clearly he has outgrown that role, but he still puts a twinkle of slapstick into his bashful gambits around the cage.

In the game itself Ron Darling is knocked out early on home runs by Leonard and Clark, but the Mets creep back into it, tying, and then taking the lead as Fitzgerald shoots a key single with the bases loaded. But it is the Giants' turn next to tie the score, after which they load the bases with no one out in sudden-death against Orosco, who gets a pop-up and then a strikeout on the suicide-squeeze try.

In extra innings Kelvin Chapman brings the Mets' coterie to its feet with a pinch double into the left-field corner, and three batters later, Hernandez brings him in with a sacrifice fly; it holds up as the winning run.

In the excitement of the comeback win I decide to attempt the next big hurdle, something I had planned to postpone for another day: a visit to the clubhouse itself. Fortunate to find an elevator descending with sportswriters to the bowels of Candlestick, Robin and I stick with the group until a guard halts my oversize baby at the end of the tunnel—only one pass and, anyway, the kid is too young; he has to wait here.

As Robin slides into a spot along the wall, I am directed toward a door. I walk through it into another universe . . . players striding about, undressed and undressing, Mookie still acclaiming the win, others grabbing cold cuts off a table, ripping open beers. My eyes dart around, again trying not to meet eyes. Being with the players in the locker room is different from watching them on the field in uniforms. In a certain sense they are still Mets, and that's what makes it disorienting. On a gut level, I respond to them as mere showering men, reading their energy and motives as I would any group of strangers. There's a sense of hazard when people mix in a social situation, especially if they are undressing. I wonder what I'm doing here.

Rusty Staub and George Foster look particularly menacing; I would not want to get in either of their ways. For no explicit reason many of the other players look unapproachable too: Heep, Gaff, Fitzgerald, Hodges. I have nothing to exchange with them.

Staub is orating in a loud voice, his uniform removed to show his t-shirt, a red hammer-and-sickle with a line drawn through it and the words: "Fuck the Russians."

I get my bearings and blend into a crowd interviewing Doc: hard-driving white male questions, good-humored homeboy answers.

Nick Peters ran into me in Berkeley a few weeks later and chided: "Richard, I was ashamed of you." Immediately I wondered what gaffe I had made. "You didn't even say hello to me in the Mets' clubhouse after that night game. You were standing there, eyes wide open, looking like a ten-year-old kid with your hand in the cookie jar." No doubt I was.

Most of the reporters crowd around Chapman's locker, those in the back asking those in front if he really is local. Foster at the next locker pretends to whisper to him: "Tell them your name. Make sure they get your name." Every now and then he turns to a newly arrived sportswriter and says—pointing at Chapman—"Don't you know who that is? That's Keith Hernandez."

Tim Leary, appearing much taller in person than even Christopher Reeve, asks me if I know the whereabouts of Bruce Jenkins, a sportswriter who happens to be an author of ours. His entreaty interrupts my introspection, and luckily I have his answer: "The American League."

"Oh, he covers the Yankees."

"You mean the A's."

"Yeah."

"How's your arm?" I slip in. Dumb question.

"The arm is [pause] great." A big spacey smile; he's said it too many times and is teasing me. "Just . . . great." Then he wanders off.

I stand and listen to a journalist make a radio tape of Dwight Gooden. As he changes his clothes, Doc answers questions in a flat diffident way. He's not even bored; he knows precisely what's expected of him and supplies the prose.

The one player who looks approachable—if this were a party at which I don't know anyone—is Ron Darling; he has a soft, thoughtful gaze. Since he was taken out of the game early, no one is hanging around his locker. He sits there, pulling on his shirt. The year before, when he was at Tidewater, I mailed him a copy of our old baseball anthology. Prompted, he remembers the book and thanks me for it.

"Do you mind talking briefly?"

"No, that's okay."

I ask him how he thinks the season is going so far: "Tonight wasn't that bad a game. I've been getting better each start. I *am* improving." Then he adds: "I made some bad pitches. I just lost my concentration. With Clark I simply forgot. I threw the ball before I remembered who was at the plate. The pitch I made to Leonard was okay. It usually gets popped up. But he's a good hitter."

I felt a sudden claw. Art Richman, who no doubt appreciates my being in his locker room about as much as my father once enjoyed my brother Michael and me sneaking extra desserts out of his hotel kitchen, has grabbed my elbow and is leading me to Frank Cashen, the General Manager. Art is going to do the right thing if it kills him.

"This is Paul Grossinger's son," he says, "you know, from the Catskills. He's a writer."

I can't say Cashen is enthusiastic or that I approve of the introduction, but Art is both helping me and making me pay for my intrusion. I ask the GM if he'd be willing to have a conversation.

"Tomorrow before the game," he shoots in quick unenunciated syllables, plowing through the mêlée.

Ed Lynch, the tall, studious right-hander, brushes past, adjusting his tie.

"Lynchie," Arthur croons, "you're on the list. Right there with George Brett, Willie, and the boys."

"What list, Art?" asks Lynch.

"My pallbearers." Then he turns to me. "They gotta treat me right, Richie, or I'll get someone else."

"Who's Willie?" I ask.

"Who's Willie? C'mon. Willie Mays."

Outside the door I find Robin, who has been excitedly watching the players leave in street clothes. "I'm just standing here and Tim Leary walks by. Then Danny Heep. And Keith Hernandez!"

I leave the ballpark unexpectedly troubled by the media event, though it's the only reason I'm even permitted to be here. Being a sportswriter among ballplayers is as parasitic as being an anthropologist among fishermen or Hopi Indians: each profession preys off and consumes symbols generated by other people's activities. Each turns indigenes into dead objects and chattel. The intellectualized distinction between observer and informant is self-serving and (ultimately) alienating.

For the ostensible transfer of information into goods, actions into assets, the anthropologist/sportswriter is tolerated as a commodity-maker, at least in the Western world. He elicits money and trinkets; he converts abject dance-steps with tridents and dormant medicine bundles into artifacts other people will pay hefty capitalist dollars for, one way or the other. But his native subjects always intuit the artificiality, extortion, and false objectivity. No one stands outside of history; history is what happens to us, regardless of our pretense of documenting it.

The summer of '67 when I spent a week on the Hopi Third Mesa collecting information about Cargo Cult religion, the locals were politely asking all anthropologists to leave, to go home "so we can do the wash," as one woman put it. The Hopis were inundated then not only with professors but entire summer schools of graduate students armed with government money to pay them to generate "data."

The fans are the ultimate source of the huge player salaries; everyone knows that. If the games were incognito, the feats, unsung, they wouldn't be worth a plug nickel. Willie Mays' catches and Henry Aaron's homers would be worthless.

With baseball, both you and the players accept that it's the daily reporting of their acts that turns their game into media, and the media that create the marketable demand and their salaries. That doesn't make it any less of a violation; it merely expiates it with collaborative greed. Once again, cash makes it tolerable.

The next day is not only a day game but getaway day, so the Mets don't arrive at Candlestick until an hour and a half before game time. Robin and I stand outside the clubhouse waiting and, when the bus arrives, the players step off one by one, most of them in sports jackets carrying briefcases: Gardenhire, Brooks, Lynch, Gorman, Orosco, Gaff, Hodges, Fitzgerald. Darryl Strawberry disembarks separately from a cab and pays the fare.

Modern ballplayers may look like young businessmen arriving for appointments, but that doesn't make their entry into the ceremony any less spellbinding—the very absence of a uniform demonstrates its power.

I wait for the bus to empty and everyone to disappear into the locker room. As the guard halts Robin again, I continue in.

Ron Darling is standing by the door. When I tell him about my son, he says, "I want to meet him."

Out in the tunnel, in spikes and uniform towering above both of us, he shakes Robin's hand and asks about school, baseball, Berkeley.

While we are talking, Frank Cashen wanders past and, although part of me thinks to let sleeping dogs lie, I remind him of his previous night's offer.

"I've got a bit of time," he says, distractedly checking his watch. "Let's find the sun."

As we continue toward the tunnel to the field, I start to give Robin instructions about meeting up later but, in the process of my calling out to him, he simply runs up and joins us. Perhaps intimidated by Cashen, the guard says nada, so we continue down the vestibule onto the field and find the sun, on the bench in the Giants bullpen.

"Is this okay?" Cashen asks.

Me and my son in the bullpen with the GM for company? Of course, it's okay. "Sure," I say. "Sure. It's great."

Since I am not sure how much time Mr. Cashen will actually give me, I decide to start with more obscure questions. I ask him why he made certain minor-league trades that might seem inexplicable to the outsider, like getting Jason Felice back from the Reds after sending him over in the Seaver deal, or picking up two players each from the Cubs for Tom Veryzer and Terry Leach. He says that many trades are made without the big-league club in mind; for instance, Felice simply was not comfortable in the Reds' system and wanted to be back with his friends on the Mets, so they worked out a deal. In other cases you move a player no longer able to help the organization, and it doesn't matter whom you get in return.

The answer makes sense in principle but, as it turned out, Felice hit over .300 with power for Lynchburg, and the two pitchers picked up for Leach (Jim Adamczak and Mitch Cook) made the Carolina League all-star team, although Cook later went to the Reds for Ray Knight—and Leach himself was back in the Met system pitching for Tidewater before the season was out.

I then ask him a few more questions about trades and player development, and he catches the subtext. I am a writer, yes, but I am a Met-fan imposter, using journalist cover to talk intimately about the team. He says he is willing to answer in depth, but his remarks have to be off the record—so during most of the conversation I put down the pen and simply listen. He then speaks about players he thinks are going to make it and others he is disappointed in. About one important prospect he complains: "He has that laid-back Southern California attitude. Everything has to be done in a certain style. He thinks he's playing hard-nosed baseball, but he's not. But because he thinks he is, it's difficult to get through to him. He's been passed by people who don't have his talent."

Among his less controversial observations are: "I think Hubie Brooks can be converted into a fine middle infielder, if he wants to do it"; "Dave Cochrane has a great future, but I'm not sure he can play third base up here"; "John Gibbons out of San Antonio is the best catcher I have ever developed, and he can become a twenty-homer-a-year player on a major-league level"; "Billy Beane is still a prospect and a great outfielder, but he is spending a third year in Double A learning to hit."

When Robin asks him if he is at all interested in Shane Mack with his number-one pick in the upcoming draft, he says, "Probably not, because we have a lot of outfielders in the system more or less in his mold—Winningham, Blocker, Dykstra, Jefferson." I mention that Marvell Wynne was another one whom he let go, and I wonder why he didn't at least try him in the majors first.

"I simply like Mookie Wilson better as a player."

"What about for left field?"

"I need more power from that portion than Marvell could give. I'm not going to get it from first base, centerfield, or my catcher, so I have to make it up in left field. You don't simply pick up random players. You try to put together a team that will work."

I wonder why he brought up Brent Gaff ahead of some other pitchers, and he explains: "Because I think he has the right temperament to be a middle-innings reliever."

Apologizing about the question, I ask him about losing Tom Seaver in the free-agent pool, adding that I don't think the White Sox drafting him hurt the Mets because it opened up a spot on the pitching staff and freed them from the pool for three years.

"That's true. But the point is: I made a mistake. I didn't intend to lose Seaver. I thought I had gone through the possibilities pretty thoroughly, and I judged what the White Sox needed and what they didn't need. I didn't take into account the ownership there and that they'd make a showbiz choice."

We drift back into history, and he speaks nostalgically of his years before becoming a baseball executive: Sundays on the beach with friends reading the box scores. It reminds me of my stepfather when I was young—the *Times* sports section spread out on the sand at Long Island, a new game about to begin, the radio on the blanket, playing Ballantine Beer jingles.

I am debating the designated-hitter rule with him when Herm Starette, the Giants' pitching coach, wanders by and advises Robin and me: "Listen to everything this man tells you. He won't steer you wrong. He's one of the great people in this game." Then to Cashen: "I guess you saw our whole pitching staff last night."

"And you saw a good part of ours. You know, people might miss it, but the thing that won the game for us last night was middle-inning relief."

Starette agrees. Then Cashen says: "Of course there's one boy on your team we'd like having in New York if you ever get tired of him: Mark Davis."

Starette chuckles. "I guess we'll keep him, Frank. It's such a shame; he looked so good in spring training, had a bad game at the start of the season; then he hurt his finger on a play at home plate, and he hasn't been able to straighten himself out. When I first heard he was available from the Phillies, I said, 'Take 'im.'"

The two begin reminiscing about their years in the American League in the '50s and '60s. They compare Tim Leary to Jim Palmer. "I remember when Palmer went down to Rochester and then Miami," Starette tell us. "His arm hurt and he didn't want to pitch. He used to throw a bit on the sidelines and just go a few innings. Then Cal Ripken decided to push him one day. He kept saying, 'One more inning, one more inning.' He got him to pitch his way through it."

Another fatherly pitching coach, my old Yankee favorite Mel Stottlemyre, drifts by and, taking a seat on the other side of us from his Giants' counterpart, joins in the conversation. They are continuing to jabber about the American League of the '60s when Cashen suddenly notices Heep and Sisk diving around in the outfield tackling one another.

"Jesus," he says to Stottlemyre. "Don't let them do that."

But instead of acting on the thought, they begin discussing players whose careers were derailed by horseplay. Eventually Heep and Sisk jog by on their way to the clubhouse. "Hey, Dougie," Cashen calls, "what's going on out there?"

"Don't you worry," says Sisk, seemingly missing the point. "He's not going to take me down."

Tom Gorman, who was peripherally involved, tries to slip past into the clubhouse. Cashen's face lights up. "Tommy Gorman, my hero," he pronounces, and Gorman's large-featured clown's countenance turns red.

This could have gone on forever and we would have stayed, but there is a game to play. The GM walks us down the tunnel, back past the clubhouse (where Ron Darling shouts, "Good luck, you two!").

It is a thousand moments I have lived or imagined living with fathers real and fictional—now as both father and son.

Back through the tunnel and outside the clubhouse door we join the crowd entering the stadium.

"Did we just do that?" Robin asks. "Did we just sit in the bullpen talking to Frank Cashen and Mel Stottlemyre about the Mets?"

It was almost a perfect day. Leading 3-1 with two outs and nobody on in the San Fran ninth, the Mets gave up five straight hits to the Giants (Terrell and Sisk) and lost 4-3. Only gradually, in the remainder of a glorious big-sky Berkeley afternoon, does it come back to me that our experience was larger than the game.

On the way down the aisle that afternoon after the debacle, a grumbling John Hernandez extended an invitation to visit him at his home in Millbrae. We got there on the following Saturday, and he demonstrated the workings of a satellite dish that Keith had bought and gotten installed for him so that he could follow the team and coach his son from afar. He asked our advice on locating games on the easternmost Galaxy satellite, but the problem was that either his system was improperly calibrated or there was a house in the way—nothing we could fix. Sitting on his living-room couch, he continued to score players and management with barbs he had me—to his mind a sportswriter—pledge would never see print.

Juan called us every time thereafter when the Mets were on the low Galaxy bird that he couldn't get. He wanted a complete account of each of Keith's at-bats because his son might phone at any moment from the dugout for feedback. Club members struggled pathetically to meet his rigorous standards of depicting stance and azimuth of swing. We just were dumb fans; we didn't see what happened in a sorcerer's way. Only Robin, with his carpenter's precision, was an acceptable reporter for Juan. The old man always wanted to know if he was there and, if he was, he said, "Put the kid on."

Early one game Robin specified the exact position of Keith's hands; then he popped out. "As I thought," Juan pronounced, and he promised better results the next time.

Keith came up in the seventh—the Mets down a run, a man on first—and put a shot into the right-field bullpen. Club members were howling and banging the walls. This loop was absurd. Certainly no one in the New York I came from would believe it. Then the phone rang.

"See, what did I tell you!" boomed Juan.

But that was what Berkeley had become for me, a kind of festival in which impossible wishes were granted and the irredeemable past was reclaimed.

One afternoon Marty Asher, the editor of Quality Paperback Book Club, made an appointment to check out our list. He was impressed by the basement publishing enterprise and our range of titles. At 4:30 he noticed a rush of people down the driveway toward the garage.

"Mets game," I explained, pointing to the dish on the listing roof.

"Goddamnit!" he exploded. "That's the last straw! You live in California, set your own hours, publish what you damn please; now you get the Mets, which I can't even do on my fucking Midtown cable."

It was the return of my childhood, vintage Grossinger's 1955. I wouldn't have been anywhere near the action in modern Manhattan. But then I couldn't have launched a publishing company there, or trained with top martial artists, or sent my kids to private schools. Berkeley felt like Manhattan without its penthouse prices, impenetrable empires, or gridlock.

6.

Arthur Richman and the boys returned to San Francisco in August. In the meantime they had reached a maximum of four and a half games in first. After that surge, they were defeated *seven* times in a row by the Cubs to fall as much as six back before beginning a slow recovery that brought them to within two games of first after Sid Fernandez beat the Dodgers in L.A. and the Cubs lost in Pete Rose's debut as manager in Cincinnati. On August 17 the Mets came to Candlestick Park for a Friday night game. Robin, Stu, and I went to the game together in Stu's car by an absurd route up and down hills through the most dangerous parts of San Francisco. We got to the park early, and I grabbed my press pass and went down onto the field.

Over at the cage the Mets are taking batting practice. In response to Junior Ortiz' attempts, coach Bobby Valentine, throwing in pitches, teases: "Send him to Yakima."

"Anything you want, Hubert," he calls out to the next hitter. When Ron Hodges bats, Foster leans over intently from his position alongside the cage and, after each pitch, solemnly intones: "Hodgo."

Down the third-base line a moving Davey Johnson is surrounded by a mosquito cloud of reporters, one questioning him, others waiting their turns. I gradually wander over that way until I am within earshot. The reporter who is speaking asks trite questions, and Johnson has little patience: "Why have the Mets improved?" "Are you having problems with Darryl Strawberry?" "Is it hard managing in New York?" Sometimes the manager just doesn't answer or answers only wearily after a long punitive pause. He responds to a number of inquiries with variants of "Those are just sportswriters' questions" and "You sportswriters think these things up, but they don't have anything to do with the game."

When the next writer follows a similar tack, Johnson begins answering his questions before he asks them: "Of course Darryl Strawberry has the tools to be a great player. Yes, he has a lot to learn."

One reporter is particularly concerned to know about Davey's use of a computer, and he says: "You sportswriters make too much out of the computer. I've been working with computers over seventeen years, so I should know how to program them. No, I don't over-rely on them. No, I don't overlook the human factor."

I did not intend to try Johnson myself but, after listening to these exchanges I imagine how much better I can do. When my turn comes, I introduce myself as a freelance writer and start by asking him if there were any players at Tidewater or Jackson who might help the Mets before the end of the season.

"I'm not concerned with things like that," he says. "I've got the best twenty-five men up here." I throw out the names of some of the better players in the farm system, and he stares at me silently. Check.

Nervously I ask: "Was John Stearns able to swing the bat the other night?"

"I should hope so. I had him in the on-deck circle three times."

"I just wondered because you didn't use him against DiPino when you had all those left-handers coming up in the ninth inning at Houston." I am instantly mortified, for I have bumbled into a second-guess. He lets me off the hook relatively easy by saying he doesn't know which game that was. But in my fluster a habitual response slips out of my mouth—I remind him that Mark Bailey hit a two-run homer off Sisk in the bottom of the ninth to win it. He says again that he doesn't remember the game, a little more sharply this time. Then: "Are you trying to second-guess me?"

"No."

"I certainly hope not." Checkmate. (God, this is shades of Elston Howard and the barber.)

Quick, think of something else. "Was Rafael Santana better than you thought he'd be?"

"Better than I thought he'd be? What does that mean? He was hitting .280 in Triple A, so I imagine he'd be pretty good."

In fact I have done no better than my predecessors and am even more pretentious in my failure. So I back out of one identity into another and, feigning guileless charm, tell him about our dish and the baseball club. He nods, waiting, arms folded. I thank him and move on.

That night Dwight Gooden and Mike Krukow dueled through nine scoreless innings, one with an overpowering fastball, the other with curve balls and changes of speed. The Mets had Krukow on the ropes early several times but failed to get runners in from third with less than two out, and the Giants almost broke through in the late innings.

In seats all around us there seemed to be a new category of fan— black people who came out to root just for Dwight, not the Mets. They danced in the aisles and gave high and low fives for his strikeouts, then left for the concession stands during Mets at-bats. It was as though he were Michael Jackson or some young break-dancer from New York.

In the tenth inning Wally Backman lined his first homer of the season into the right-field stands with Mookie Wilson on base, and we stood there cheering until we were hoarse. Stu ran into the aisle throwing his arms up and down. "One and a half games out—take that, Harry!"

Leaving the stadium, he said to us: "I don't care about anything else. All's right in the world. National debt, nuclear proliferation, no problem; the Mets have won." We were walking back to his car when Robin noticed that the moon over the Bay seemed unusually large. "Maybe it's falling," he said.

For a second I too was concerned. The moon was enormous, but then I realized that if it were really swollen, there would be tidal waves and an earthquake, and I pointed that out to him.

"That sure would ruin a Mets victory, wouldn't it?" he said.

"Nothing ruins this Mets victory," Stu added. But I remembered to recommend a different route back to the Bay Bridge.

Guilty winners, we were trying to hold onto the momentum, but one and a half was as close as the Mets were to get to the Cubs during this last great run of '84.

We arrive at Candlestick early for the Saturday afternoon game and go right to the clubhouse. While Robin waits outside, I continue in. It surprises me to see the players smoking, eating candy, and drinking soda and beer before the game; I naïvely assumed that athletes stayed away from sugar, nicotine, and chemical additives—it is disconcerting to watch stars peel open chocolate bars. The clubhouse set is tuned to NBC with the pre-game show for Game of the Week. The announcer begins talking about the race in the N.L. East, and a number of Mets cluster around the set in various states of uniform, street clothes, and nakedness. He must be describing Dwight Gooden, for players are whistling and cheering at an image of Dwight firing away.

"Can't hit that, right?" someone calls out.

Gorman and Sisk, right in front, drink from their cans and laugh. I look at Dwight as he stares at himself on the tube. He seems half-bemused, half-serious; there is no way he can possibly have caught up with himself yet.

The Mets suddenly let out a loud cheer for a replay of Backman's home run. I look around at their faces: they are so accessible and, at the same time, utterly closed to the outside. They know instinctively how to keep their privacy in public; they have perfected remoteness in intimacy: Strawberry, Berenyi, Orosco, Lynch. They are young, some of them almost childlike—young and intense. Strawberry's deadpan classic look is brooding yet buoyant. The boy in old minor-league Giants' photos is gone from George Foster's ancient face. He is a hardened warrior now, the scars of his career in his empty eyes.

Because baseball is a game, one forgets that it is also a play—the players are actors; otherwise they would be players year-round, all of their lives like worker ants. The façade is that they play only the avowed game, within its geometry, rules, and boundaries, but of course they also play themselves—they play themselves playing baseball and embody insensibly its ritual acts.

The network switches to the Cubs, the debut of Pete Rose in Cincinnati: a hit to the outfield followed by a crashing slide into second base. A bunch of players burst out laughing. "Slides and no one's covering the base," someone jeers. "Look at that slide. There's no one near him."

Now the announcer says that they will be back after a message, for the next segment—"The Beanball Wars." Jay Horwitz, Mets' public relations director, nudges Ed Lynch, who gives a friendly shove back. The remaining players beeline from their lockers and crowd for position around the set. Even Tim McCarver is there, right in the center.

Pascual Perez hits Alan Wiggins with a pitch; the room is filled with whistles and hisses. Then Perez is up at bat and the pitcher drives him off the plate. Just as he falls away backwards, Hubie Brooks wriggles in front of the TV in imitation of Perez' almost feminine quality. Then he playfully pats me on the fanny. I would hardly have believed myself standing beside Hubie in the Mets' clubhouse, having him express conviviality while hooting at Game of the Week. Now Perez is posturing beside home plate protecting himself by waving the bat.

"Put down the bat," shout several players at once. "Put down the fucking bat."

Perez hits again, and you can feel the heightened tension in the room. Behind me Jesse Orosco is pushing to get closer, holding an unopened bottle of wine in the air. I hurry out of his way and find myself looking back at the crowd around the set. Perez is finally hit by the pitch and the team erupts in a cheer.

The tinny TV image is the same one we get in our Saturday living rooms; here, though, the set is dwarfed by players around it. They are collectively the real source of energy, but on the screen they are reduced and packaged and put inside a tube, their actions tagged. In a few minutes they're going to go onto the field and play their own game. They are going to continue to spin the thread for these machines to grind into second-hand myth. It's not who they are; they know it's not who they are, but everything in their upbringing enjoins them to go along with it.

The actual Mets are more touching and vulnerable than the baseball-card Mets. They are not statistics or national heroes; take away the tube and the addiction of millions, and they're a bunch of mostly small-town guys recruited to play on a company team, not that different from the first nineteenth-century squads that set out from Eastern and Midwestern cities to represent neighborhoods.

The segment ends and they drift away, back to getting dressed. Rafael Santana is wearing a Licey t-shirt. Jesse Orosco has opened his bottle of wine and is guzzling; handlettered on the back of his t-shirt: "The Scum Bunch."

Ron Darling is the starting pitcher today, and I head over to his locker. I expect him to remember me, but I am cautious. You follow them but they don't follow you. They go from city to city; you track them from one position like planets. We talk only briefly; I wish him good luck. Then I find myself suddenly touched by the person rather than ballplayer to whom the person has given his name. Looking dreamily in the air, he is wearing a white t-shirt with a black outlined ghost and the words: "I Ain't Afraid of No Ghost." That free-connects me to a recent event. I tell him I wished someone could have magically rescued him from that afternoon in Chicago when the Cubs knocked him out; he hit a batter, the fans booed, and he left the mound to a virtual Boschian hell of crazed faces cursing him all the way into the dugout.

Though the fan in me wanted him to stay in there at all costs and prevail, the human being in this room seems to have no place in that Wrigley madhouse. He is much closer to Robin's age than mine, but he is full-grown, an adult, so he is halfway between us. "It was a nightmare," he says. "Sometimes you just find yourself there and it gets worse and worse, and you can't find any way out." Then he realizes how introspective that sounds and he catches himself, the professional athlete again: "I guess you have to expect that sometimes when you go up against the best hitters in baseball."

I wander over to where a few of the players sit watching the beginning of the Angel-Oriole game. "Where was that pitch?" asks Jerry Martin, like any fan. Staub shouts to Hernandez across the room: "When you struck out the second time, I said, 'Better watch out, old man's in the stands.'"

"I know," says Hernandez, tying a shoe. "Juan's in town, on the war path, big trouble."

Everyone has left the Oriole-Angel telecast except Hubie Brooks, who sits against a concrete post, his eyes more on the ceiling than the TV. He is idly rubbing a styrofoam cup along his lips and scratching his cheek.

I see that as a semi-autistic call for privacy, my reporting of it as an invasion. People's sensations of themselves, their interior familiarity, are what are hard to keep here—to have something that feels like yourself while you space out the unrelenting media version of your situation. I have always believed in Hubie's integrity, though I have no way of certifying it. On a gut level he is one of my favorite Mets, so I am stealing a moment of his privacy to make him real. I have defended him as a coming great player for years, but he has a legion of detractors. I hear that Bill James, that arrogant armchair expert, puts Hubie down on just about every level as a bad player. So I'm glad Hubie has had the kind of year that shoves it right back down Bill James' throat—not only average but homers; not only average and homers, but game-winning hits; not only hits and power and coming through in the clutch, but playing hurt and adjusting his style to deliver for weeks with a bad wrist; not only playing well and from the heart but shifting to shortstop late in the season when Santana got hurt, and making game-saving plays.

Yes, Hubie is sort of spaced out: he may dive to catch a strike-three bunt foul or run into outs at third base after driving in runs with a big hit; he may take too long with a throw and then sail it over first—but that kind of doggedness seems at the core of his individuality. People can't always improve in a straight line, eradicating all their faults as with a vacuum cleaner. Hubie seems to need his idiosyncrasies to play as well as he does; he thrives on the complications he generates.

At the end of last season someone in the Mets' management, at least by hearsay, accused him of having a bad attitude. "They don't know me that well," said Hubie. "What makes them think they understand me? My own mother hasn't figured me out yet."

Right on, Hubie. They are rough on letting black players have complex personalities; stereotyping comes so easily. Hubie is an interesting and difficult man and a complicated player, worth appreciating no matter what he does.

In order to talk to Hernandez about his father I have to run the gauntlet of George Foster, who is trying to convince me that Keith's brother Gary is Keith. "You want to talk to Keith? Here's Keith."

I finally get a brief exchange with the real first baseman. "Everyone loves Juan," he tells me. "But that's because he's not their father."

After I leave the locker room, Robin and I walk around the stadium to the entrance. He imparts how he saw Terrell, Heep, and Berenyi race into the Giants' clubhouse. "I wondered who they were going to talk to. And then they came out, and one of them was wearing the Crazy Crab costume." That player, possibly Terrell, then went around attacking his teammates with his claws.

When we get into the ballpark and down to field level, Walt Terrell or Danny Heep as Crazy Crab is running around the outfield tackling Met players before fleeing back into the tunnel. Lucky that Frank Cashen isn't on this trip.

Standing on the field by the cage, I am aware of the sounds the players hear: "Wally, nice shot last night."

Backman doesn't look up.

Then just as he is entering the dugout a fat uniformed Met fan comes charging down the aisle and in a big voice booms out, "Wally Home Run Backman!", giving the thumbs-up sign. The player can't resist breaking his stoneface with a smile. Sometimes a spectator is actually funny.

Behind the batting cage Frank Howard joins a closely staring Bill Robinson. "You ain't observin' shit," says Howard, giving him a playful shove.

Only a few Giants are left on the field as the Mets take it over. Strawberry and Brooks entertain one of them by the dugout, and Wilson and Hodges tell jokes and horseplay with Joel Youngblood behind the batting cage. As the guard completes its change, Youngblood is the only Giant left. He is busy describing to Wilson how hard it is to pick up Gooden's pitches. He holds up the bat like a gun and aims it. "You only see the littlest bit of the ball." He makes a mark the size of a dime. While they are fussing over Gooden's fastball, Youngblood notices that all the other Giants are gone. He lingers for a nostalgic second with his old teammates and then starts back to the dugout. Halfway there he turns around and looks back, "You guys, be good. Now don't get psyched out."

It was about the sweetest thing that he could have said.

I stand behind home plate trying to understand Strawberry's swing. It's harder to follow than anyone else's. It isn't just the bat on the ball; it's as though something more nuclear is happening. He sweeps through the strike zone with such a swift but subtle arc, capturing more area than most players. His hits leave their own acoustic tingle.

Now Foster stands by the side watching Hernandez in the batter's box. After a couple of swings Keith asks, "How many pitches?"

"Pitches," says Foster. "You did say pitches?"

On Strawberry's next turn he gets under the ball and hits it high in the air to medium right field. Foster runs out in front of him in the cage, holding up his hand as though to watch a ball disappearing into the horizon. "It's, it's, it's," he keeps saying, continuing to raise his hand with each repetition. As the ball drops and is lazily caught by a pitcher running in the outfield, Foster flips his hand, as though about to give five to Strawberry, then lets it fall away suddenly and turns around and takes back his spot behind the cage. Almost mesmerized, I wonder what I am watching, but we don't get to choose our obsessions.

Darling starts well that Saturday, but he is wild and throws a lot of pitches; Wes Gardner replaces him in the sixth, and the Giants hit him hard and take the lead. The Mets come back to tie it on a pinch hit by Rusty Staub, but Gaff sets up the winning run with a wild pitch in the ninth.

In the row behind us Juan Hernandez is laughing to keep from crying. He punches his fist in his hand, as though to say, "I told them to get rid of this bum."

On Sunday, the day of the Mets' last appearance in San Francisco (a doubleheader), I make a final trip to the locker room. Art is clearly getting tired of seeing me in this role. "Up early, Richard," he says.

Public and Private Baseball

Ron Darling is sitting in front of his locker; he asks me how my piece is coming, and I tell him my insights about public and private baseball, the anthropologist as observer. "When I talk to you," I add, "you're of course just another person, but then there's this other version of you out on the mound, so when I go sit in the stands I'm just one of eight million people."

"Or six hundred here."

"No, I mean all the people who read the box scores and follow the games. You're a name and a number in that world, but if it weren't for that we wouldn't even be talking."

"I don't always like the role," he says. "And there's another thing. What about greatness? They decide who's going to be great and then that's that. Look what it's doing to Dwight and Darryl."

"It's a media event," I add. "They invent you to serve themselves, like the way they collect withholding tax; they want your money right away, not at tax time, because they've already spent it. Same thing with greatness. They want to capitalize on you before you've actually become anything. In a sense they steal it from you because they've used up everything else. You're left being some movie character, like Robert Redford playing a ballplayer."

"It doesn't leave much room for development when they say you're great. You either do it...."

"And when you do, they've already said it."

"They've made the mold, and you can either fill it or fail."

"It's like with Gooden," I say. "They're always digging up ridiculous new records for him to break—number of rookie strikeouts, strikeouts for a teenager, ten or more strikeout games. These things have nothing to do with what he's actually pitching for and, when they trump them up, they rob the game of its integrity. What space is there just to grow into something different, like himself?"

"But I still feel it's okay playing baseball," Ron Darling abruptly inserts.

"It wouldn't work if it were the roller derby. Everyone sees through that."

"Or wrestling," he adds. "I tell myself sometimes that baseball is so old, it's like history; it must be okay."

Looking at Ron Darling sitting there working on his glove, I picture the stolid players of the '50s, many of them with winter jobs to get over the March hill; disappearing into the working-class players of the '40s; then flowing into the first organized teams representing cities, barely professionals, at the turn of the century; back to the old-time uniforms and small gloves of the 1880s, the bases laid out on the Civil War battlefield; before that, club-ball and rounders in England, field games with bean-filled balls and nets between Indian groups to mark the equinox, openings in a pre-Columbian wilderness.

The diamond within the circle of baseball summarizes thousands of ancient games and extinct tribes, peoples who have disappeared by becoming us, pitchers who threw before there were balls, and fielders who caught according to the rules of nondecimal systems.

There is something about Ron Darling as a half-Chinese, half-Irish pitcher from Hawaii that is both nineteenth-century and indigenous. Modern baseball may cheapen its own currency through its concupiscence and self-promotion, but the overdrop of history is still there and gives it the texture that the media then hammers out into its own hysterical metal. Myths may be a threatened resource in 1984, but they have not yet faded or vitiated entirely. The pretense of empty records and fake history is sustained latently by the old fields and decades of grassroots players who carried out this game.

Debra Heimerdinger, a freelance photographer, shot a whole portfolio of odd moments between plays and before games, unfamiliar images of players on the field, their gloves and bats, loose balls, awkward stretches, nonfluid motion at the core of a pitcher's delivery, a forgotten dangling hand after a completed play. We published them as a book called *Waiting Game: Photographs of the Oakland A's*—baseball between and outside camera clichés.

She sent a finished copy to the Oakland Coliseum, and an infuriated Sandy Alderson had her press pass taken away and tried to ban the book because it seemed to him an unflattering portrait of the team he was trying to sell.* She had represented his product as drab, action-less, dreamlike, but real—and management only wanted to see a designer jeans ad: Rickey Henderson in a cloud of dust, the umpire's arms outstretched. *Safe!*

Yet for all the great players and the cumulative intensity of the pennant race, there are billions more instants of hollow repose, of day-dreaming out from the game, and of gods battering away at the stale repetitious images through the irresistible force of their archetypes.

As I keep intuiting, the confusion of public and private here is a fundamental confusion of *our* identity with *their* identities, and underlying that is the almost epochal displacement of our compassion for each other, our failure of community and sanctuary.

When I suddenly recognize a ballplayer's humanity, it is like finding my connection to the root and, yes, it is uplifting. But then I have to go toward embracing that humanity in everyone, I tell myself, not just fame and not just the bias of my own team. The Dalai Lama doesn't root for the Tibetan Guerrillas exactly. The Pope can't be a Yankee fan.

We are demoralized by news of famine in Africa and slaughter of boat people at sea by Asian pirates. We hear about new brutalities and abuses of the innocent every day. In the process of celebrity adulation we are corroding our authentic emotions for each other and our ethics as well. We have turned the possibility for true comradeship and empa-thy, real shamans and warriors, into star-creation and hero-worship. The entertainment industry and media have exploited our weakness into its own billion-dollar empire, converting our guilt into a collec-tive neurosis. Instead of rooting for life on Earth, we root for teams. Instead of looking for humanity in everyone, we seek it in these play-ers because they are already universalized and particular, and it is eas-

---

*That was said between the lines; his outward excuse was trademark violation.

ier to serve their public personae than the terrifying blank wall of tens of thousands of starving Ethiopians.

This is a dangerous lapse in modern life, and its consequences are not determined because we do not know yet what will be required of us in this century or the next. Don't think for a moment that the Soviets have avoided it because they are ideologically non-capitalistic. Even as they suppress the cult of personality, they manufacture Olympic athletes, generals, and astronauts, and scorn the black and Latino masses they feed with arms.

The result is an undiagnosed but profound and hollow cavity in the clubhouse and in the game itself, a loneliness in the midst of crowds. I can feel it, and I know I have been averting it, in fact just about my whole life, and I will evade it again.

A pennant can still bring a wave of euphoria to a city, but it would take the spirit of a Papago ballgame to nurse that fire through the great winter and transform it into a new harvest of brotherhood and sisterhood in the spring. Until then, we must make do with what we have, Ron Darling, Hubie Brooks, Keith Hernandez, and the boys.

7.

Brad Wellman's two-run homer off Jesse Orosco in the ninth inning of the first game of the Sunday doubleheader was a turning point in the Mets' season. It broke the momentum that had brought them to within a game and a half of the Cubs. During the subsequent week they lost twice in San Diego and returned home on Friday to play a doubleheader against the Giants. San Francisco came back from a five-run deficit in the first game and won two more before they were finally halted on Sunday (Brent Gaff going most of the game in relief and Kelvin Chapman hitting a grand slam).

This set the distance between the Mets and the Cubs at roughly where it would land despite a roller-coaster of subsequent rallies and fades by both teams: six games. After those eight losses in ten tries the Mets put on their last great surge of the pennant race. The Sunday win was followed by a sweep of three close games from the Dodgers and then four out of five in three days from the San Diego Padres over the weekend.

This Mets revival at the end of August had all the makings of the gods of '69, but the Cubs had the curse of '69 driving them, its powerful counter-hex making them virtually impregnable. If the Cubbies hadn't been flying too, the Mets would have been back at their heels, ready for another miracle. But, in the greater skirmish of tribal magic and team totems, the zodiac was on the Cubs' side this time. If Don Juan Matus could come to Los Angeles in 1980 disguised as a plump young Yaqui pitcher (to tease Carlos and answer Tommy Lasorda's prayers to the Big Dodger in the Sky), then the ghosts of the '69 Cubs, led by Ron Santo and Leo Durocher, could visit 1984 as Odin, a thunderbolt-bearer named Rick Sutcliffe who materialized in mid-season to lead them to the Eastern Championship.

That the Mets had their own ancestral spirits and magic at work was evident on September 1 against the Padres. Having already split a doubleheader the day before and won the first game that day, Davey Johnson handed Calvin Schiraldi the ball for his first major-league start in the second tilt against the Padres' number-one pitcher, Eric Show, a self-declared right-wing ideologue. The Padres got to Schiraldi quickly and had a 5-1 lead in the bottom of the fifth. The Mets had no one on base, two out, and the pitcher due up when they sent out an old warrior, John Stearns, who had not (as per my earlier ill-advised queries of Davey Johnson) been to bat in over two years because of injuries.

In an interview after the game Stearns said that, although he had envisioned that moment hundreds of times over the period of exile, he was tranquil, almost without feeling at the plate; he did not even remember hitting the ball, but he stood on second base clapping his hands in triumph after lining a double up the left-field alley. Backman followed with an infield single. Herm Winningham, starting his first major-league game, stung a two-strike pitch to the opposite field and, after a couple of walks, Hubie Brooks cleared the bases with a shot off the base of the center-field wall. He was thrown out by twenty feet, trying for third, but the Mets were up 6-5 and went on to clinch the game. John Stearns' first at-bat in two years had sparked five two-out runs.

The next day, in a tightly played 2-2 game that went into extra innings, Hubie made a series of wonderful stops and throws from the strange shortstop position. He handled the pivot on a game-situation double-play—as Backman fielded and flipped to him crossing the bag—and turned it against a fast runner ("our whole season right there on that play," Keith Hernandez said later). It kept them in the game until they could outlast Goose Gossage, who labored five long innings—George Foster poling a two-out flare to right in the twelfth and Mookie Wilson racing home with the winning run.

The Mets and Cubs were now both white-hot and headed for a showdown. But the Mets were also ripe for ambush. Ever since Hernandez had beaten the Cardinals on the field in New York in July and referred to them as a second-division team, St. Louis played the Mets extremely tough, winning the last seven skirmishes between the clubs. The ballpark in St. Louis was just the right antidote for any Mets' magic: a shopping mall with pinball machines. The ball bounces off the hard rug, the Cardinals run the bases like flashing colored lights, the organ plays beer commercials and other junk-music jingles.

The Mets lost two in St. Louis and another in Pittsburgh before coming home to face the Cubs.

On Friday night, before a national-television audience, Dwight pitched a one-hitter, and the Mets prevailed 10-0, ending their own seven-game losing streak against their rivals. Although the pennant race was all but over with, Gooden's performance that evening, more than any other in the season, served to establish the 1984 Mets' renaissance in the imagination of fans across the country. He pitched a flawless game from a center of poise so striking that for one night he was the Natural, the child-man representing the 'hood, the hunter with the rock. Old baseball shined through media hyperbole. It was like pubescent Sam Cooke singing the stuffin' out of gospel, the Soul Stirrers harmonizing behind him. Doc was to follow this ballad with back-to-back sixteen-strikeout performances and close the season as the most dominating pitcher in baseball—a huge jump from the Triple-A World Series in Louisville. We were already gazing at 1985.

Rick Sutcliffe, the man of 1984, stopped the Mets just as cold the next night, adding a bomb of a double. Ron Darling set down the Cubs on Sunday, but the Mets lost three out of four to the Cardinals and Pirates again, this time at home, and then the first two over the next weekend in Chicago. When Bruce Berenyi finally two-hit the Cubs on Sunday, it was the first victory for the Mets at Wrigley all season.

The ghosts of Chicago '69 had seized their opportunity for revenge. It's too bad they waited only fifteen years; they could as easily have waited 150 or 1500.

The Sunday win broke the spell and also set the Cubs into their one big losing streak of the season. But Gooden blew his second sixteen-strikeout game on a balk in Philadelphia, and it wasn't until the following weekend against Montreal in New York that the Mets began to make up any ground: they swept back-to-back series against the Expos and Phillies but, as Gooden beat the Expos on Sunday, the Cubs were sweeping the Cardinals, setting up their pennant-clincher on Monday night. Cub fans, their friends, and bandwagon-jumpers swarmed the satellite-dish club on those final days, some of them celebrating after as many as thirty years of personal disappointment and chagrin. Now it was us on the outside, only imagining Jesse Orosco coming in from the bullpen to face Kirk Gibson, Darryl Strawberry going up to bat against Jack Morris.

At season's end, the pleasure was in watching Winningham, Christensen, Beane, Mitchell, and Gibbons on the Mets, though it was with the sadness of knowing that the games were dwindling down to the finale, the equinox approaching winter and the death of the 1984 Mets. The season would end in sacrifice and silence (if not defeat). The ceremony was over, its symbols sown. The Mets had won back their dignity, their fans, and their destiny; no more could modestly be asked for.

The players must go home, live, dream, change, survive, and come back to the myth, which will also change with the constellations of the night sky. They will continue to evolve during the winter, privately, as whoever they were, but the characters they played will go into hibernation, the implements of baseball stored—and the Northern Hemisphere itself, the civilized and developed world, will turn through another dangerous winter before the props are unpacked in Florida in the spring.

The game as myth repeats its themes: new players arise in preexisting roles, even as Osiris was transformed into Horus, and Mars replaced Ares. On the 1984 Mets Darryl Strawberry played Darryl Strawberry, not as olympically as the media and fans demanded him to play it—he wasn't the second coming of Henry Aaron or even Richie Allen—but he did it well and transformed the role. Hubie Brooks developed the character of Hubie Brooks. Ed Lynch had trouble performing his character, so his status in the game is in jeopardy. There is no way to explain why one season Danny Heep executes four pinch homers, the next season none. There is no way to foresee the nova-like ascension of a young character played by Dwight Gooden. For years to come, ghosts of Herb Score and James Rodney Richard will haunt this actor until he plays past them, pennant by pennant. And there is no way to know what surprising figures will bumble onto stage next year like extras from *Godot*.

In the meantime the collective mythical being constituted by the Mets rests at a turning-point moment in its evolution, with the possibility of making something more enduring than '69. To that end Herm Winningham, Randy Myers, Barry Lyons, Kyle Hartshorn, and Stanley Jefferson wait in the wings.

But when Herm Winningham flies out to end the season, this is the moment of the longest wait till the next game. There is an unexplored sorrow in this, but it is the way everything is: darkness stretches between night and morning, consciousness and unconsciousness; it fills the interstellar space between epochs, suns, and lives. Baseball is wonderfully ordinary and we don't usually think about it in cosmic terms. We want its gentle thread of continuity waiting for us again in some form next spring.

If life on Earth survives, the players will be reincarnated by their ka-souls on sunny practice diamonds and, within this episode of American life, the ceremony will go on.

8.

Postscript: December 10, 1984

The months following the season brought little fresh baseball except for the assembling of our new North Atlantic Books anthology, *The Temple of Baseball*.

"You should talk to Steve Boros," novelist Barry Gifford told me in late October. "He and I have been discussing things, and I think he might have something for your book."

So I dropped a postcard to the recently fired A's manager, and he called me a few days later and suggested a meeting time and place: Friday, 2:00, November 9, Cody's Bookstore.

That afternoon Miranda and I trekked up to Telegraph, purchasing giant cookies on the way. Steve arrived with his wife and kids, and they broke off to go Christmas shopping while we headed back to our house. He was curious to see the East Bay Satellite Baseball TV Club, so we went right down the driveway to the garage, where Robin met us. In the winter the space was barely habitable: a dank outdoor room with towels over the receiver and dish drive, roof tar all over the ceiling failing to stop the leaks (hence, plenty of damp spots on the stone floor). "Here's your temple of baseball," Steve joked, as he gazed at the pictures and the schedules of a season past. "I like the green paint."

That afternoon we began an interview and also talked about the Mets, especially Jeff Bettendorf (whom he had managed earlier in the season when both were with the A's) and Bruce Berenyi ("you've got scouts combing the bushes all over America just trying to find big strong kids with his kind of arm"). I also recalled Steve's days as a Tiger third baseman during the 1961 pennant race against Johnny Blanchard, Roger Maris, and the Yankees, and he was pleased I knew that piece of his history.

"I followed those games from summer camp, rooted against you, I'm afraid."

"It hardly matters now who won. We played the game, right?"

I showed him the current issue of *Inside Pitch* in which Steve Schryver, the Mets' minor-league director, had said: "When someone asks them where they learned to play ball, you hope they'll say it was back when I was at Lynchburg or Columbia."

His response: "That's the kind of tradition I want to develop too."

Steve was warm and expansive and, when he headed back up to Telegraph, Robin remarked, "Isn't it strange that we had to root against him last season so that now we can root for him?"

It would have been nice if he were moving on to the Mets, but his next job was assistant farm-system director for the Padres.

Robin and I kept checking the radio all that week of the winter meetings, and finally on Friday was it reported that the Mets had made a transaction with the Tigers (to be announced later). Robin passed the day nervously at school, but he could have saved expectations; we had already guessed it. When he got home and looked at me eagerly, I simply said, "We know the Mets too well."

"You mean it *was* Terrell for Howard Johnson?" I nodded.

On December 10 I was cooking dinner when the phone rang. It was the poet Tom Clark.

"Just wanted to know what you thought of the trade?"

"Which one?"

"Gary Carter."

I paused for a moment, and an old wave of apprehension passed through me. "Not to the Mets?"

"That's right."

"Oh no."

"You don't like it?"

"Well, for whom?"

"I think it's great. They're going for it all."

"For whom?"

"Do you care?"

"For whom?"

"Okay. Hubie Brooks. . . ."

I felt a sting of disbelief, as though Tom had told me that Hubie had been killed. "A guy named Youmans, you probably know who that is. Herm Winningham. Mike Fitzgerald."

I was speechless, stunned, weighing in my mind now whether such a thing was possible against the unlikelihood of Tom teasing me in this way. Finally I said, irrelevantly, "Youmans was the guy they were actually scouting when they found Gooden."

"Well, I'll let you go," Tom said. "You know, it's like being born."

Robin's vigilance was astute enough that he was already approaching me with a look of alarm. I told him the Mets players first to make it a little easier, but he was heartbroken. He just kept saying, "They couldn't . . ."

Maybe they couldn't. I called Stu. He hadn't heard of such a trade, and he warned me to hold everything because people had been telling him fake deals all week. He would call New York to make sure.

Two minutes later he was back on the phone. "It's for real. A blockbuster. Gary Carter for four players. I just don't know. I kind of wish they hadn't." Both of us had Hubie Brooks pencilled in as the shortstop on our 1985 Mets.

My feelings and thoughts were in a tumult. I kept picturing Hubie that first night in San Diego, Hubie in the locker room at Candlestick, then turning the double play against San Diego, interviewed by Ralph Kiner after the game.

I said angrily, "Well, we might as well go out and get Cal Ripkin, Jr., to play short and Jack Clark for right field. We'll move Strawberry to center, sign Jim Rice for left. We'll put an All-Star team out there and beat everyone."

"Yeah," said Robin. "And it won't be the Mets."

After dinner he went upstairs and took a shower. But instead of putting his Met cap over his wet hair, a custom of his, he was discovered sitting reading on the floor in his room with a much darker blue cap on, an unfamiliar white-outlined gold serif M on its front.

"What is that?" Lindy exclaimed.

It was Margarita's Mexican Lunch, the cap of the Berkeley softball team that slugger Bob Pearce had given me in honor of my piece on him. I hadn't seen it for over a year.

"I'm in protest," Robin announced.

Later that night Steve Boros called to console me, but I told him about the cap and suggested that Robin was the one who really needed consoling.

"You'll get over it," Steve told him. "That's the way baseball is these days. Trades are cold. You'll get that Mets cap down off the shelf before the spring and, if you don't—well, I've got a Padres one for you."

"Look at it this way," I said, as I tucked Robin into bed, "sometimes the world is stranger than you can imagine, and that means more than the ways in which it disappoints you. What would you have thought if I told you at the beginning of the season that Hubie Brooks would have a great year, finish the season as the Met shortstop, get traded to the Expos, and that Steve Boros would call and console you?"

He laughed and then turned over to sleep.

By the next evening I found that Stu had made the adjustment quickly: "What a trade! When I came in to work this morning you should have seen the long looks on those Cub fans. They couldn't face me. 'Earliest clinching of a pennant,' I told them. 'December 10.' Then I said: 'That sound you heard yesterday was Dallas Green's jaw when he got the news. Then he called Rick Sutcliffe and told him—'Hey, forget it. We can finish second without you.'"

Robin and I would never make that adjustment. The Mets team we cared about, that began on a night in San Diego years ago, was extinct; it would never play in a World Series—not when Gary Carter was facilely substituted for Hubie Brooks. If this group of Mets won the division, we would root for them of course, all the way there and all the way through the post-season, but something would be missing. It would be a Faustian victory.

"I didn't realize how perfect it was," Robin said, "how they represented everything right. They were the perfect team for us. I didn't appreciate it until it was over."

By next season, yes, it will almost be forgotten. Teams, just like people, die a little bit at a time—and by the time you win, it's probably too late, at least in this existence.

I had tricked myself into thinking the Mets were different, but how could they be? They were the Yankees' shadow and just another powerhouse in the white macho Eastern Division.

"Poor Hubie," said Robin.

HUBIE BROOKS OF

TIDES

The September-October 1973 Mets

(from *The Slag of Creation*)
Year of Writing: 1973

1.

There are so many songs, so many singers, so much has been lost already, and these few records are what I hold onto, from all I once had—their grooves awakening to the needle, always. Playing 45s on a late summer evening—Gene McDaniels singing: "If I Were a Tower of Strength"; Robin, holding "blanket" and sucking his thumb, suddenly perks up: "He says, 'I don't like you. I don't need you. I don't want you.' And he goes out the door. He's *mean!*"

I realize that he can hear the words, and they mean something different to him, as they will continue to, until the end.

I'm not a teenager anymore.

Lindy is sitting by us on the couch, blue jeans, no socks, tapping rhythm, pregnant.

The songs are the same, but we are changed, deflected from them so that their intensity is greater. Sam the Sham, the Pharaohs: *"Hey there Little Red Riding Hood,/You sure are looking good...."* Al Wilson and *"You knew damn well I was a snake/Before you took me in...."*; The Four Seasons: *"Big Girls Don't Cry...."*; Jimmy Rodgers: *"Tell'im what the*

Wizard said," then *"people talking/with-out speak-ing; it's all so beautiful!;* and *I know I'm gonna miss you/for a long long time."*

Landscapes flicker and merge, a holograph in purples and violets, responding like a sine wave with an alpha tailwind, as in an old comic book of Mars. The orchestra has horns, woodwinds, and pianos, the crowd is dressed for the symphony, but instead of sound, colored notes come out of their instruments and blend in the air.

All of this was begun by an invasion of "The Monster Mash" from CHUM (Toronto), interfering with the final inning of the Mets' 1-0 win over San Francisco on WHN (New York), both 1050 AM: *"It's a grave-yard smash . . . Bonds dives—can't come up with it . . . Boswell rounds third . . . the winning run . . . , it's the Monster Mash."* At first damning the loss of signal, I realize that I can embrace both . . . and I leap from the game to the turntable and put on Del Shannon *("And I wonder/I why why why why wonder. . . .").* Then we sit there, the two of us, plus child, plus child in embryo, in an unpredictable lesion of creation:

"My little runaway,/My run run run run runaway. . . ."

2.

Cold winds evacuate the fire, summer heat vanishing through the starry sky. Each morning the thermostat registers a few degrees less until, at 61, the first flush of hot air fills the pipes, and the metals of the furnace stir on signal from the diode, breathed through our memory of when the hulk was last filled, in June says the postmark in my winter coat, as I reach into the pockets as though someone else's.

This is the time, as summer ends, of the quiet rundown of the base-ball season. I sit in the living room with the ballgame, rooting gently for a few Met wins while attending to September rookies in the line-up—a sense of autumn in the swift breeze and roused branches. . . .

Suddenly, beginning with the second game of a doubleheader in Montreal, everything changes. The Mets are still in last place, but they have won the game on absurdly daring base-running and a diving catch of a bunt by Tug McGraw. It can be '69 again.

Part of me doesn't want to get into it; I am at peace with calm and cold September nights, orange trees, the rhythm of the game like the wind thru parchment. I don't want to break my hibernation, but I also don't want to betray the tension and heat that underlies the listening, that kept the game alive during fallow years, all the way back to 1952 when it began.

I'm here, hovering in anticipation, hoping for an early lead, after which I will settle back into reading *Don Quixote*, as long as the Mets hold it, until the crush of the late innings. Spanish medievalism and windmills, a disappointment of dragons and crusading armies, the dangerous reversal of sign and object.

There are no other fans. People go about their lives in northern Vermont far from the crush and ceremony of the city. I listen thru the night air, the game half blotted out by the Toronto rock station, warbling between a faint distortion of the announcer's voice and a billow of clarity that seems to be right in the room as though the broadcast tower were out on Route 2 by the Barre skating rink.

In the daytime, reception is impossible; a New Hampshire station overrides it with banal jingles. But how is what I want to hear not equally banal? Its grace becomes (like the signal) something that I can barely make out, the score an obscure but cogent message, a momentary link between Plainfield and New York. Reversal of sign and object again.

If I'm moved by something, it's not baseball, but the game brings me there without explanation. If I were in the city, the Mets would be sociological space, a frolic of fans, a dance of urban totems. Here, in this house, in my remote life, able to let it fall hundreds of miles away with the click of the dial, it is a channel, a tuning in—airwaves more than baseball.

The code pours out of the radio, and I join in, yelling and clapping, commanding the whole downstairs like a revival meeting.

"It's like a gift," Lindy says, as vibes dance thru the house. "You have something none of the rest of us can have."

Brief hiatus when the Pirates win a big Monday night game after knocking out Seaver. The next night maybe it's over; the Pirates have a two-run lead in the ninth. Then Beauchamp pinch-hits successfully and Millan triples, tying run on third. Tense two-strike pitch to Hodges, a sub-.200 catcher in the Texas League, brought up to fill in for injured players—he doesn't strike out; he *singles*. This is like nothing else! A few more base-runners, then Hahn is up, a 3-2 count, and I yell to no one in particular, "This may be the pitch of the season," Hahn himself a refugee from Tidewater when the Mets ran out of outfielders. Line drive over short, two more runs.

They barely hold it thru the bottom of the ninth. Apodaca makes his major-league debut, called from his home in California after the minor-league season; he's wild. Capra replaces him; it's a one-run lead, bases loaded. Sanguillen pops up a 3-1 pitch. You can listen forever to games, but this is what you wait for, and you can't be deaf when it's happening

It's a month-long climb from last to first. My dreams are filled with the halved and broken names of the Mets' pitching rotation, Soosman and Keaver, as old high-school friends wander thru abandoned stadiums and subway stations; a hypnogogic motif wedged between dreams of how George Stone, the fourth man in the rotation, is twelve and three, imagined again and again thru the trade in which the Mets got him and Millan from the Braves.

The next night in New York, the Pirate-Met battle continues. Cleon settles matters with his second home run of the game. A night later they find themselves a run down in the bottom of the ninth, two out and a man on first. Duffy Dyer, without a hit in a month and without an RBI most of the season, lines the ball up against the wall, and the tying run races in.

Later, in extra innings, with Sadecki mowing them down like clockwork, the Pirates suddenly get a two-out baserunner and follow it with a line drive by one of their own rookies, Dave Augustine. It sounds as though it's going to go over the fence, but the ball lands on the top of the railing, bounces back into the hands of Cleon, and he throws out the runner at home. The next day thousands of New Yorkers claim it was *their* psi-waves that stopped its flight. I see the play on the news that night and realize that *something* must have gotten in the way. That ball was a game-winning home run before it hit an invisible barrier.

Bottom of that inning, two strikes on him like before, Hodges outbattles Giusti again and drives in the winning run.

This is too good to be true; they're not only winning, the rhythm is fantastic, a three-week wipeout high. They're doing it in a run of one-in-a-billion cards, which is the way a statistical madhouse like baseball works. Tug McGraw chanting "You gotta believe!" has become the same as David Bowie's "And I want to live!" Against nuclear war, against Vietnam armies, against corrupt politicians and depletion of natural resources, against the coming dark ages, against the romantic orgy and its biofeedback machine: *I want to live!*

The next night Seaver and the Mets and a full house at Shea, and me in Vermont, blow them right out of the ballpark. The Mets are in first place! The following afternoon they find themselves on national TV, the first time the game comes as a visual rather than cosmic sound. In some ways it's not as good. Kubek and Gowdy try to own the phenomenon, but they're latecomers, as usual, to every set, too phony-dramatic, missing the subtle and exquisite. Still it's a joy to see the team. Garrett homers and Matlack shuts out the Cardinals—they hold first place, honoring the adage: it's one thing to get there, another. . . .

And it must be a dance (though I can't hear the music), and since I can't dance slower it must be faster, faster, until it ends. Is this what it's like? Is this what I want it to be like?

3.

A few days later David* and I take the car up East Hill to the top, hoping to pick up the Mets from across the mountains, from Chicago where they are trying to hold on. There is nothing but static as we trail dirt road into dirt road. Leaves glow yellow and red; the brilliance of Earth, blue the color of, as light pours from the hills; the eroded colors, the mountains in faint clinging intelligence against the hierarchy of creation itself. Then a sliver of baseball clarity from the decay of language in atmospheric radiation, a filament of intelligent life on the planet.

We come back down with the win, anticlimactic beyond any game, in the magnificence of the interference and the staggered, tilted geography in which it happens, the oblivious farms adding to the galactic drama, wagons heaped high with hay.

The rain falls, the leaves grow more brilliant before fading; the sky dwindles, and winter appears on the horizon. The Monday after the season should be over, the last game is played in equally rainy Chicago. The stray tabby is sick, so we take it to the vet. In the center of Barre, daytime reception improves to unprecedented clarity, so Lindy and Robin check out the thrift shop while I drive around town looking for the optimum position, settling finally on the Grand Union parking lot.

The season ends not in New York City, where the change in mood and energy might be palpable, but thru a modulated din, in a granite town, where a continuously-operating machine by the railroad tracks seems to boost reception.

The skyline is old and white; the stores are still dressed in 1950s façades. Customers, elderly, from a granite renaissance long past, leave the Grand Union with their bags—two outs to go. Traffic pours down the concourse, past the construction, where a few people stand watching because a whole building is being leveled. School children rush

---

*Writer friend David Wilk.

thru streets like mercury, past the old folks sitting on the benches holding their canes—one out to go.

The Mets struggle from a 5-0 lead to win 6-4 and, with the game,
the Eastern Division of the National League.

There is no response in Barre. Like Cocteau's Orpheus, I sit alone
in the car dialed into another world.

We leave town with second-hand maternity clothes, two toy trucks,
and three vanilla ice cream cones. We sit in the three-dimensional sun
outside our house while a measureless calm rises thru the maples to
the sky.

4.

Game Seven of the World Series against the A's

In the center of Plainfield it is like an old warehouse, the cold October sun silent in the almost-bare trees. The big kids sit on the stone
wall by the church, their legs kicking, their hotrods revved, talking
and silent before the absolute winter.

The image sits there too, a boulder inert and frozen, in my head the
fire of the last World Series game, about to begin on TV, from childhood October glory, flames illusorily blown into the city of my youth,
this last game a memory before the winter of the outermost declivity
of my life. A false excitement time will vitiate, if not my body, my
bones, and bring me back as a frog, in the brutal calm condition, set, in
a single pale sun, kin to Ice Age darkness, against the stone wall, numb
to the senses that brought them into being, that they will bring themselves into being, again and again.

This is an omen of what my heart is made of and how empty this if
I pursue it, a cold and profound pre-game warning, the graveyard on
the hill above, where the wind blows.

Mets at Parc Jarry, July 5, 1973

Year of Writing: 1973

In Parc Jarry I feel the yearning for something lost. Before baseball. Before even childhood. Because baseball, I have abandoned, and reclaimed, abandoned and reclaimed so many times, it is both the gaiety of the life I have not lived and the opiate, along with others, that keeps me from living it.

But Jarry is the old forgotten baseball innocence, Montreal itself the Norte American city that never was, at least not in the U.S. where the game was invented and the big leagues are now the whole global show. The President of which is El Presidente of the world. Behind which Montreal lingers in the northern sun-splash like an aging monk, lingers at a different archaeological stratum. Though it has its plazas and ceremonial architecture. Squares with fountains and cubic institutional mass. And gardens. And narrow irregular streets. *Vieux Montréal.*

The arc lights are brilliant, gems of the modern century; they turn the field of late afternoon from a dwindling arena of shadows into a proscenium. Grass and sod shine, and the players awake from afternoon naps and loosen their reptilian limbs. The light is new each moment, as if peeling of the gem reveals only a more precise and atomic stone within.

Only once, a flutter, does the power fail in the hot dormant evening. The stage is stricken like a ghost; the players begin to awake with a start; then the circuits revive and tragedy is postponed.

The day begins in the early morning in Plainfield, the tickets from my desk drawer: July 5, *Les Expos*. I run Robbie up the hill to Center School, and we launch out in the station wagon, through the farmlands of northern Vermont, sea-blue forever skies, interstate into southern Quebec, egg and butter farmhouses, urban outskirts, onto St. Catherines, lunch at a Chinese restaurant.

Beneath a planetarium roof thick with stars, the wail of quasars. From Rue de Notre Dame to Eglise—churches, shops, endless parks and neighborhoods. We cross the Jacques Cartier Bridge to the aquarium. It is like walking through the Solar System illumined. Just as they hit the boundary, giant fish suspended beyond gravity whip their tails.

The Montreal airport is an insane international event. David arrives from the tailwind over the Atlantic as simply as from a teleportation tunnel. He is flying from "David Bowie's Last Concert," teenyboppers with sparkle and sequins on their faces, to the French-American baseball game in post-Northern Vermont. He brings us a poster of Bowie, one leg bare, the opposite arm bare, man and woman both, in a hermaphroditic spacesuit, a Flash Gordon belt of lightning across his chest.

We have beers and roast-beef sandwiches in Dominion Square by the fountain. Heavy talk of imperial America, England, Canada, Watergate, North Carolina farms David would like to buy, Vermont floods. Outer space or world culture?

"This is as good as London," David smiles, leaving his fat shillings as a tip for the waitress he has charmed by his bad French of which I am jealous.

Colored flags dance out an international semaphore we find again on Laurentian as we head for Jarry thru the Hebrew neighborhood, kosher butchers, Semitic alphabets; then Greek letters, Italian names, until the city breaks down into parks and pasture.

Most of the people are not there for *Les Expos* but to play on their own amateur diamonds and tennis courts, or to walk with one another: children and baby carriages. The stadium sits in the center of this temple complex—no wonder they still play the old game.

The sun sets and the sandlot fields pass into night (except for one with the small light towers). I have the sense that the players and strollers on those fields will wander into the bleachers, but they don't. A crowd sweeps away the extras.

Inside, Lindy asks loudly why I switched from being a Yankee to a Met fan.

"If this were Chicago," I yell back, "you'd have just gotten us all killed."

CBC is there with its twisted pack of electric lines and plugs, but they seem a minor occasion, like assigning a single crew to a street riot. Perhaps the game is being sent to the bars of uptown, downtown, midtown, and suburbia, to Joel Oppenheimer and Fielding Dawson at Max's Kansas City. But they know nothing of this gentle evening scene and the shouts of the kids in the fields beyond, how the blue-white strobes of Jarry light the whole plaza, while the Mets, despite their losing streak, despite the nineteen runs given up by pitching staff two nights ago, despite blowing Seaver's 5-0 lead the night before, goof and jive about the field. Only poor Yogi is solemn, but he's getting paid for that.

Jim Fregosi plays first base with exaggerated dance steps; then he pitches batting practice with elaborate arm motions and dramatic facial gestures, putting his hand on his hat, lifting one leg, and yelping every time a ball is hit out, kissing the baseball every now and then before he tosses it up, boogying to the organ music I have found so irritating on the radio, except that here people are doing little jigs in the aisles.

The sense of drama is gone; the Mets are not going to win anything; they are out of the race. So it is just baseball, and they are men playing it, despite and because of the intricate system of drafts, minor leagues, waivers, and trades that has gathered them here. They are guys with a job, which, for their fans, may be everything. But *they* did not invent baseball. The Cooperstown-style history they make, imprecisely called their "immortality" (which is true for each play and not just Henry Aaron's home runs), is overwhelmed by the job of living and being on time.

Teddy Martinez fields fifty balls at short that will never be assists. Wayne Garrett smashes a few light bulbs with a line drive against the scoreboard, causing Jim Fregosi, who has lost two infield jobs to him, to prance wildly. This is Montreal, not Shea, and they are playing the same game the kids are playing on the Algonquian fields around them. The condition is early Norte Americano, the real Cooper's town: sand-lot America, Frontenac's Kebec. Long before the coaches arrived with their stopwatches and pep pills and machine-drilled cadres and base-ball academies.

The old city has not been lost, and the new city has not yet been born.

Buzz Capra, who has lost three games on home runs this week, is juggling baseballs with Harry Parker. Jim Gosger and Don Hahn are telling jokes. Jim McAndrew, last man on the staff, is doing even fancier juggling tricks while a cluster of fans applaud.

The Mets are condemned to New York and the Big Time and those intense sports writers who follow them like a summit conference. The scribes who hooked me on it back when I was a kid.

Any way you look at it, it's a matter of attention. The global problems are too many and too complex to have any bearing. The farmers will never get back the money from the floods; the government will go deeper into debt; the victims of violent crimes will be paid only in precious karma. None of these, or the wind, will appear in the line scores. The trees and clouds stand in material proof of another energy, of a stasis that overrides this one. The farmers do not care; their tax relief is problematic, their lives short like baseball seasons. Our lives are just as brief.

The ecstasy of '69 is still palpable, clam-digging for dinner while the Mets were winning the pennant, ocean waves and early stars.

It is as though we are doomed to make the wrong things serious, for reasons even Galileo suspected as he weighed the motions of moons in times of political crisis. Psychology and physics are both physics.

George McDougall, the madman down the hall from me in college, said many times, "I don't go to games to enjoy them. I go to see my team win. Then I enjoy it."

Suddenly for me it's not true, and I feel cheated by the years I have put in on pennant races and standings. Part of it is sour grapes, with the Mets in last and going nowhere (George's Cubs are back in first, though George has moved to Puerto Rico, out of listening range, in pursuit of a career in politics). Part of it is the wish to be free at last, to know where and why the urgency goes. I reach into twilight and feel only a hollow behind the life, the silence of everything that rides on meaning. I wonder: "Will this stay, or will this move too?"

Music enters the sky, the air darkening and heavy clouds gathering beyond the bleachers, as the stands fill with bilingual chatter, and jets operate between Dorval and Europe, above the ceremony.

Canada has its own preoccupations, like the number of French players you can have on a hockey team and still win, the pronunciation of American and Latin ballplayers ("John Boccccaaa-belllll-aaaa!"). There is a subtle spoof on the whole thing, i.e., Gene Mauch's sense of incredible self-importance as he manages *Les Expos*, which the fans seem to mock by joining in his cause with a fierce rooting both sincere and ironical.

When the North American corporations take over, a lot of this will be blown on out. Already the PR men have dressed the usherettes in bright colors and short skirts. They plan a domed stadium. Already this has been touched by the banality of Mr. Curt Gowdy and others who sell baseball and the American way of life on every pitch. I recall the more perfect voice of Mel Allen, who loved and understood this game and was fired after the Yankees' glory years, for mediocre salesmen who hawked it without gravitas or history.

The darkening sky grows ominous: dark purples and violets thrown out of twilight with long streaks of brown, the sun setting in brilliant orange over third base, right in our eyes, while the Expos take batting and infield practice and the kids in the bleachers scream. George Theodore, the Stork, looking like a classic hippie with his big glasses, signs autographs behind the Mets' dugout. A father with his young son sitting in front of us is howling at the players already; he probably can be heard on the other side of the ballpark.

Now is game time, but the game doesn't begin right away. The Montreal Commission of Public Transportation, represented by its officials in a green bus, drives down the right-field line and arrives at home plate to present an award to its favorite Expo, who turns out to be Bob Bailey. He comes out of the dugout and receives a statue entitled "Human Activity" by a well-known local sculptor. It is presented to him by the leading official in both French and English; then he poses for the photographers with the artifact, the bus, the lot of them. It's like a New Wave movie on the American star in Francophile Canada.

The American National Anthem is played, and an American couple on vacation in Province Quebec, sitting a row behind us, sings it very loud. I'm mum, waiting for it to pass. The Canadian Anthem follows, a more haunting and ancient tune, reminiscent of beaver and kangaroo totems, England in Canada, Australia, Hong Kong, E.M. Forster in India looking for Stonehenge. Sub-Arctic caribou hunters are in my head, the Abenaki, and Champlain himself, hero of this riff, joined in harlequin suit to David Bowie and Wayne Garrett, here in the forgotten republic of the North Atlantic, of the cod and the lobster, quahog and larch—the fans singing, some in French, some in Anglais, sun halfway down, its colors rubedo, tribal, sub-incisionary.

A cloudburst in the bottom of the first gives *Les Expos* three runs when Wayne Garrett heaves a wet ball into the Met dugout and, after a fifteen-minute delay and the tarpaulin, rain still mixed with moths in the lights, Jon Matlack grooves one to Bob Bailey. Fans pound the metal benches into submission.

The game is one-sided; the Expos have base runners in every inning; the Mets go quickly. Only a running catch by Willie Mays in deep centerfield keeps the score close. After a couple of innings the Mets begin getting base runners. Millan pokes a single every time he's up, but no runs score until Rusty Staub, playing before the fans that named him Le Grand Orange, first baseball hero of this city, shoots one out in right for a run.

All thru the early innings huge planes leave Montreal for Europe, Asia, and Africa: Irish and Italian airlines, BOAC, Air Canada, 747s low over this game in the wilderness of the body of light. It's not destination-Nebraska or Atlanta. It's Dublin, Rome, New Sydney, Zaire, the Indo-European natal culture, baseball cast against it as a single linguistic riddle in the global village, the voodoo church, the international city Montreal is, New York still is not. The exact and detailed baseball statistics sheathe, in general numerical seriousness, the import-export diaries of the world, the continual migrations. The jets are the outer determinants of the game, their wings lit, their position fixed as they approach and leave the earth beneath the clouds.

In the seventh inning the Mets load the bases on a pinch single and a couple of walks; Staub dumps a single into short center and, against the great relief pitcher, Mike Marshall, pinch-hitter Theodore hits the first offering softly through the left side; then a wild pitch; then Garrett singles in two more. Too little too late. But these are the first clean runs I have seen live in eleven years, absolute and tingling in the rain-cleared Quebec air.

Beating the crowd by half an inning, we rush thru the night, down the dark avenues counter Laurentian, back into the city, over the bridges, sleepily across rural Quebec, checked by a senile customs official, onto Vermont 89, Route 2, home, in the silence of the cosmic broadcast.

METS

CATCHER
JESSE GONDER

Mets-Cubs, September 15, 1971

(from *The Book of Being Born Again into the World*)
Year of Writing: 1971

Durocher starts Burt Hooton, just up from Tacoma, a couple of months out of college. It's late in a very bad year. Second game of a double-header. Mets lost the first one, 6-2, Koosman bombed out early. Capra makes his first big-league appearance, goes four strong innings: the Goat.

McGraw takes the mound for the nightcap, his first start in two years, and the last one was against the Cubs also I believe, back in early '69 when nobody knew what was going to happen, and it was just a matter of stopping a Chicago winning streak, holding the league together.

McGraw is hit hard—the Cubs get two runs early—but goes to his screwball and settles down. Meanwhile Hooton is striking out every-body, no hits, inning after inning, throwing what *The Sporting News* called a nickel curve, or "the thing," in its article on the Pacific Coast League two weeks ago when he fanned nineteen Eugene Emeralds, the most since 1905.

The game grows. Baseball crackles on the radio and is alive.

Warm Indian summer, moths at the window. No end, but no begin-ning either. To baseball, or history. One season after another. Last year the Cubs beat out the Mets for second place. This year the Mets folded in July.

Yet on this mid-September night a classic match emerges with no pennant at stake. Mets hitless to the seventh. First man goes out. Jorgensen lines a single to right; Singleton !boom! a home run to the opposite field: 2-2 tie. Beautiful. Don Rose pitching in his first major-league game. In September the whole extended Mets family plays. Rosters at forty: endless pinch-hitters, relief specialists. The manager becomes a virtuoso, a juggler of the future. Let's bring in everyone, all the kids, the '70s and the '80s, and throw zeroes at the Cubs till dawn. Let's stick it out till we learn who the Mets are, what baseball is. Let's win more than one game.

Rose is shaky but gets thru two innings, and that's what'll go in the box score forever.

From here, there is news of riots at Attica, the unknown ball-clubs and cities in this nation, obscurities we will hear from, that will decide everything, making up more than an underground geography or the slugging Tidewater Tides, to seize the Rockefellers and Oswalds and lay on them that beautiful spirit of negotiation: "We're here, you see: deal with us." Any way you slice it, it's life. The women on the outside are weeping for a time that's not yet born. The men who are not allowed to be men are on the inside managed by dwarves. Grown animals, herded out of history, return with a bang to where they always were.

And even then you knew you were looking at dead men. Old films of an episode concluded. With no uncertainty they would be shot with their hands up, the guards in the middle, useless pawns in a higher war.

You are watching dead men play this game, even while they are alive. You are watching the stars of the future. And the dark reptilian tragedy of the past.

How we'd like to smash Durocher one more time for good measure. A game to grow on. He sends up Billy Williams to hit against Frisella in the ninth, and Mr. Williams puts one out in right: 3-2. In the bottom half, John Milner, The Hammer, gets his first major-league hit, a single to right, the Mets' third. He's stranded on first.

The sun is passing thru the center of the Earth, from which: no messages yet, though we man the stations, no messages from *Mariner*, pulled into Mars orbit. And yet it is happening, the star and its planets passing thru a critical yet invisible transformation. The academic robes are on fire, the moths red with flame.

It's a slow death in autumn, George down the road hammering all night in moonlight the boards of his home, expanding on the concept of materialism, and he's one of the last, the metallic echo empty in the night air. There is no way out for him. He will die there.

Toward midnight, Maine time, the Giants and Dodgers will fight for an ancient pennant neither of them owns, far from New York, and even further from meaning, though to Hoyt Wilhelm, who has pitched on both sides, it is literal, coming back at fifty to throw these few last knuckleballs. In Maine, professional wrestling rules. Further to the north: the same, plus hockey and cock-fighting.

We could come back at another time, captain, but it wouldn't be the same.

Wayne Garrett Dream

(from *The Book of Being Born Again into the World*)
Year of Writing: 1971

Asleep.
I awake on a green field.
I am playing ball.
You have been reborn.
Where am I? Why can I still remember?
My other life. This one I am living.
You have been reborn.
The coach hits baseballs at me; I think they are too hard.
I dive to my left and right and somehow field them.
How can I? How can they expect me to play?
"He'll do," coach says. "He's getting better every day."
Words used by the Mets to describe Wayne Garrett before they
    drafted him.
The forest all around this field. I don't even know my name.
I don't want to play.

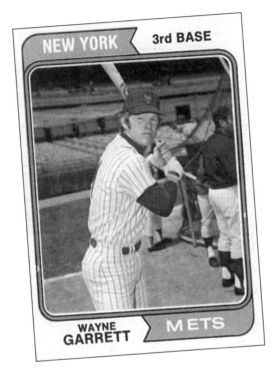

NEW YORK   3rd BASE

WAYNE
GARRETT   METS

Second Dream of Wayne Garrett

(from *The Slag of Creation*)
Year of Writing: 1974

John Todd of the New Alchemists, farmer, sailor, torch-bearer, is confused with Rusty Staub of the Mets—their blondness, their Montreal
roots. And Wayne Garrett, figure of an earlier dream, is found far from
baseball, on a commune tilling hay, fighting monocrop, bringing back
amaranths and wildmen and biodiversity. A solar cell atop a log fort
decodes the sun. The Mesolithic ice is melting. Windmills pump shit
from tilapia-filled ponds into greenhouses. Pelton wheels direct water
through snail- and algae-purified cisterns into yurts. Two pyramids
rest beneath a UFO charioteer on the horizon.

Wayne Garrett is Pico della Mirandola/Thoth or myself in the center of my dream, the railroad tracks out of Harlem and Manhattan
leading nowhere, civilization ended, no more scores, no more games.

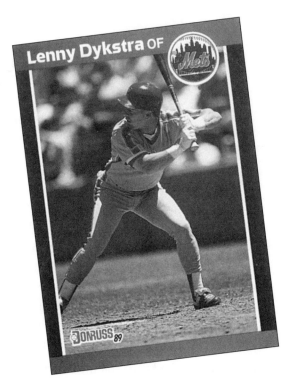

An Interlude During Which Enoch Stanley Sitting in His Rooms in Southwest Harbor Watches the Mayor of New York Get Dunked with Champagne by Rod Gaspar

(from *Book of the Cranberry Islands*)
Year of Writing: 1969

The nation returns to New York, and it is the end of the Middle Ages, as the Middle West, and the Green Bay Packers, and the St. Louis Cardinals, and the Cleveland Browns, and the Detroit Tigers, and with it an end to Southern California grape-growers and John Birchers and Ann-Margrets and Art Linkletters. It's the New York Mets and the New York Jets, invented in the early '60s, not the giant Yankees or the yankee New York Giants, but the children, the grandchildren, who are the grandfathers, the hidden black-power backstreets Iroquois-Indian New York.

It's the nation again looking back to the City, not for Babe Ruth and Joe DiMaggio and Marilyn Monroe, but Tom Seaver and Charles Olson finally winning those 25 games for the East Coast, taking the Cy Young away from Lyrical Poets, Organ Grinders, and Denny McClains ruling Detroit. And among retired ballplayers in L.A., it's Rod Kanehl and not Chuck Connors, cowboy in Africa, who's victorious at last. Rod Gaspar, reserve outfielder, called it in four straight, like Namath. And nothing scares your Vice President from Maryland, Mr. Spiro

Agnew, more than the New York Jets with long hair and Mr. Beaver Falls Alabam' Joe Namath knocking off the Baltimore Colts *in football,* e.g., a tribe of hippies, an entire underdog unregarded league wiping the establishment. And the New York Mets, at best a threat to the Republican Party in the '80s. . . . Hell, half the kids in the country throwing harder than Bob Feller are coming from Texas and Minnesota and Iowa to compete against the Baltimore Orioles and the U.S. Navy. Nothing scares Mr. Agnew like this, not the moratoriums, not SDS, not the Vietcong; he can handle those, he thinks, but here in baseball and football he is totally exposed, the world turning back to New York and cheering Jerry Koosman and Tommy Agee and Cleon—away from Dave McNally with his seventeen straight wins, and Earl Weaver, and Leo Durocher, that other fascist Napoleon from the '40s and '50s of Ron Santo, and Italian gangs beating up black kids.

Weeb Ewbank wants to put in the subs, but the players won't have it. "We're smashing the NFL!" they scream.

"What," says Weeb, "smashing the NFL? I used to win championships in the NFL."

But Bob Dylan could care less about who Pete Seeger used to pitch for or the Irish Rovers.

"Johnny Unitas looks silly with that crewcut," George Sauer says. "I mean, it's funny-looking. He should let his hair grow. He'd look good." That's how much vision has changed, pure blasphemy; shouldn't happen that Al Weis on successive days in Chicago hits home runs, angering the Cub announcers so much they yell down at the field, "You can get this guy out with a curve ball." Yeah, and with tear gas and napalm. That's what they used to think, in Berkeley, and North Vietnam, that they could smash a fourth-rate military power with the all-stars, beat the Russians in hockey, and deliver ultimate campaign speeches. But McNally didn't get him out with a curve ball—twice he didn't—once in the first win, once in the last, a guy with the lowest batting average on either team.

It's a new world age, so that Dylan just has to sing, not even "the times they are a-changing," and the Mayor of New York can get dunked with free publicity by Rod Gaspar. And Art Shamsky, and Jack DiLauro and Wayne Garrett, all of these players whose names are hidden behind the Bart Starrs and Jackie Kemps and Richard Nixons, with George Atlas buying space on the backs of comic books—and even David Eisenhower wears a Baltimore button, knowing on which side his own chances lie.

And they do it, like magic, right before the eyes of Mickey Mantle, Joe DiMag, Teddy Baseball, who know it can't be done, and Mrs. Babe Ruth, who knows it can. Mantle says he's even beginning to believe in astrology and the Age of Aquarius now, as Swoboda dives blindly in the path of the ball, and meets it, like his fate, and the country's—"the World Series of Injustice," Abbie Hoffman declares, but he's on the wrong side, in Chicago with a Cubs button because "C" stands for conspiracy too. We've outgrown the Chicago Cubs and the Chicago police, the Uncle Toms and the *Pueblo,* and Mayor Daly, and Ken Holtzman. The blacks in San Francisco want the Willie Mays Tot Lot changed to the Malcolm X Tot Lot, "'cause we don't groove on Willie Mays anymore."

The eyes of the nation are on New York, not Haight and the *Oracle,* but Max's farm in Bethel and the Woodstock Festival, and Tommy Agee grabbing the pellet in the tip of his glove as he runs into the wall. The concert in the mud has been coming for a long time—the Rolling Stones in the Labrador air, hidden beneath the obese bar graph of the middle class and the popular appeal of Lyndon Johnson and George Wallace and Vince Lombardi.

What do we do with the enigma of our heroes? Many of the New York Jets are from Texas, and Wayne Garrett was drafted from obscurity in the South to hit the Pennant-winning home run and still doesn't understand New York but thinks it's a great town to play ball in. And Emerson Boozer is back, and Matt Snell is back, and Nolan Ryan is back striking out the side with the bases loaded, his inevitable velocity feat. And Tug is a new man, greeting hippies in the stands, even after a stint in the Marines—and all hell is about to break loose in the Army high on pot.

Tom Seaver pats a fuming Leo Durocher on the fanny as Leo returns from his umpteenth spat with the umpires, tells him, "How about another Schlitz, Leo," the exact words we hear Leo say on Game of the Week, which won't even show the New York Mets all year even as the *Times* won't review Charles Olson and Robert Duncan—but this is the year of the *Maximus Poems,* and the return to origins. Robert Frost is dead because he never lived, Donald Hall reduced to offerings at Allen Ginsberg's altar—and Casey Stengel, the Charles Olson of the game if anyone is, is brought back to national glory, and no kidding, just like Charles at Berkeley, running "faster than Peter Rabbit," caucusing for President with Ginsberg his "Secretary of State for Love, baby" because "the cause is creation, and not in any big shit sense." It's Casey who's running tonight—along with W.C. Williams and old Ezra Pound—first manager of the team, who says, "The Mets have come on slow but fast."

And it's true. We all have.

And Gaspar will throw out the one runner he must. Shamsky will hit, as in the mythical past one night in Pittsburgh. The wheel turns, the possible returns. "To hell with liberalism," shouts the dean at Hampshire College. "Let's shoot for the noosphere!" And James Brown owns the world. Not Civil Rights but Stan Brakhage's *Dog Star Man,* Kenneth Anger's *Scorpio Rising,* an age when the Africans will arise from Zulu myths not ward politics. These are the perfect fixed points in the living room around which all others move. Namath hits Maynard; Swoboda drops a double inside the line.

Monday afternoon Jack DiLauro "strikes out" Koosman on the lawn at Gracie Mansion, Olson takes a job at Storrs, is "in like Flynn," the old president of Black Mountain returned.

And maybe Lindy and I, with *Io* and Robin, will return to Amherst where it began, and begin again without the old fight.

Bobby Pfeil is crying, after seven years in the minors. Wendell

Seavey is king of the lobstermen. It's a new age. It's gotta be. You can see it, Enoch. There's no one else alive. It's ourselves.

Endnote

This piece stands as a kind of spontaneous hymn, a 1969-version rap, written soon after the Mets' World Series victory. I have adjusted it so that its references are not completely obscure. However, for those who want to follow the "plot," these updated facts would help:

Charles Olson, author of *The Maximus Poems* and various other avant-garde works, represents the most radical branch of American poetry and cosmology, heir to a cutting-edge lineage blending Herman Melville, Ezra Pound, Alfred North Whitehead, and William Carlos Williams. An outsider to both academic and literary cabals, Olson nonetheless became president of Black Mountain College in North Carolina in the 1950s. A bureaucrat in Franklin Delano Roosevelt's Democratic Party before he was converted by the muse, he turned a legendary performance at the Berkeley Poetry Festival on July 23, 1965, into his own Presidential convention—Robert Duncan and Allen Ginsberg among those in his audience of poetic delegates. At the time of the Mets' World Series victory, Olson had just been hired with much hoopla to lecture at the University of Connecticut in Storrs; he died unexpectedly in 1970 after only a few months on the job.

While the Mets were playing the Orioles, I—more or less a disciple of Olson's then—was offered my first teaching job at Hampshire College, a new experimental school starting the following year in Amherst, Massachusetts. I had gone to college in the town of Amherst and, while battling the establishment there, managed to score funds to start the interdisciplinary journal *Io* with my wife-to-be, Lindy Hough. The "noosphere" line was uttered by Hampshire's Dean of Faculty in a manic phone call extending the offer. A few months later I was deemed too controversial and the invitation was rescinded. (The noosphere is the purported ring of consciousness surrounding the Earth's lithosphere, atmosphere, and biosphere, a term coined by French priest and anthropologist Pierre Teilhard de Chardin.)

I was just beginning fieldwork in Maine as the Mets finished the 1969 season. Enoch Stanley, a retired sea captain and fisherman, held court on a bench in Southwest Harbor while discoursing on his favorite team, the "Maine Mets." Wendell Seavey, the premier fisherman out of Thurston & Company in Bernard, Maine, was the "informant" on whose accounts I would base my PhD thesis. In 2003 and 2004 I collected Wendell's stories and published them under the title *Working the Sea*. Although his family had been fishing in the North Atlantic since the sixteenth century, gentrification and old age forced him off the sea and out of his niche, his home, and his community, and he is presently a greeter at Wal-Mart in suburban San Antonio, Texas. So much for the noosphere of 1969!

PS: That "Army high on pot" in '69 was publishing anti-war magazines and fragging officers by 1973.

The T'ai Chi/Baseball Star-Dance

(from *The Slag of Creation*)
Year of Writing: 1974

After a summer of no baseball at all, the poets from South London-derry come to town, rouse me, and in ten minutes I am patrolling the outfield with Mark the Snark while Shepherd Ogden in his West Virginia sweatshirt (name and number on it) smacks them out, high and tiny, into the sky. I start to do the usual baseball warm-ups, but I find myself in a combination of them and t'ai chi—needle at sea-bottom, cloudy hands. Is this what baseball was? All the time? Simply chi?

I am proud to stand with Shep and his brother Lash on this muddy field. The game comes alive, and I feel speed and breath. Unknown ancestors, human and animal, run with me. Dancing across intermontane flatlands mixed of rocks and mantle among centerfield weeds, I throw the forever-daylight back.

Chi, with its Asian and medicinal lineage, its surety of a life current in a body of veins and arteries, is a clue to the sequence of motions. Baseball isn't neutral either, not while I'm sensing, while I'm scooping, while I'm flung beyond myself, glove to webbing, stumbling as I snag the missile of disintegrating time, running it out of impossibly oceanic sky.

This is Vermont and October, and I have not honored how big the Indian games were on the Plains, their bumpiness and scars, not just the halcyon village green; how far-flung the spaces, the chase of sewn and bound objects of hide and beans, the flow and slink of deer and beaver and weasel, oscillating in the center of creature selves. I collide with the orb for the moment it is solid, the sun intense but fallen, the leaves red and ochre, the cold breath of those who have lived into the eleventh month of their thirtieth year.

Mark says, "When you catch the ball, it's like you're catching the whole world," and so opens for me a wonder I have suspected all along, greater than my knowledge, that I have fled, forever a child.

I love the field of play, its grassiness and that it is prairie; I love the ball as a pinpoint, connection, sting. There is rhythm and pellet and breath and deep awe of sky, where daylight is an inner phenomenal splay. I lie bare and arms open, before the powers of this creation.

And though the ball is not a planet, and a meteorite only in a lark, it is a sky totem for the way it loses itself in the blue and then comes down on the parabola I measure without thought, that precise occluded moment at which we come together and I "grasp sparrow's tail" of what I can yet become.

I am Mickey Mantle and Gil McDougald, Don Hahn and Teddy Martinez. I want scar-tissue to open, fear and desire to mesh, where autumn is more brilliant than left field, and the only spectator is fire in my blood, imaginary applause of iron running in my ears. Did I think I was playing some kind of adult game all those years, when I was dancing openly, making baseball liturgy and myth? In a few hours this gravity well will be night-blazed with history, strung out in eternity with the faces of those who would be our gods, as at twilight Mars sings, and a hundred stars appear sultry, subtly, plus the billion that do not, like the suffusion in liquid/life once was, coacervate warm on the dilute robes of the missing dakini.

All these things, stars and cells and deer and Pawnees and rough sewn objects, stand for creation. They make their way into my baseball piece always, by stealth and association, and leave me silent, a player on some remote field where the game has either ceased or not yet been invented, because everywhere else I am a historian, a gimp astronomer—here alone am I magician and prince.

Let the trees like giant men enter into their discourse with the stars.

We will stay small and shy and imperfect, for we are approximations anyway and, if we are babes, these are our rightful toys.

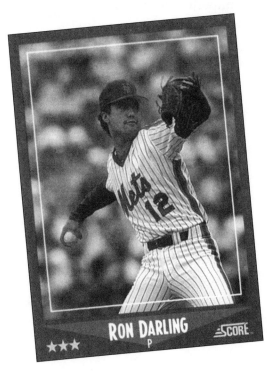

RON DARLING
P

GAME NO.   ENTER GATE

52   B

106   D   3

BOX   SEAT

PHILADELPHIA
AUG. 2,1979
THURS.8 05PM

FIELD BOX

ADMIT ONE - SUBJECT TO THE
CONDITIONS ON THE BACK HEREOF

"MR.MET"

RAINCHECK

6.00

The Ultimate Game

Year of Writing: 2006

My involvement in scores and seasons and the teams I follow (Mets, Jets, Nets, and Ottawa Senators) seems juvenile and inexplicable at times, and certainly a colossal waste of time. Yet I can't seem to stop. The games of the day draw me to them as surely as my writing or livelihood. They are part of my existence, a commitment and a practice, though I hardly understand why. Perhaps it is that the dramas, resolutions, and morning box scores give me a distraction from my own game, the one I have to play every moment without respite. I create a shadow version, a counterweight to my life.

To call the games "entertainment," as marketing people do, is to miss their function. Either that, or everything is, in one way or another, entertainment—entertainment or survival—to a cat or beetle too.

Yes, games are real and absolute, when they are happening, because during the ritual, the ritual is all. Yet winning or losing finally serves only to wind the clock, to keep time running. Once a season is done, it fades. The past is a hollow bucket, a rusty spoon. Championships—the ostensible aim—grow vapid and redundant over time. They lose their value, their gloss; their ecstasy fades, even before the tickertape falls.

The victories of the Yankees of my childhood, each one a cherished amulet back then, stand in opposition to the Yankees of the present era, against whom I staunchly root. Those old Andy Carey-Tony Kubek pinstripes were as essential to me as eating and sleeping at the time; their rosters and scores were part of my imagination and every breath

I took. Yet when I changed loyalties, the Yankees became colonial usurpers and their history the history of the empire. They were bullies, using moolah to entice players and assemble the rosters that meant so much to me during my childhood. Yet, despite present disillusion, the old victories can never be taken away. They're mine forever, too.

As much as I care while the spheroid is in play, I don't care at all. I root not for team legacy or ultimate victory but the continuity of scores, which allows me to forget myself without forfeiting urgency or the sense that the drama counts, that there is cruciality here.

No wonder people in the '50s called it the World Serious and bore the heavy radios of the day through the streets of New York to track its drama. Amid our melodramas and throwaway culture, something might as well be serious. Something that means nothing. We are already ghosts in a ghostworld, strangers in a stranger land. At least the games are more real than that. At least they allow us to enter the lion's den, in suspenseful interludes while the clock is running and the orb is under rules.

Watch how coaches and managers drill their charges, how ferocious, even sadistic, they are, how legitimate they consider their tyranny and command. War by proxy is still war. What did that demon Green Bay Packers coach Vince Lombardi say? "Winning is not life or death. It's more important." But he missed the point: it's not winning; it's the "game." Winning—or its attempt—is the only credible excuse to play.

A friend remarked recently that it's too bad players don't come from the cities they represent so that we could get the full patriotic benefit of symbolic battle as a stand-in for violence, what sports are apparently intended to be, e.g., their cultural role. Having evolved well past such a neighborly society into a global marketplace, we must adopt mercenaries who seek their destiny in foreign lands.

The Mets, mostly Midwestern, Southern, Scottish-Irish, and Californian in their salad days, are now Dominican, Venezuelan, Puerto Rican, Korean, and Japanese. The Senators are Slovakian, Swedish, Russian, Czech, and German as well as North American. The Nets are

Slovenian, Croatian, Serbian, and of course biracial. But that doesn't diminish my commitment or my affiliation with them. Quite the opposite: it allows me to embrace a multicultural totem.

As much as a vehicle of ancient tribal loyalty, games are for me a container for the primitive rage of my childhood, gestated in a family that was only *against* things, never for anyone, that hated more than loved, that wished ill on others routinely. They experienced clandestine joy at another's failure or demise, precisely what a fan does every day. They competed so hard that they cannibalized their own members without knowing it.

The radiation of that has to go somewhere, be stored in some form, has to be kept smoldering in a safe vessel through its half-life, because otherwise it would get out and contaminate everything, namely the rest of my life. The habit of it must be fed in proxy form. Better to "waste" time rooting innocently and eternally for victories and their artificial highs—because the joy liberated by them is simple and untarnishable, and harms no one. Better to root against the abstracted opponent than real friends and rivals.

The lesson I seem to have learned most effectively in growing up is how to measure and contain damage by preserving it in pure and primeval acts, by honoring their forms and sigils unconditionally. That is why I am such a rabid and compulsive fan. The aesthetic of the games actually bores me. I am not a baseball or basketball aficionado. I am a fan of energy, momentum, redemption, but especially the triumph of the underdog. In fact I lose some interest during stretches when my teams do too well, or then I root for some underdog player instead of the team.

The sporting events onto which I project my intense interest, from the standpoint of the constellations, matter no more than tournaments among South American indigenes or Australian outback children—or even wind driving untold spores between unregistered goal posts.

There is a purer archetypal game to which most fans are oblivious. The ball or puck is a trope of an atom or world: disperse space to concentrated energy, smaller surface to greater volume. It is also ovum, buckyball, droplet in gravity, radiolarian, moon of bound fibers against bat of gravity, perpendicular section of tube trajected along ice of Callisto, pellet hurled against Stone Age fibers into nettings of harvest time, oblique conic slices sewn together and hurled or punted through trees. Each ball transfers energy and attention to and from the position of the electron, completing and breaking a circuit, scoring a point, making a goal (however it is counted).

This unfinished game goes all the way back to Cro-Magnon, *Homo erectus*, and *Homo africanus*, to primates playing with one another and shaping implements, sticks and rocks. The original ball was a stone, and the pitcher was primevally a hunter. The addition of batters and fielders to the equation shows an awakening of consciousness, self-reflection providing the existential act at the roots of culture, the recognition that "I" is a mirror, that not all acts are "actual," not all selves are egos, not all plays are necessary or dangerous. So from the symbolic act are born the rudiments of play and the game.

The first symbol fused from the dreaming mind into an artifact was probably the notch on the primitive pebble tool, which became the groove on the hand-axe, the point on the spear. It gave rise to another lineage of symbols: the score. Scoring literally created scores, a scratch on flint or chert, a mark on caribou bone becoming a lunar count, then a numeral, then a nascent algebra. It sired the scorecard and the box score.

In the end, I believe, these false games will be renounced and purged, and the foes on all the teams will embrace and thank one another for the fierce engagement. Until then, I keep the hearth fires alive.

Index

Payson, Joan, 51, 52, 53
Payton, Jay, 3, 37, 39, 60, 63, 124
Pearce, Bob, 252
Pelfry, Mike, 42, 58
Peña, Alejandro, 35
Pendleton, Terry, 74
Pennock, Herb, 14
Perez, Oliver, 8, 9
Perez, Pascual, 235–36
Perez, Timo, 6, 37
Perez, Tony, 154, 175
Perez, Yorkis, 35
Person, Robert, 4, 60, 63
Peters, Nick, 198, 222
Peterson, Rick, 56
Pettitte, Andy, 126
Pfeil, Bobby, 282
Philadelphia Phillies, 155
    1979 season, 199
    1980 NLCS, 152, 157–58
    1981 season, 88–89
    1982 season, 76, 90–91
    1984 season, 247
    1987 season, 108
Phillips, Jason, 60, 61, 63
Phillips, Mike, 28, 55
Phillips, Steve, 6, 54, 57
Phoenix Coyotes, 46
Piazza, Mike, 34, 37, 40, 41, 51, 55, 63, 127
Pierce, Billy, 184
Piersall, Jim, 11, 186–87
Pittsburgh Pirates, 9, 149, 155
    1960 World Series, 152

1969 season, 24–25, 153
1971 season, 190
1973 season, 3, 25, 153, 258–59
1984 season, 246, 247
Pittsburgh Steelers, 4
Powell, Boog, 144
Powell, Grover, 162
Pratt, Todd, 3, 36
Puleo, Charlie, 162
Pulsipher, Bill, 37

Q
Quebec Nordiques, 46
Quisenberry, Dan, 92

R
Raines, Tim, 108
Rajsich, Gary, 91, 205, 208
Ralston, Peter, 50
Ramirez, Manny, 12
Randle, Lenny, 11, 27
Randolph, Willie, 1, 2, 3, 62, 156, 192
Ranew, Merritt, 15
Raschi, Vic, 14, 182
Ratelle, Jean, 43
Reardon, Jeff, 29, 72, 162, 208
Reed, Jack, 13
Reed, Rick, 37
Reed, Steve, 57
Relaford, Desi, 60, 63
Remlinger, Mike, 60, 63
Renna, Bill, 13
Renteria, Edgar, 12

Index

Taylor, Sammy, 16

Teilhard de Chardin, Pierre, 284

Terrell, Walt, 30, 208, 229, 239, 250

Terry, Ralph, 184

Teufel, Tim, 31, 53, 168, 176–80

Theodore, George, 268, 269

Thomas, Frank, 21

Thomas, George, 14

Thomas, LeRoy, 14, 155

Thome, Jim, 12

Thompson, John, 39, 126

Thompson, Ryan, 4, 33

Thomson, Bobby, 167

Thon, Dickie, 193, 216

Thorogood, George, 125

Throneberry, Marv, 11, 22

Tibbs, Jay, 205, 207

Todd, Jackson, 29

Todd, John, 277

Torgeson, Earl, 13

Toronto Blue Jays, 158

Torre, Joe, 198

Torrez, Mike, 29, 210, 216

Traber, Billy, 57

Trachsel, Steve, 40, 56

Trammell, Bubba, 6

Tresh, Tom, 13, 23

Trevino, Alex, 201

Triandos, Gus, 182

Tudor, John, 74

Turley, Bob, 75, 182

Turner, Bake, 44

Turner, Jim, 44

Turner, Ted, 92

Twitchell, Wayne, 29, 199

Tyner, Jason, 6, 13

U

Unitas, Johnny, 280

Unser, Del, 27, 158, 192

Upledger, John, 114

V

Vail, Mike, 27, 205

Valentin, John, 41

Valentine, Bobby, 29, 38, 231

Valentine, Ellis, 29, 208

Valenzuela, Fernando, 108, 155

Valo, Elmer, 13

Vargas, Jason, 58

Vaughn, Moe, 38, 54

Veale, Bob, 87

Ventura, Robin, 36, 37

Veryzer, Tom, 204, 226

Viola, Frank, 34

Virgil, Ozzie, 90

Vizcaino, José, 35

W

Waful, Donald, 103

Wagner, Billy, 41, 67

Wagner, Leon, 155

Wainwright, Adam, 10

Walling, Denny, 167

Washington, Claudell, 125

Washington, Herb, 5

Washington Senators, 14

Weaver, Earl, 209, 280

About the Author

RICHARD GROSSINGER is an anthropologist and publisher who has authored or edited over twenty books, including five anthologies of baseball literature. Grossinger and Kevin Kerrane co-edited *Baseball I Gave You the Best Years of My Life*, the first anthology of its kind, and one that includes work from contributors as diverse as Jack Kerouac, Bernadette Mayer, and John Updike. *Baseball Diamonds* and *Into the Temple of Baseball* followed, both edited by Grossinger and Kerrane. For over thirty years, Grossinger and his wife, Lindy Hough, have run North Atlantic Books.

MIKE VACCARO has been the lead sports columnist at the *New York Post* since 1992, after previously working at the *Newark Star-Ledger*, the *Kansas City Star*, and at newspapers in upstate New York and Arkansas. He is the author of *Emperors and Idiots*, the definitive history of the Yankees-Red Sox rivalry, and *1941: The Greatest Year in Sports*. The winner of over 150 journalism awards since 1989, he is a graduate of St. Bonaventure University and lives in Hillsdale, New Jersey, with his wife, Leigh.